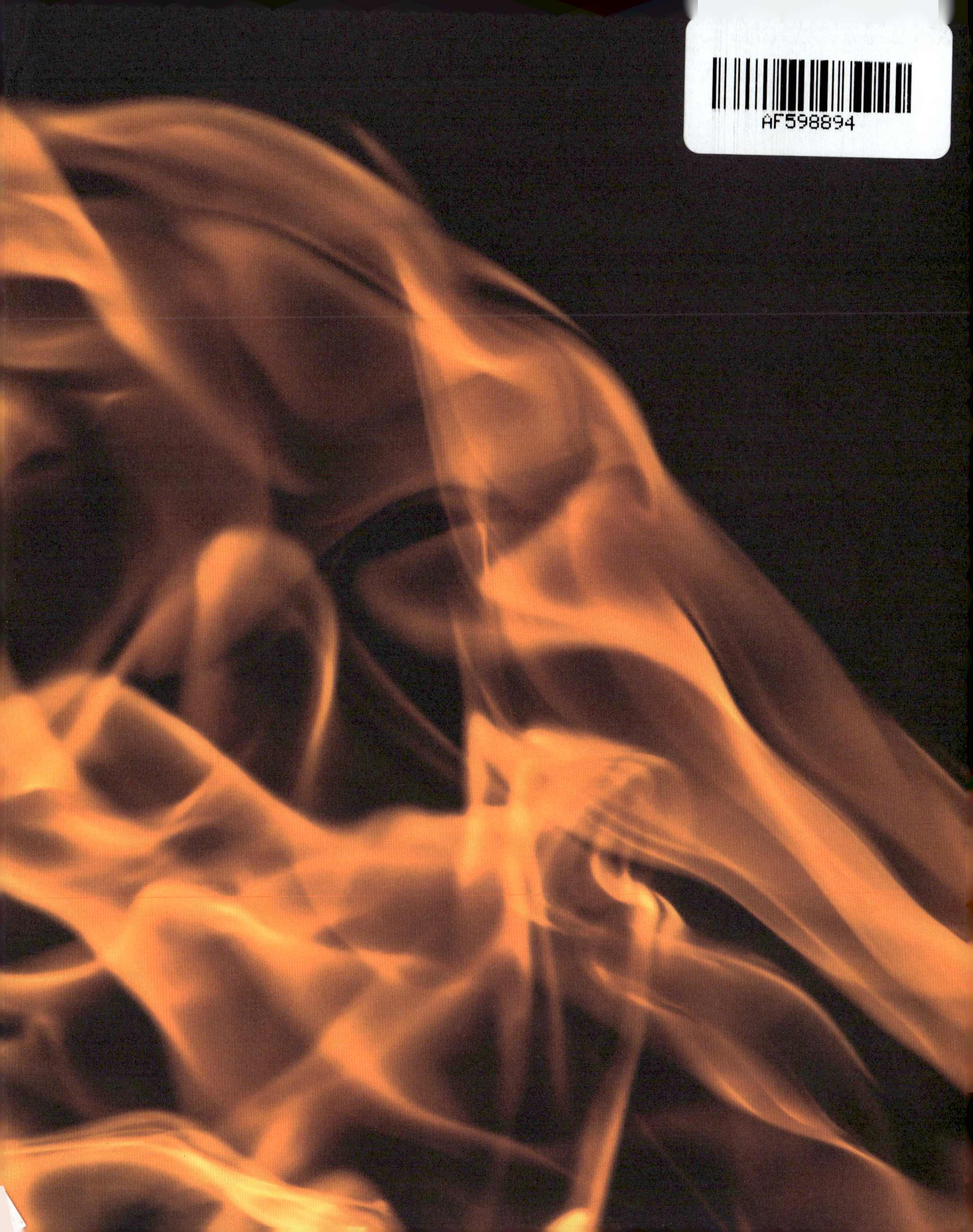

LOADED

LOADED

GUNS IN CONTEMPORARY ART

SUZANNE RAMLJAK

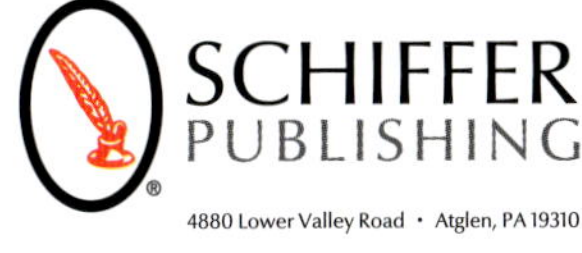

4880 Lower Valley Road • Atglen, PA 19310

Other Schiffer Books by the Author:
On Body and Soul: Contemporary Armor to Amulets, ISBN 978-0-7643-4647-7

Other Schiffer Books on Related Subjects:
Open Aperture: The Evolution of Photography in an Abstract World, Paul Matte, ISBN 978-0-7643-5540-0

50 Contemporary Women Artists: Groundbreaking Contemporary Art from 1960 to Now, John Gosslee and Heather Zises, eds., foreword by Elizabeth Sackler, ISBN 978-0-7643-5653-7

Disrupted Realism: Paintings for a Distracted World, John Seed, foreword by Katherine Stanek, ISBN 978-0-7643-5801-2

Library of Congress Control Number: 2020952749

Front cover image:
Willie Cole, *Medicine Man*, 2010
cast resin, flocking, paint; 23¼ × 17¼ × 11 in.

Back cover image:
Nancy Fouts, *If you hear the word "art" . . . reach for the gun*, 2011
cast replica gun, wood, glass, hammer; 15 × 12¼ × 2¼ in.

Type set in Agenda/Bodoni

ISBN: 978-0-7643-6278-1
Printed in China

Published by Schiffer Publishing, Ltd.
4880 Lower Valley Road
Atglen, PA 19310
Phone: (610) 593-1777; Fax: (610) 593-2002
Email: Info@schifferbooks.com
Web: www.schifferbooks.com

For the artists and seers,
who are tending the flames . . .

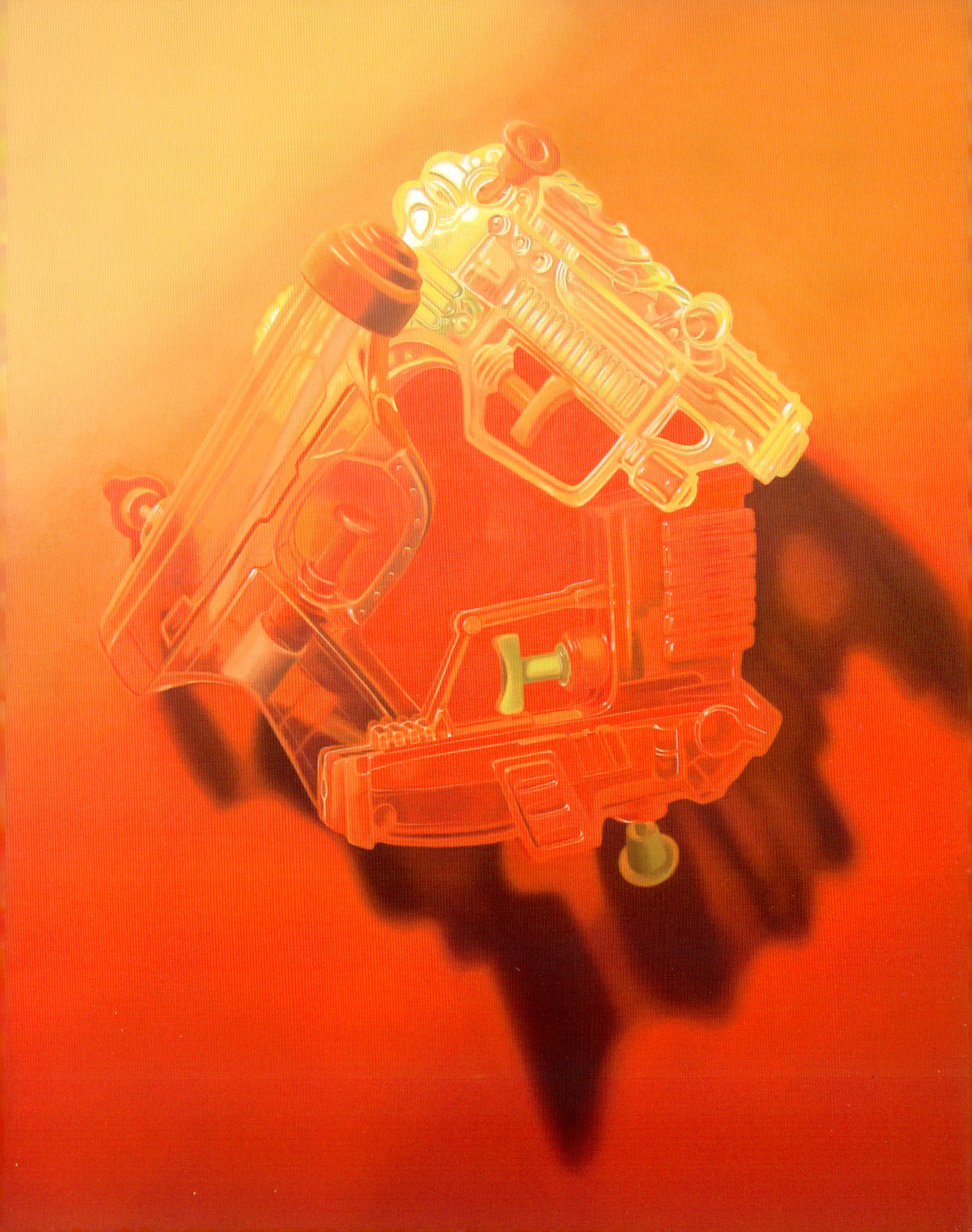

CONTENTS

Shannon Cannings, *Ring of Fire*, 2018
oil on canvas; 60 × 48 in.

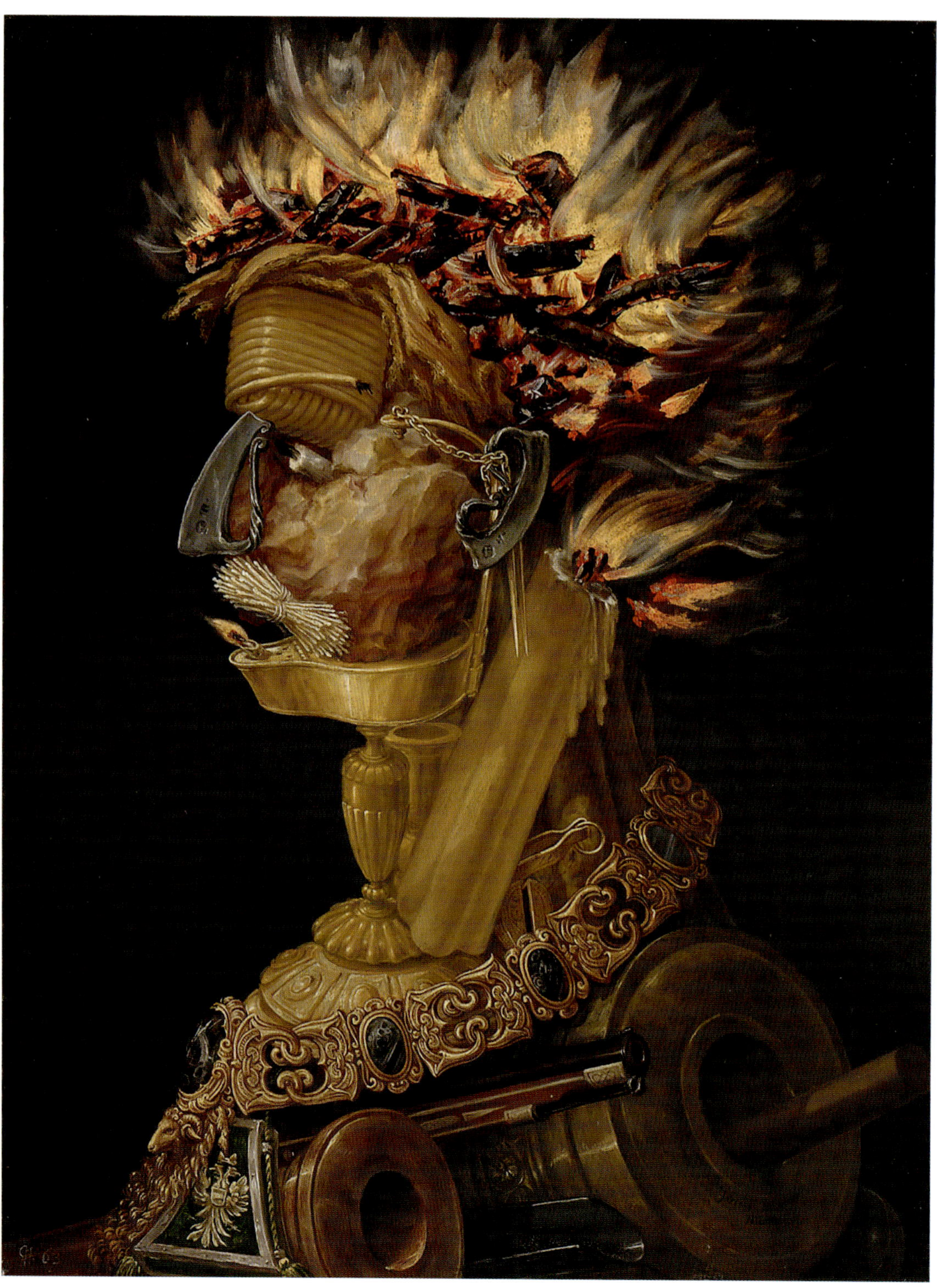

INTRODUCTION

FIRE IN THE HAND

Suzanne Ramljak

The subject of guns is a volatile one. As the term "firearm" suggests, a gun is an instrument designed to cause and contain combustion. Each shot is a mini explosion. Therein lies the power and allure of guns. Therein also lies their menace. The emotions and associations roused by firearms are conflicted, even contradictory. Where one person sees danger, another finds security. While a gun signals weakness to some, it is the epitome of strength to others. Destroyer, protector, savior, betrayer—guns have come to represent all of these traits and more.

Feelings aside, we can ground the exploration of this heated topic in a couple of basic facts. As a form of weaponry, firearms exist for a distinct purpose. Their exquisite engineering is geared to a singular end: to forcefully propel projectiles. A reliable gun delivers a bullet to its target, whoever or whatever that may be. Guns do not discriminate. Firearms also embody a ferocious eloquence; they speak knowingly about matters of life and death. A fear of dying, however latent, underwrites our relationship with guns. It is hard to dismiss their threat to our mortality.

History is written by the victors, as the saying goes, and art history is also shaped by the powerful. Throughout the past, images and sculptures have been created to celebrate the mighty, whether hailing from church, state, or the private realm. Guns have increasingly earned a place in the visual-arts pantheon, deemed a subject worthy of contemplation and portrayal. By surveying depictions of firearms in contemporary art, this book will reveal the compelling role they have come to play within our lives and imaginations.

To appreciate the cultural significance of guns, we must go back to prehistory and the taming of fire. This naturally occurring process, ignited by volcanoes and lightning, is a consuming force that can reduce organic matter to ash. Early humans began preserving these spontaneous outbursts one million years ago and gained the means to produce fire on demand around 7,000 BCE. Campfires became social foci as well as communal projects for the maintenance of flames, marking the dawn of civilization.[1] Domestication of fire was a game-changer in human evolution, transforming every conceivable aspect of life (fig. 1). Fire's heat and light countered the cold and dark, extending geographic

FIG. 1.
Giuseppe Arcimboldo. *Fire*, 1566. Oil on wood. Kunsthistorisches Museum, Vienna.

range to cooler climes and illuminating the night. Fire also aided the clearing of land for planting and hunting and enabled cooking, which prompted changes in diet and physiology. Indeed, fire usage has emerged as the distinguishing trait of our species. While other animals employ language and tools, only humans know how to handle fire. *Homo sapiens* is also *Homo ignis*, creature of the flame.

Although we have mastered the production of fire, the element itself remains innately dangerous, demanding vigilance and reverence. Accordingly, fire worship and ritual are culturally widespread, found in religions from the Israelites to the Inca. In the ancient Greek myth of Prometheus, the Titan steals fire from the gods and gifts it to mortals. Such thievery held consequences for all involved; Prometheus was bound to a rock and tortured by Zeus, while humankind was punished by Pandora, the original woman, who spread suffering across the land.

The Prometheus myth can be read as a cautionary tale, showing the risks of hubristically grasping at godly power. It is also a story about the mixed blessings of fire, which brings both progress and peril in its wake. This duality is stressed in Johan Goudsblom's seminal study, *Fire and Civilization:* "The possession of fire has made human societies more productive and more formidable but has also increased their capacity for destruction and made them more vulnerable. As a part of the apparatus by which people control nature, the control of fire has always been, and will always continue to be, enveloped in social control and self-control."[2]

Encounters with flames have become more rare, but fire invisibly lurks within our high-tech culture. One means of access to this primordial force is through the use of guns. As noted, the bond between fire and guns is evinced in language: "firepower," "hold your fire," "firing squad," and "fire at." Their ties go beyond semantics, however, and encompass vital capacities. Everything that pertains to fire—domination of nature, destructive potential, a need for caution and requisite social cooperation—also holds true for guns. Echoing Goudsblom's passage, gun scholar Jim Supica affirms the Janus face of firearms: "Guns have been used to implement both the highest and basest goals of humanity—to put food on the table, to provide personal protection, to enforce or defy the law, to defend or acquire territory and treasure, and to liberate or to enslave."[3] Firearms, like fire, have a deeply torn character.

Whereas fire control dates back one million years, guns appeared on the world stage less than a millennium ago. The genesis of firearms began with the invention of gunpowder in China, during the ninth century. The first weapon to enlist this explosive powder was the fire lance. Although crude, these spear-like arms combined the three basic components of a gun: gunpowder, a tube or barrel, and projectiles. The early fourteenth century saw the emergence of firearms proper, in the form of portable hand cannons (fig. 2).

With the introduction of the matchlock in the fifteenth century, ignition mechanisms became integrated into the gun's structure. Performance was enhanced by other design features, including barrel rifling for improved range and aim. By the sixteenth century, armies across Europe and Asia were equipped with firearms, which also accompanied

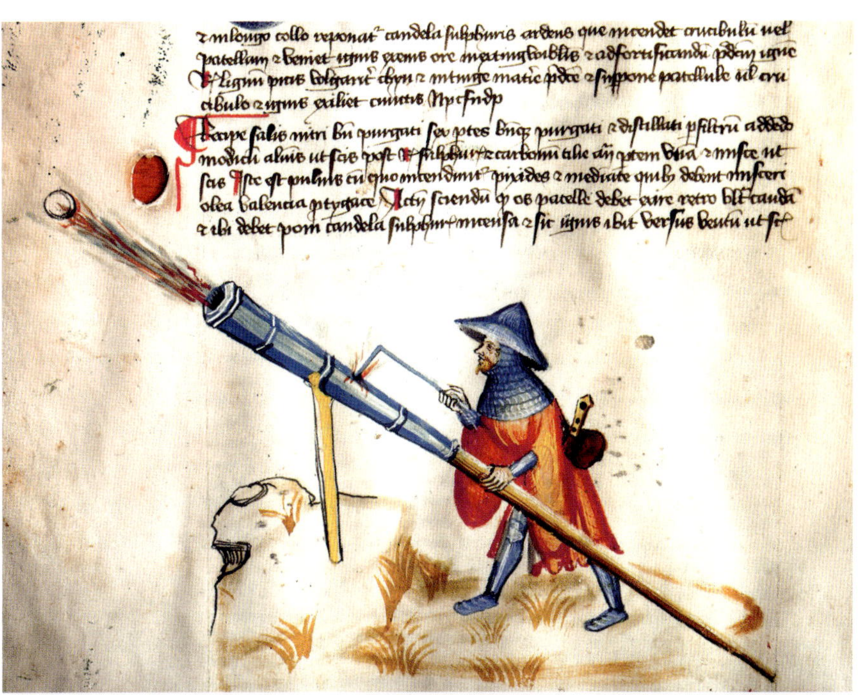

FIG. 2. Konrad Kyeser. Illustration of soldier firing a hand cannon, from the *Bellifortis Manuscript*, ca. 1402–04. Göttingen State and University Library.

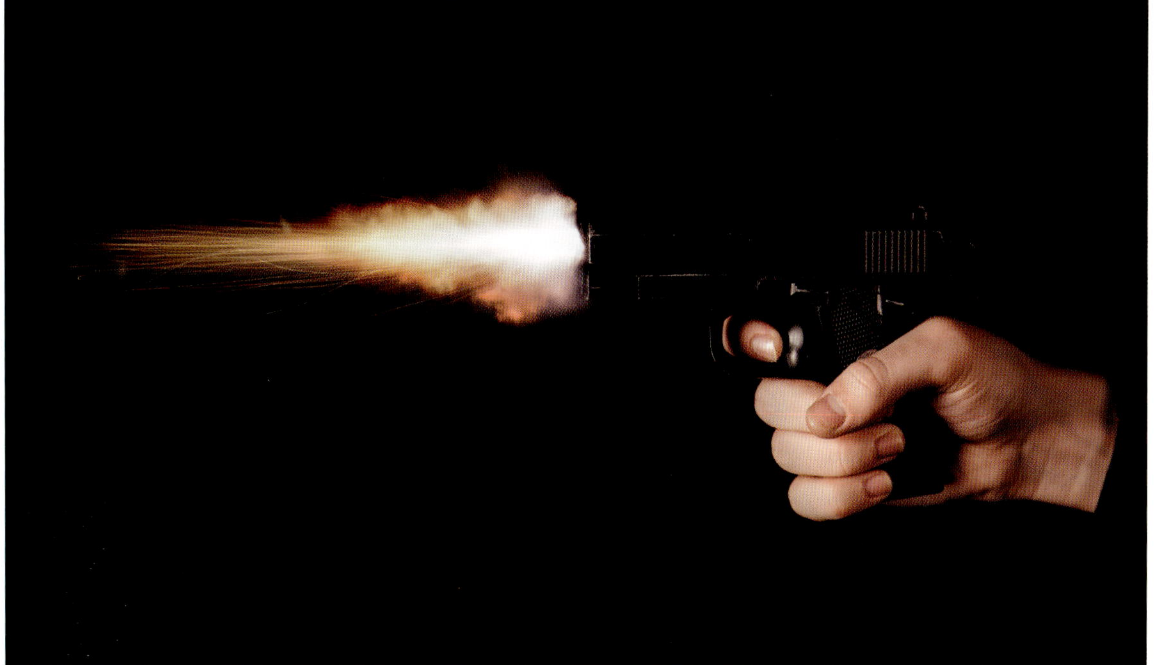

FIG. 3. Frunze Anton Nikolaevich. Flash from the shot of a modern firearm.

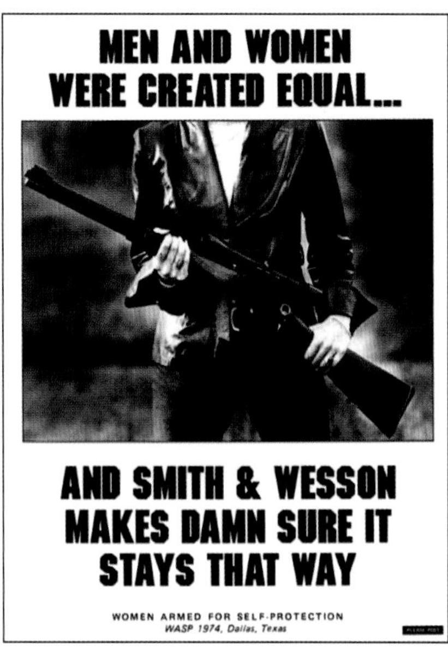

FIG. 4. Women Armed for Self-Protection flyer. © WASP 1974.

explorers on their New World journeys. And during the 1700s, guns replaced swords as the weapon of choice for duals. The world became held at gunpoint.

With industrialization in the ninteenth century, firearms joined the ranks of other mass-produced goods, growing ever more affordable and accessible. The majority of households in the United States held at least one gun by 1900.[4] Further technological advances over the last 100 years have resulted in lighter and more-durable materials—with aluminum, rubber, plastic, and other synthetics replacing traditional steel and wood. And the quest for more-efficient autoloading guns continues up to the present. Firearm variety abounds, with hundreds of gun types currently on the market. In the space of 500 years, guns have evolved from clumsy military weapons to readily available consumer products. As one writer put it, "Anyone with a little property . . . can have literally the most powerful force on earth, to take life both in wilderness and in society"[5] (fig. 3).

There are now more than one billion firearms in global circulation, with 85% in civilian hands.[6] Nearly half of these are owned by citizens in the United States, the most heavily armed nation on the planet. Guns have become a ubiquitous fact of life, populating our material and symbolic landscapes. Like it or not, they are here to stay—there is no putting the gunpowder back in the bottle.

Current debates notwithstanding, the question today is not *if* people may have guns, but rather who gets to own a killing tool. While there is consensus that criminals should not possess firearms (though they defy the law by definition), little agreement exists about who has a given right to be armed. Equality is trickier when it comes with a license to kill. It is notable that guns themselves have been called the "great equalizer." This leveling effect has been reflected in firearm promotion, as in a nineteenth-century slogan from the Colt Manufacturing Company: "God created man,

Sam Colt made them equal." A similar pitch, touting a rifle, was used by the Women Armed for Self-Protection (WASP) group in a 1974 flyer: "Men and Woman were created equal . . . and Smith & Wesson makes damn sure it stays that way"[7] (fig. 4).

While a gun in the hand may balance the scales of physical power—between two men, or between a man and a woman—equal access to firearms is a divisive issue. In the US, many deem gun ownership a birthright, guaranteed under the Bill of Rights' Second Amendment, reading: "A well regulated Militia, being necessary to the security of a free State, the right of the People to keep and bear arms, shall not be infringed." Whether this right was intended for individuals or a militia remains contested, and even the nation's founders did not endorse guns for all, denying firearms to African Americans, slaves, and Native Americans, among others.

The interplay between race and weaponry is still fraught, as gun control and people control are invariably entwined. The right to possess firearms, regardless of race, class, or political persuasion, was tested in the 1960s by the Black Panther Party, who publicly carried arms to defend against police violence.[8] As the movement's cofounder Huey P. Newton declared, "An unarmed people are slaves or are subject to slavery at any given moment."[9] This claim, from Newton's essay "In Defense of Self-Defense," underlines the primary motive behind most gun ownership—defense of person and property.

The most common reason given for possessing a firearm is protection and self-defense. Over 60 percent of US owners report having a gun to counter attacks, rather than for hunting or sport.[10] Fear for one's personal safety fuels the enormous gun industry. In spite of sharply falling homicide rates and violent crime in recent years, both progun and antigun adherents remain united in insecurity. Gun advertising promotes this sense of threat, brandishing messages of danger and preparedness such as "It's a Jungle Out There" (Springfield Armory Co.), "Arm Yourself"® (Mossberg), and "Be Your Own Protector" (Wilson Combat).[11] Through such messaging, civilians are urged to pack a piece for peace of mind.

When it comes to gun ownership, as in other matters, perception often eclipses reality. Of those who choose to carry a gun, most will never use it to defend themselves. If one did face a life-threatening encounter, performance under pressure is a dicey prospect. Even for trained police officers, the number of unintentional shootings is alarming.[12] Further, those murdered by guns are usually shot by familiars, not strangers. And the majority of gun deaths in America are actually from suicide, not homicide. Medical professionals view firearms as a certified health risk, correlated with accidental death and injury. Nonetheless, most people feel that a gun makes them safer, and it is hard to argue with feelings. Fear rings louder than words.

Understandably, statistics won't hinder individuals from keeping guns to safeguard against offenders, especially in an age of mass shootings. What is less comprehensible is the desire to amass multiple firearms until one's home becomes a veritable armory. Such stockpiling of weapons is not an isolated occurrence. Of the nearly 400 million guns in the United States, approximately half are held by just 3% of owners.[13] Among these so-called super-owners, many are collectors, or those who require assorted firearms for work or sport. For others, their arsenals are built on distrust of the government or other social groups and are based on the belief that safety comes from a surplus of arms.

Although relationships with firearms are often emotional, not rational, many well-reasoned solutions are offered to curb gun ownership and abuse. These cures for what is seen as a major social ill run the gamut from economics to education. One prevailing account of gun violence points to mental illness as a prime cause. As an antidote, psychological services are prescribed to minimize aggression or depression, and to cultivate better coping skills. Tied to psychology are educational remedies, calling for more information about the risks and liabilities of gun ownership. Another approach involves economic strategies to reduce poverty and resource disparity. Then there are efforts to restrict firearm access, making it more difficult for harmful individuals to acquire a gun. On the opposite end, others support an increase of guns to outweigh the weapons already in troublesome hands. While there is some validity to all these positions, none has managed to rule the day.

To gun enthusiasts, talk of problems and illness can itself sound problematic and ill conceived. Instead of paranoia they would speak of pleasure. A Ruger revolver ad teases this notion with a label that reads: "WARNING: Shooting the Wrangler is fun. Plan extra time at the range and don't expect any left over ammo."[14] There is no doubt that shooting firearms is an enjoyable, even thrilling, activity. To fire a gun is to feel an explosion in your hand and running throughout your entire body. Add to that the satisfaction of hitting targets on the range or in the field and you have an agreeable, if not addictive, experience. For those driven by such love and desire, there is even a fitting Greek term—*Hoplophile* (*hoplon*/arms and *philia*/love).

The gratification that firearms provide is often couched in sexual language, particularly that of males, with shared words such as "cock," "shaft," and "shooting a wad." The kindred shape and projectile function of guns and male genitalia are made explicit in Robert Mapplethorpe's 1982 photo *Cock and Gun*, which profiles both rigid forms in tandem.[15] Guns are commonly viewed as phallic structures, an aspect graphically displayed on these pages. Then there is the anatomy of actual gun violence, which is decidedly male (fig. 5). The vast majority of homicides are committed by men, who are also behind almost all mass shootings.

Aside from the close alignment among masculinity, violence, and guns, women have also taken up arms for the same reasons as men. Over the centuries, guns have been enlisted by women for hunting, recreation, self-defense, competition, and military and police careers. Although they have demonstrated equal prowess with firearms (witness Annie Oakley's superstardom), the sight of an armed woman can still be unnerving and upend traditional feminine standards of nurturing and gentleness. A gun-toting woman comes fiercely equipped with the force and destructiveness inherent in the weapon, embodying an arresting clash of gender norms. As shown in Laura Browder's valuable history *Her Best Shot: Women and Guns in America*, "Our fascination with the armed woman is an expression of our societal ambivalence about women's equality with men: we are titillated, but we are afraid."[16]

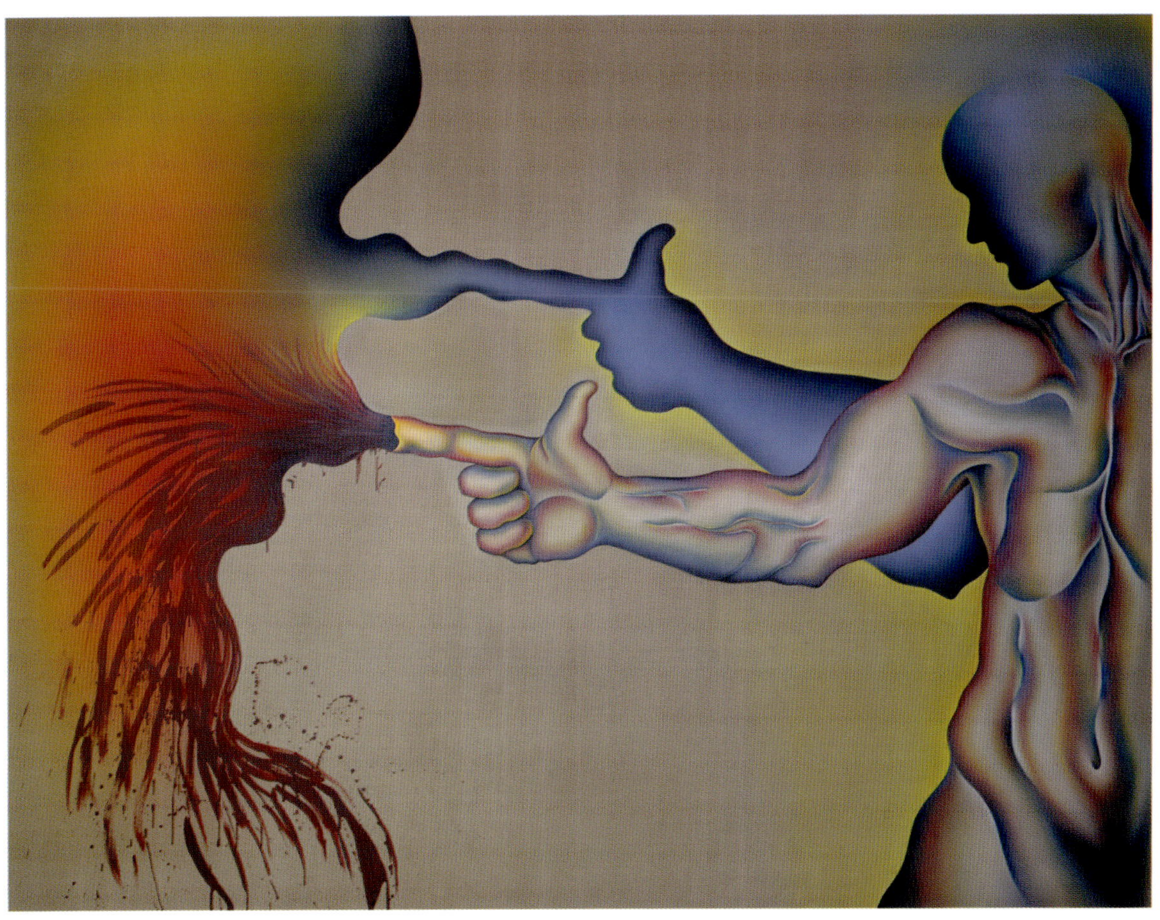

FIG. 5. **Judy Chicago.** *In the Shadow of the Handgun* from the PowerPlay series, 1983. Sprayed acrylic and oil on Belgian linen; 108 × 144 in. Collection of Elizabeth A. Sackler. © Judy Chicago / Artists Rights Society (ARS), New York; photo © Donald Woodman / ARS, New York.

Even without a shooter, male or female, guns have a tangible agency all their own. The very presence of a firearm is found to alter human behavior and stimulate violence. According to one social psychologist, "The finger pulls the trigger, but the trigger may also be pulling the finger."[17] Just as spiders and snakes instinctually signal mortal danger, spurring a fight-or-flight response, guns instantly register as life threatening, albeit based on training not instinct. Known as the "weapons effect," this dynamic has been confirmed in dozens of studies since first identified in 1967.[18] Experiments repeatedly show that the proximity of a gun, or merely its image, generates aggression by priming hostile thoughts and appraisals. Beyond being interesting social science, these findings have real-world consequences in law enforcement, where violent interactions between police and public are fueled by the weapons effect.[19] Though inanimate, guns communicate, and what they say is deadly serious.

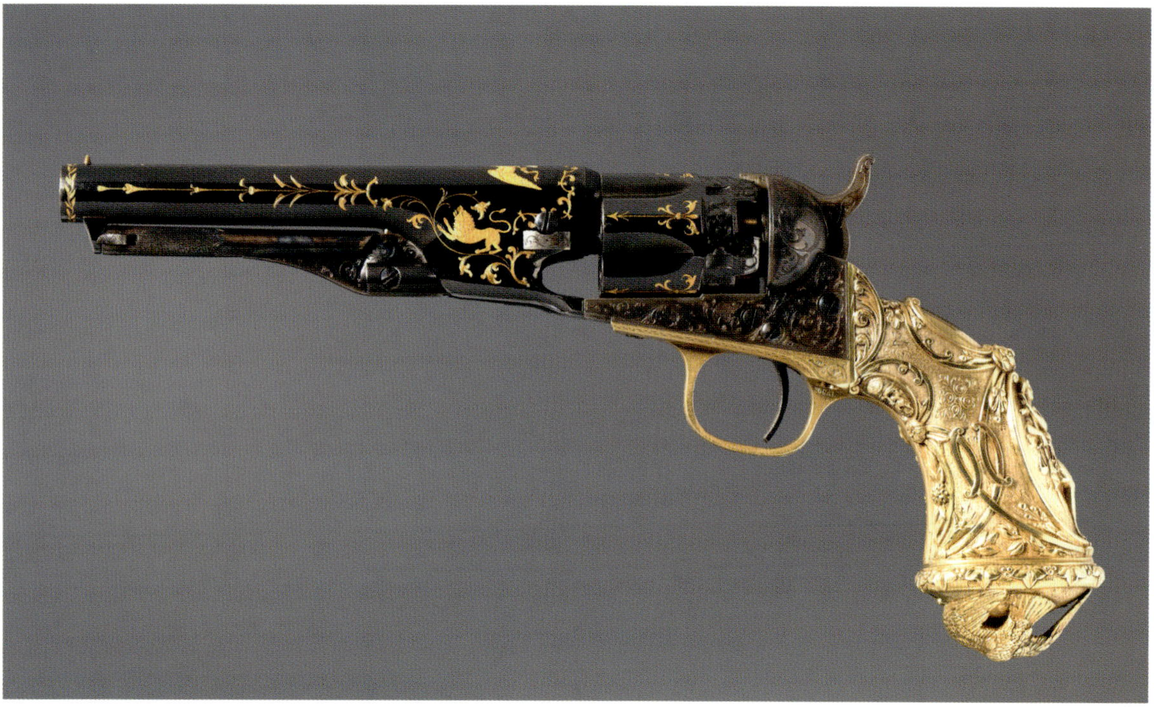

FIG. 6. Colt's Patent Fire Arms Manufacturing with grip designed by John Quincy Adams Ward. *Colt Model 1862 Police Revolver, Serial No. 38549*, ca. 1868. Steel, gold, brass. The Metropolitan Museum of Art, New York

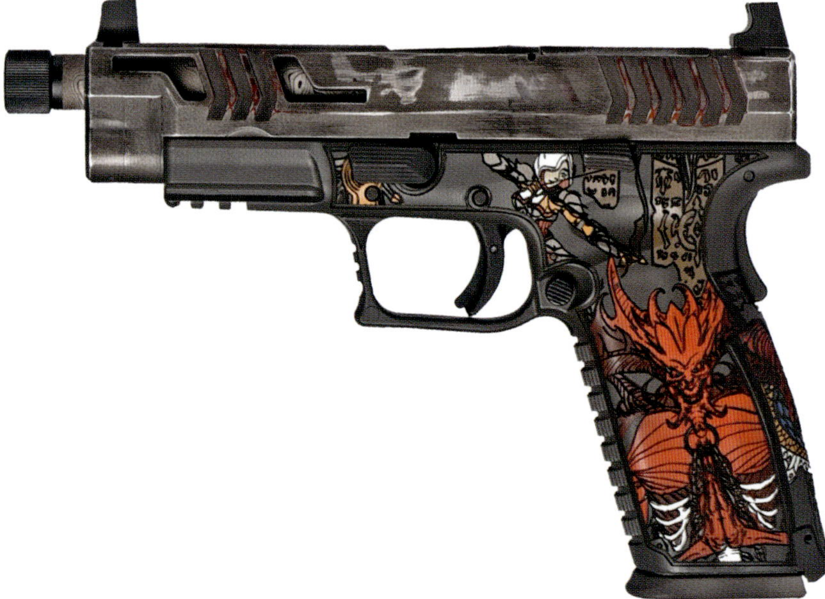

FIG. 7. **Cody Dennis / Odin's Workshop, Detroit.** *"Diablo" Pistol* (customized Springfield XD-M OSP 10 mm), 2019. Photo courtesy of Andy Grossman, Athlon Outdoors from *Ballistic* (April/May 2020).

Our keen visual sense, suffused with a will to survive, has attuned us to the threat of a gun's silhouette, alike that of a poisonous creature. Guns also carry an aesthetic charge due to their formal properties. Throughout history, firearms have been elaborately crafted and prized as items of luxury, beauty, and ceremony. In such instances, guns themselves *are* the artistic object, rather than the subject of art. Museums and private collections are filled with gorgeous weapons, whose fine workmanship, decoration, and precious materials far transcend the object's function (fig. 6). This tradition of custom-made or bespoke firearms continues within modern gunsmithing (fig. 7).

Guns can still pack a solid visual punch, even when lacking fancy styling or imagery. In the article "Guns Are Beautiful," Stephen Marche argues for a link between aesthetics and gun use within the US.[20] "Guns are works of art," writes Marche, and "one of the primary avenues by which ordinary Americans experience beauty." He further maintains that the demographically diverse gun owners in this country are united by artistic appreciation. Whether or not aesthetics is the common denominator in today's gun culture, a strong case can certainly be made for the sensual appeal of firearms.

Past artists were duly attracted to guns, embellishing or designing them, as did Leonardo da Vinci with his multibarreled firearm of the late 1400s. Within historical painting, guns appeared in the context of activities such as hunting, sport, and war, or in portraiture. The gun in Thomas Gainsborough's celebrated portrait *Mr. and*

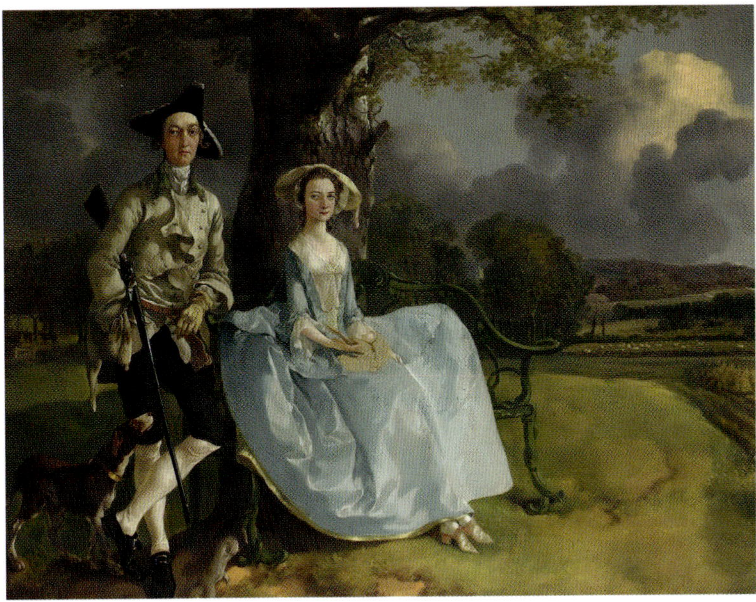

FIG. 8. **Thomas Gainsborough.** *Mr. and Mrs. Andrews* (detail), ca. 1750. Oil on canvas. The National Gallery, London.

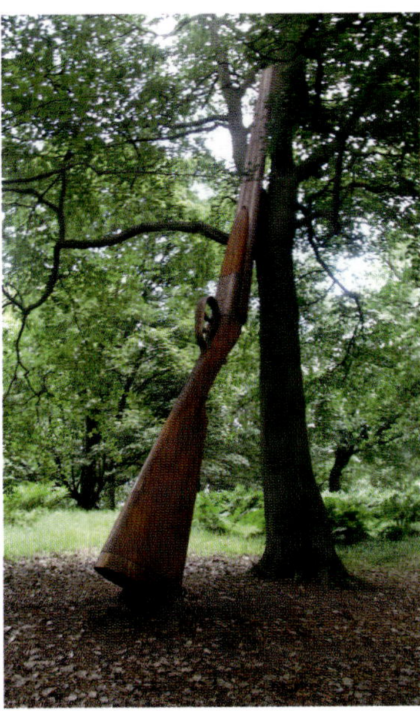

FIG. 9. **Cornelia Parker.** *Landscape with Gun and Tree*, 2010. Cast iron and corten steel. Installation view at Jupiter Artland, Edinburgh, Scotland. Photo: Ann Shaw.

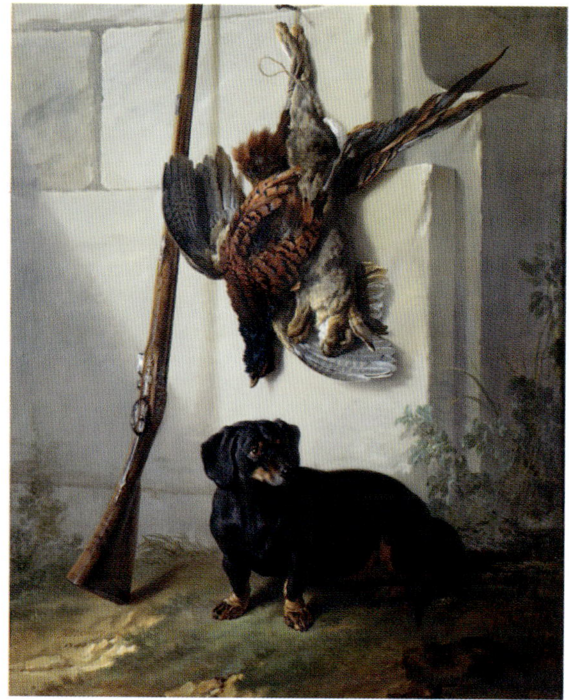

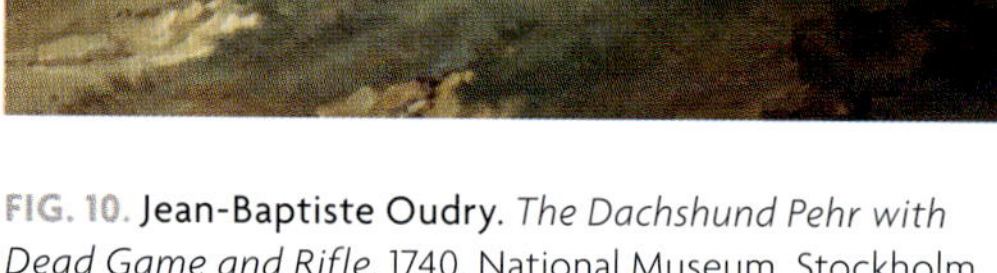

FIG. 10. Jean-Baptiste Oudry. *The Dachshund Pehr with Dead Game and Rifle*, 1740. National Museum, Stockholm.

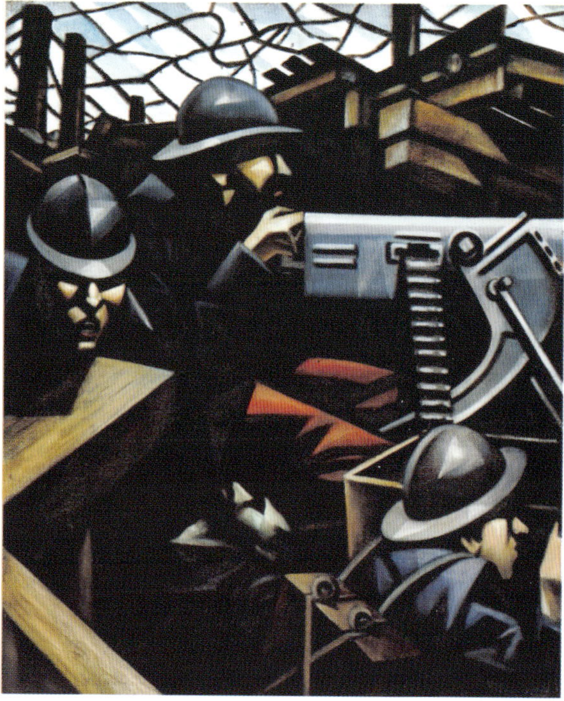

FIG. 11. C. R. W. Nevinson. *La Mitrailleuse*, 1915. Oil on canvas. Tate Britain.

Mrs. Andrews (ca. 1750) casually accompanies the aristocratic couple, signaling their leisurely pursuits and dominion over the land (fig. 8). Contemporary British artist Cornelia Parker's riff on this painting extracts and enlarges the gun into a public sculpture set in an actual landscape (fig. 9). Through the eighteenth and nineteenth centuries, one would be hard pressed to find a gun isolated like this as a work's sole focus. Even in the genres of still life or "after the hunt" paintings, firearms are featured as useful tools, surrounded by the bounty they helped procure (fig. 10).

Within art of the early and mid-twentieth century, depictions of guns remained embedded in cultural events or battle scenes, especially those of the two world wars. On the eve of WWI, Italian Futurist artists extolled the speed and force of modern machinery, including the liberating violence of weaponry. The Vorticist movement, active in Britain from 1912 to 1915, borrowed the fractured syntax of Futurism to address a broader thematic range, and with less zeal for the role of firearms (fig. 11). During the interwar period, the Surrealist movement sought to sow ambiguity, if not inanity, in an effort to disrupt the complacent status quo. In his *Second Surrealist Manifesto* of 1929, the movement's leader, André Breton, provocatively declared, "The simplest Surrealist act consists of dashing down into the street, pistol in hand, and firing blindly, as fast as you can pull the trigger, into the crowd."[21] Breton's notion of an incendiary and counterculture act has sadly become a regular occurrence today.

While guns continued to make cameo appearances in art after WWII, they were largely sidelined amid postwar devastation and the rising tide of abstraction.

Firearms as a discreet artistic motif arose in the 1960s as part of the iconography of modern life. Gun imagery was widely circulated via mass media and television, which by 1960 was a fixture in 90 percent of American households. TV injected war, murder, and local shootings into people's homes and minds, and firearms become a staple of daily visual fare. With westerns and hit TV shows such as *Gunsmoke* and *The Rifleman*, the gun morphed from instrument into icon. Guns made a bold debut in Pop art, rendered by Roy Lichtenstein, Claes Oldenberg, James Rosenquist, Andy Warhol, and others who culled imagery from popular culture (fig. 12). Warhol first treated the subject in 1963 with his *Triple Elvis*, a fetching mash-up of pop music and westerns. Twenty years later, Warhol's *Guns* series (1981–82) featured solitary firearms, akin to the pistol used in the near-fatal shot he took from a would-be murderer.[22] Art of the era assumed more heat against the backdrop of bullet-riddled events, including assassinations of John F. Kennedy and Martin Luther King Jr., nationwide riots of 1967–68, and the Kent State student shootings in 1970, while the escalating war in Vietnam generated its own gallery of gun-strewn art.

During this period, guns became not only subjects in art, but also a creative medium, used in performance events or to produce new work. Influential in this vein was Niki de Saint Phalle's series of *Tirs séances* or "shooting performances," begun in 1961 with the artist and other participants firing rifles at mixed-media paintings.

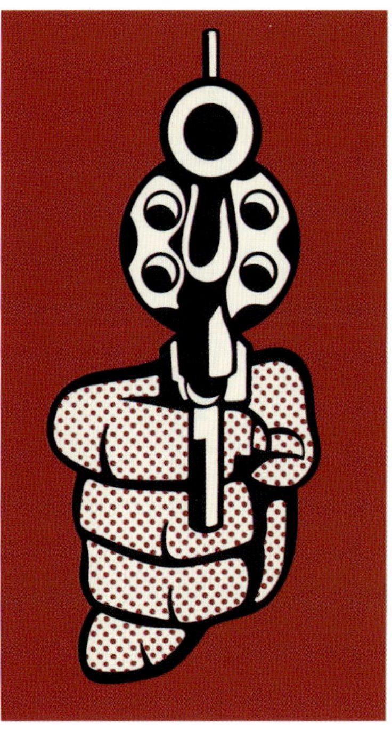

FIG. 12. Roy Lichtenstein. *Pistol*, 1968. Color screenprint.

The most sensational example in this gun art genre is Chris Burden's *Shoot* (1971), for which he hired a sniper to publicly fire a bullet through his arm, yielding a portrait of the artist as gun violence victim. Burden's spectacle, replete with his own blood, was one of many unprecedented artistic modes of the 1960s and '70s, decades that expanded the canon to include Earthworks, Conceptualism, Installation, and Video Art.

Pluralism still reigns within contemporary art, and there are now as many ways and reasons to represent guns as there are artists. Along with the varied approaches, there exists a quantitative dimension that parallels the surge of firearms in our zeitgeist. The proliferation of gun imagery, and the number of artists engaging this theme, testifies to its gripping significance. Firearms have stepped into the cultural foreground, taking a commanding role in our collective drama and discourse.

Although this book includes works by nearly 100 artists, it is not an inclusive survey of gun-related art. Chosen artists were those who intently probed the subject, offering fresh insight into the meaning and function of guns in our society. Not surprisingly, many of today's most prominent artists have turned their attention to this pressing topic, interpreting it through diverse genres and media including painting, sculpture, photography, and installation. With few exceptions, all of the featured work was made in the twenty-first century. While more than half of the artists are from the US, this collection includes examples from a dozen other countries and is not about guns in America per se. And, even though men are responsible for the majority of gun violence and ownership, female artists just as readily embrace firearms in their work, and women compose over 30% of the selection.

Ultimately, this project does not take a firm stance on gun possession or use. What emerges in the process of studying firearms is their inherently dualistic nature. Guns are both positive and negative, protective and destructive, empowering and enfeebling, supporting peace and war, life and death. While this central ambivalence cannot be captured in statistical data or in the volley of media sound bites, it thrives within the complex forms of visual art, which can simultaneously convey contrasting visions. Indeed, the array of work presented here unfolds a striking diversity of viewpoints on guns, some praising, some damning, and often both at once. Together the perspectives highlight the inescapable duplicity that burns at the heart of firearms.

The panoply of works in *Loaded: Guns in Contemporary Art* is arranged in sections based on genre or subject. The first group, "Shooting Gallery," presents gun-slinging figures of every social stripe, revealing how our perception of guns can be swayed by *who* is wielding them. "Playing with Fire" offers a subset of shooters, showing children with firearms and gun-related toys, which are ubiquitous from an early age. The works in "Killer Portraits" portray the inanimate object as imbued with agency while also pointing to the tradition of *memento mori* still lifes. "Disarmed Firearms" displays manipulations of the gun that seek to neuter its destructive force. Targets and victims of gunfire get their due in the "Gunned Down" section, which reminds us of the consequence of these deadly instruments. In "Gun License," artists approach the subject in an uncensored manner, freely conjoining firearms with religion, sex, and other hot-button issues. And "The Armory" holds configurations of amassed and stockpiled guns that speak to the obscene quantities and hoarding of arms in our culture.

Despite any inherent vice, the virtue of these showcased guns is that no one will suffer or die in their viewing. Such depicted firearms might prompt unease and dismay, but we remain safe within their presence. Their violence is vicarious. And just as the taming of fire spurred civilization and a cooperative drive, artists' conceptions of firearms ignite essential aspects of our humanity. Like fire, these guns shed both heat and light on what it means to live in the crosshairs (fig. 13).

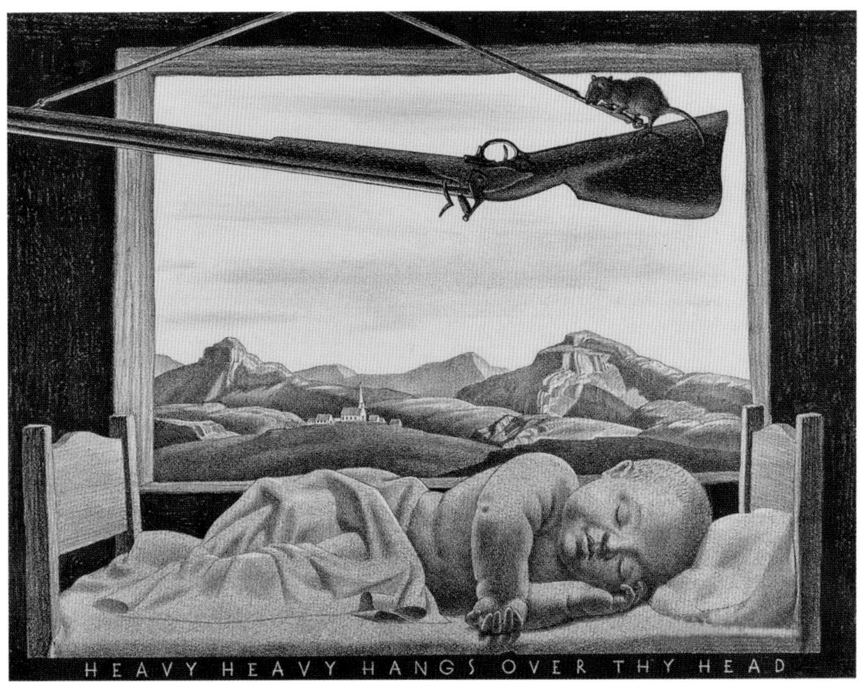

FIG. 13. Rockwell Kent. *Heavy, Heavy Hangs over Thy Head*, 1946. Crayon lithograph on paper.

NOTES

1. Estimated dates of fire domestication by early humans, or *Homo erectus*, are mainly based on archeological findings of campsite remains.
2. Johan Goudsblom, *Fire and Civilization* (London: Penguin Group, 1992), p. 11.
3. Jim Supica, "A Brief History of Firearms," in *Guns* (Surrey, UK: Taj Books, 2005), p. 6, and reprinted as a resource by NRA National Firearms Museums on www.nramuseum.org.
4. Historical firearm ownership statistics from "How Many Households Had Guns in 1900?" at www.extranosalley.com.
5. Stephen Marche, "Guns Are Beautiful," *Esquire*, March 2013, pp. 106–08.
6. Global firearms ownership estimates from World Economic Forum, www.weforum.org.
7. The flyer was issued in 1974 by Women Armed for Self-Protection (WASP), a Texas-based progun feminist group that sought to arm women in self-defense against domestic and sexual violence.
8. This tension surfaced again in 2014 with the "Hands Up, Don't Shoot" protests to resist violent shootings of black people by law enforcement, and more recently in 2020 with the "Black Lives Matter" protest movement spurred by several murders of black citizens by police officers.
9. Huey P. Newton, "In Defense of Self-Defense," in *The Black Panther Newspaper*, June 20, 1967.
10. Pew Research Center Survey of US adults conducted March–April 2017, on "Americans' Views of Guns and Gun Ownership."
11. Promotional slogans from advertisements published in October and November 2019 issues of gun magazines, including *Guns & Ammo*, *Ballistic*, and *Recoil*.
12. Martha Bellisle, "Accidental Shootings Show Police Training Gaps," Associated Press, December 9, 2019.

13. From "The Stock and Flow of U.S. Firearms: Results from the 2015 National Firearms Survey," by Deborah Azrael, Lisa Hepburn, and David Hemenway, Harvard University and Northeastern University.
14. Ruger firearm company advertisement for the Wrangler® single-action revolver, printed in October 2019 issue of *Guns & Ammo* magazine.
15. Robert Mapplethorpe created a number of iconic photographs with weapons and firearms, including *Self Portrait* (1983), with the artist holding a submachine gun, and *Gun Blast* (1985), which shows the trajectory of particles after a bullet is fired.
16. Laura Browder, *Her Best Shot: Women and Guns in America* (Chapel Hill: University of North Carolina Press, 2006), p. 232.
17. Leonard Berkowitz, in Leonard Berkowitz & Anthony LePage, "Weapons as Aggression-Eliciting Stimuli," *Journal of Personality and Social Psychology* 7, no. 2 (1967): 202–07.
18. Berkowitz and LePage published the first study demonstrating that the mere presence of a weapon increases aggressive behavior. These results have since been replicated by several research teams.
19. Alan Yuhas, "Mere Sight of a Gun Makes Police—and Public—More Aggressive, Experts Say," *The Guardian*, August 5, 2015.
20. Marche, "Guns Are Beautiful."
21. André Breton, *Second Surrealist Manifesto*, 1929, in *Manifestoes of Surrealism*, trans. Richard Seaver and Helen R. Lane (Ann Arbor: University of Michigan Press, 1969).
22. In 1968 Valerie Solanis shot and critically wounded Andy Warhol, who suffered great physical consequences and was forced to wear a surgical corset for the rest of his life.

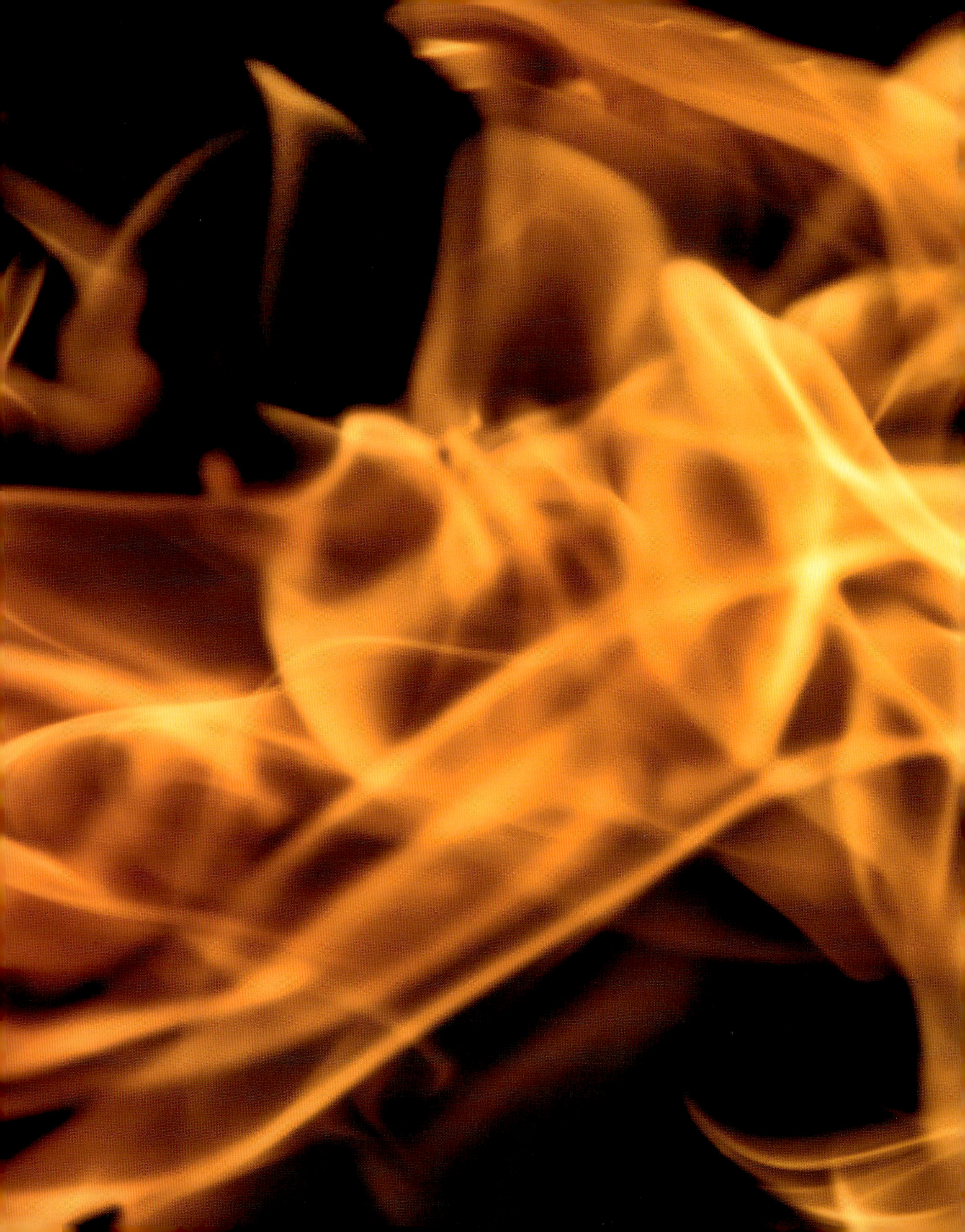

SHOOTING GALLERY

The well-known saying "Guns don't kill people, people kill people" shifts attention from the weapon to the person who wields it. Often voiced to counter gun control, this claim seeks to pardon firearms of any guilt, passing blame on to the shooters. Although people are not killed by guns per se, they are certainly killed with them as prime accomplices. In the end, gun toters are responsible for the fired shots, and it matters whose finger is on the trigger. The person behind the barrel also affects our sense of imminent peril. Each encounter with a shooter tests our acumen at judging demeanor, as if our lives truly depended on it.

This section's works showcase a motley cast of characters who have taken up arms for various reasons. Among the gunslingers are hunters, soldiers, adventurers, criminals, and even nonhumans, each equipped with fire in the hand. Guns have been called the "great equalizers," which grant everyone the same lethal power. While skill remains crucial for hitting one's target, firearms give us all a fair shot, or at least the chance to hold others at gunpoint. As enacted in westerns and detective films, whoever has the gun rules the room, with commands like "Freeze!" or "Stick 'em up!" It behooves us to attend to armed individuals, because people do kill people.

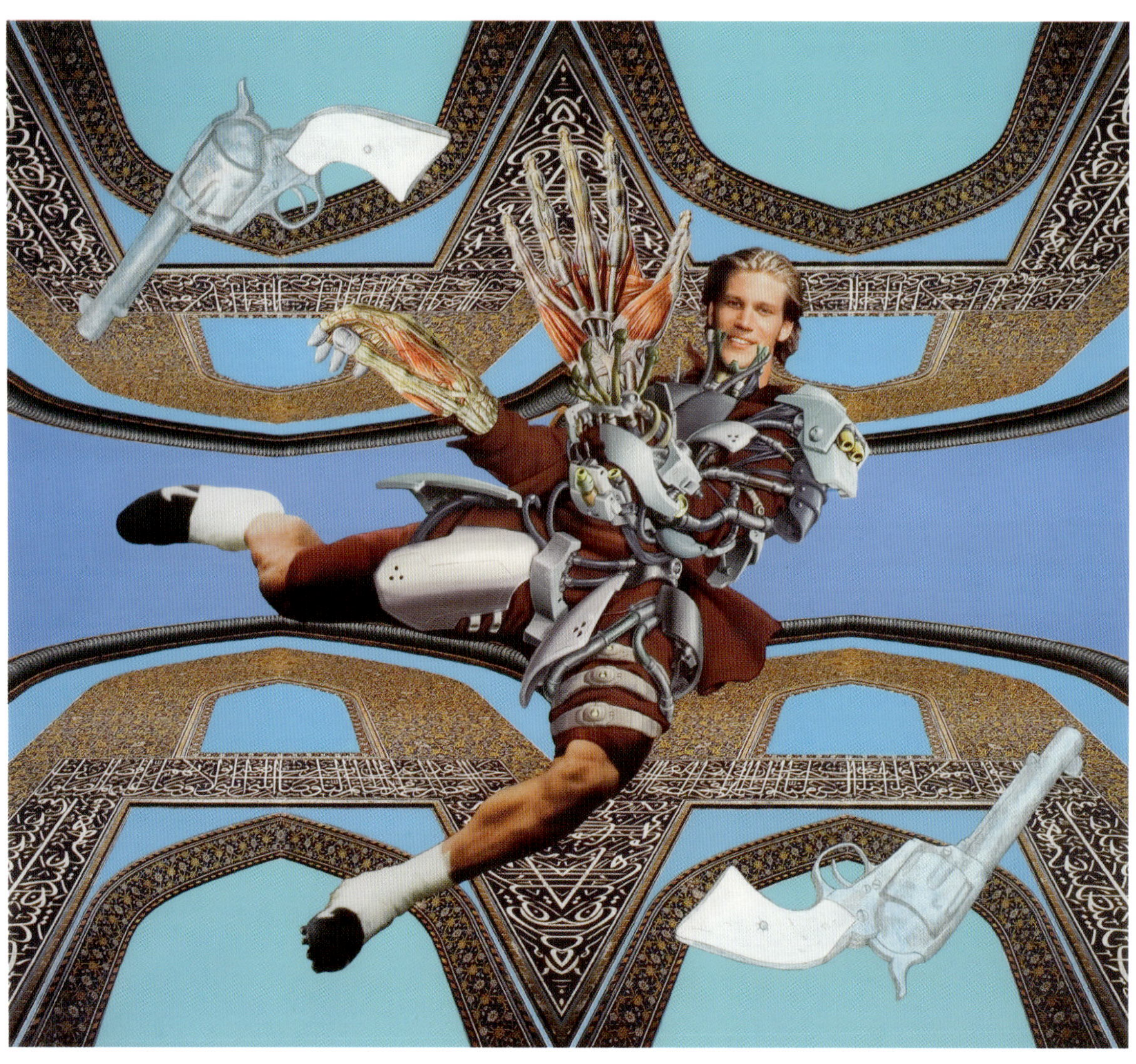

Jerry Kearns
Shooter, 2004–07
acrylic and ink on canvas
35½ × 40 in.

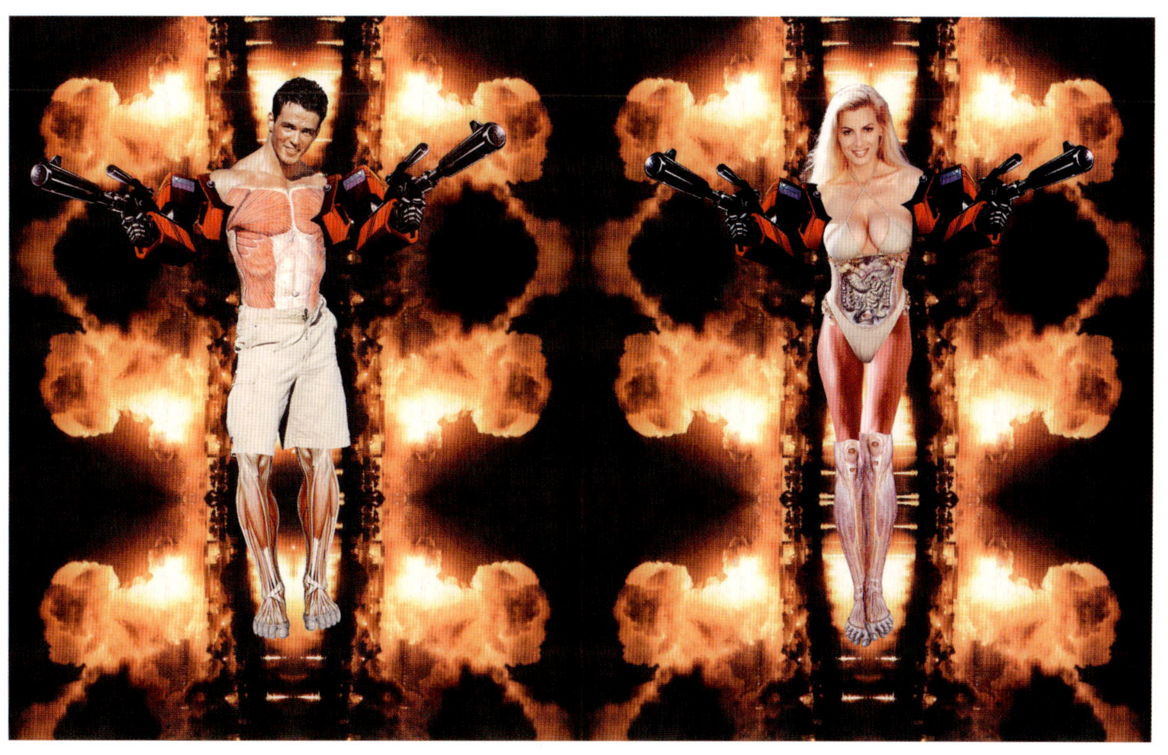

Jerry Kearns
Jack and Jill (diptych), 2004
archival ink on canvas
36 × 58 in.

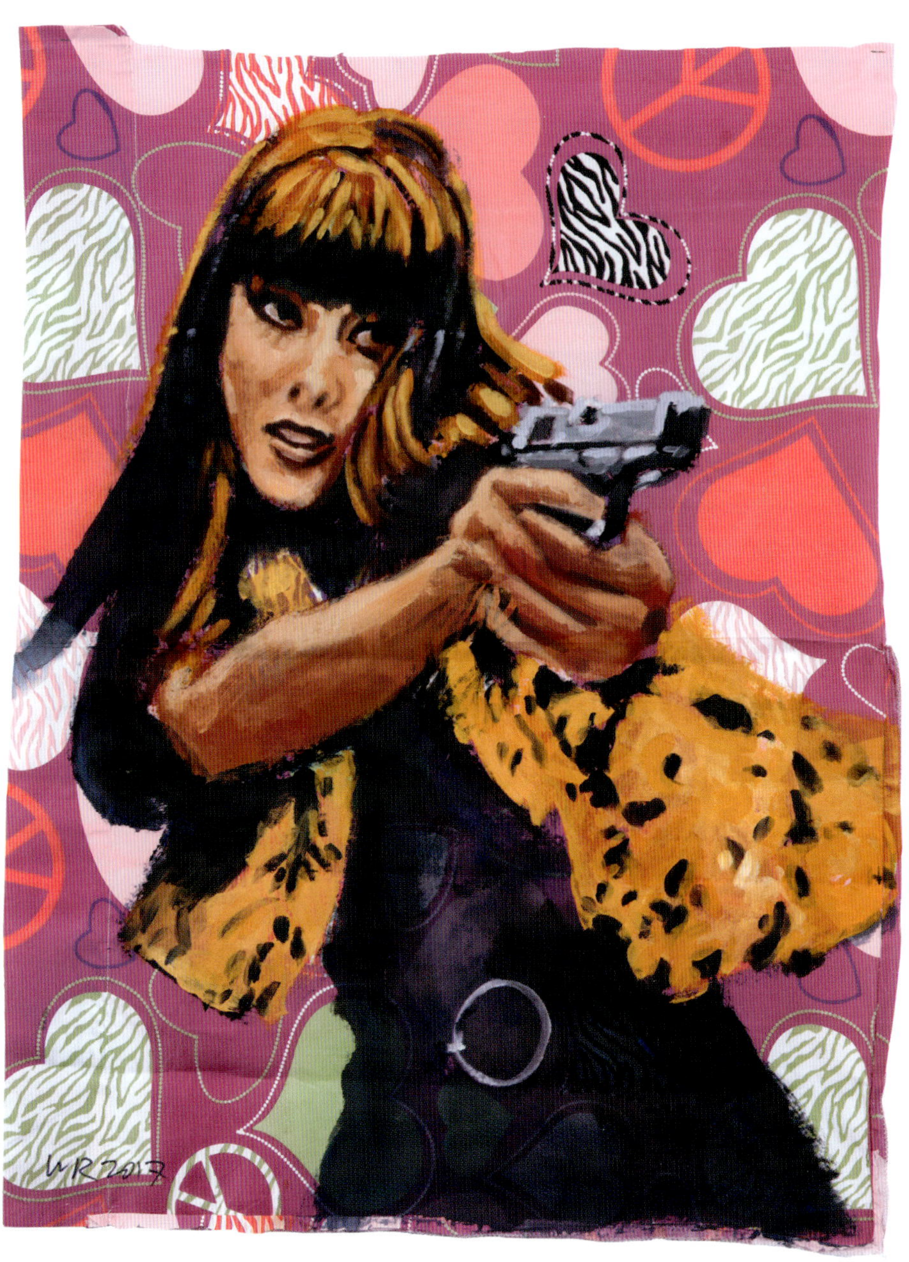

Walter Robinson
Smokin' Aces, 2017
acrylic on pillow case
40 × 31 in.

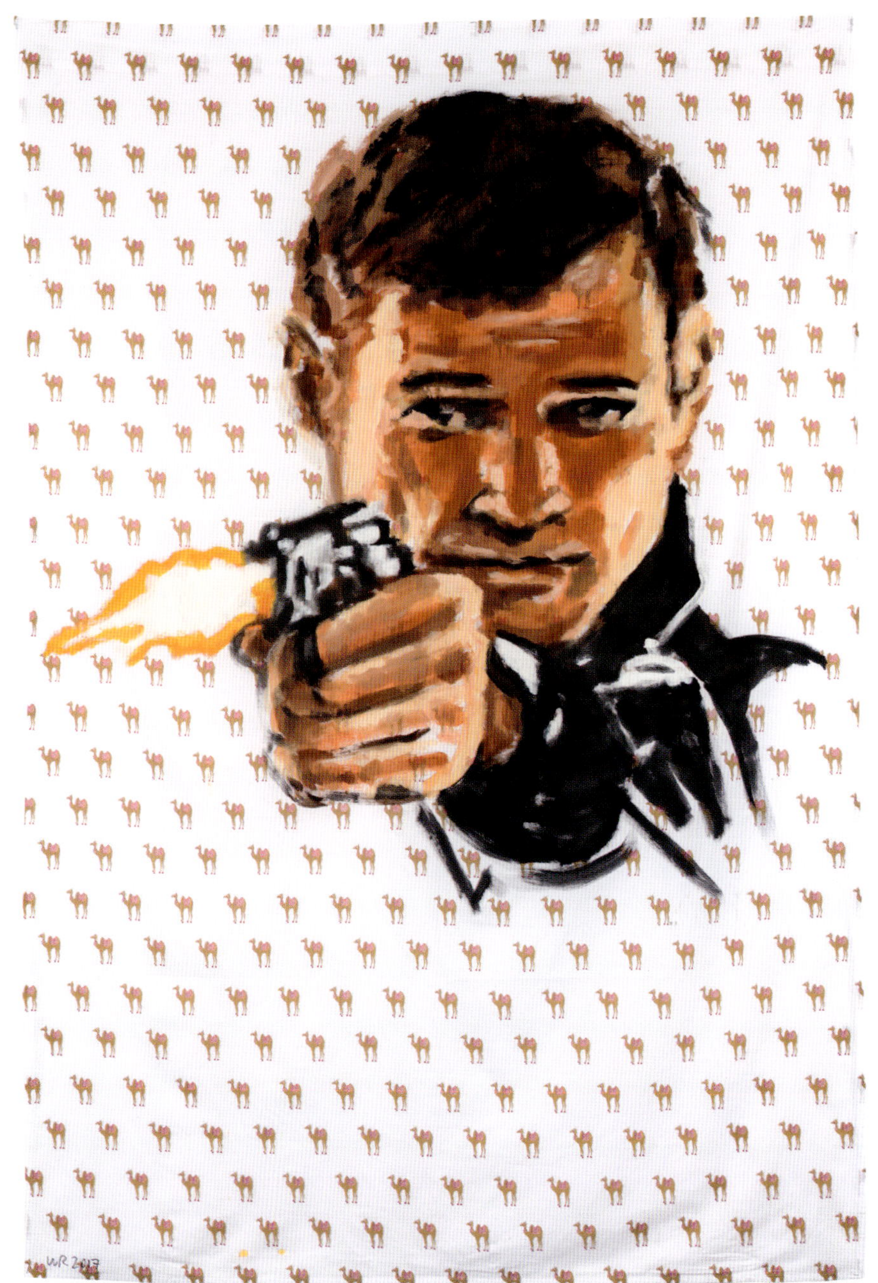

Walter Robinson
The Executioner Blood Vendetta, 2017
acrylic on bedsheet
100 × 60 in.

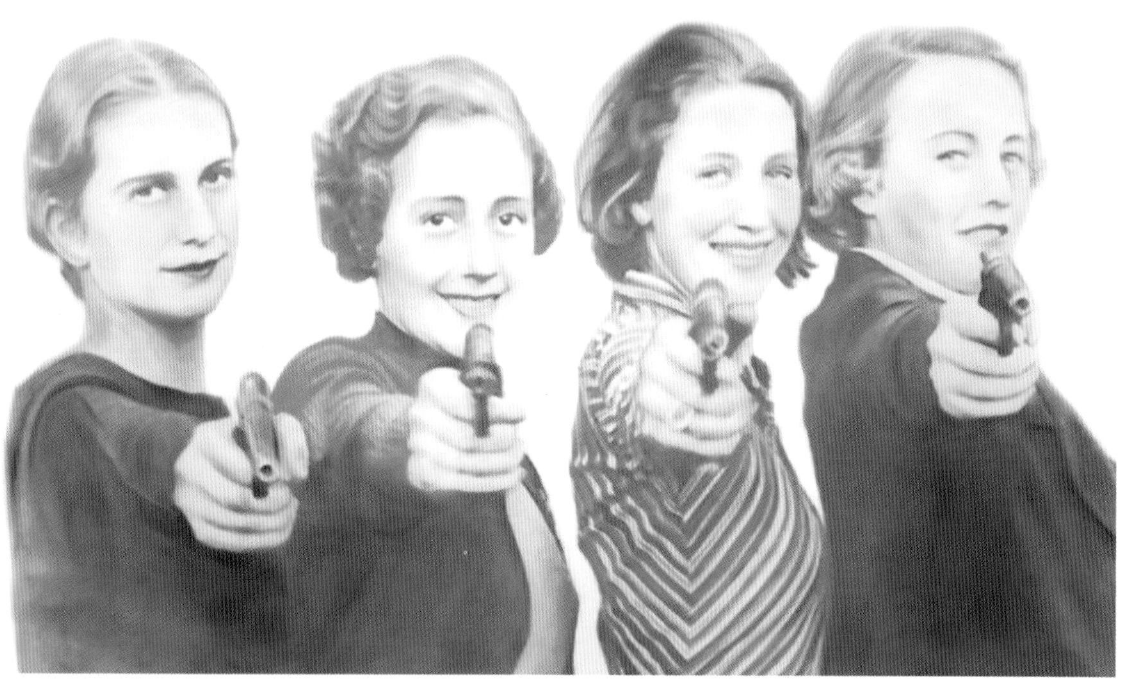

Brigitte Zieger
Women Are Different from Men 10, 2010
drawing with eye shadow and glitter
45¼ × 32 in.

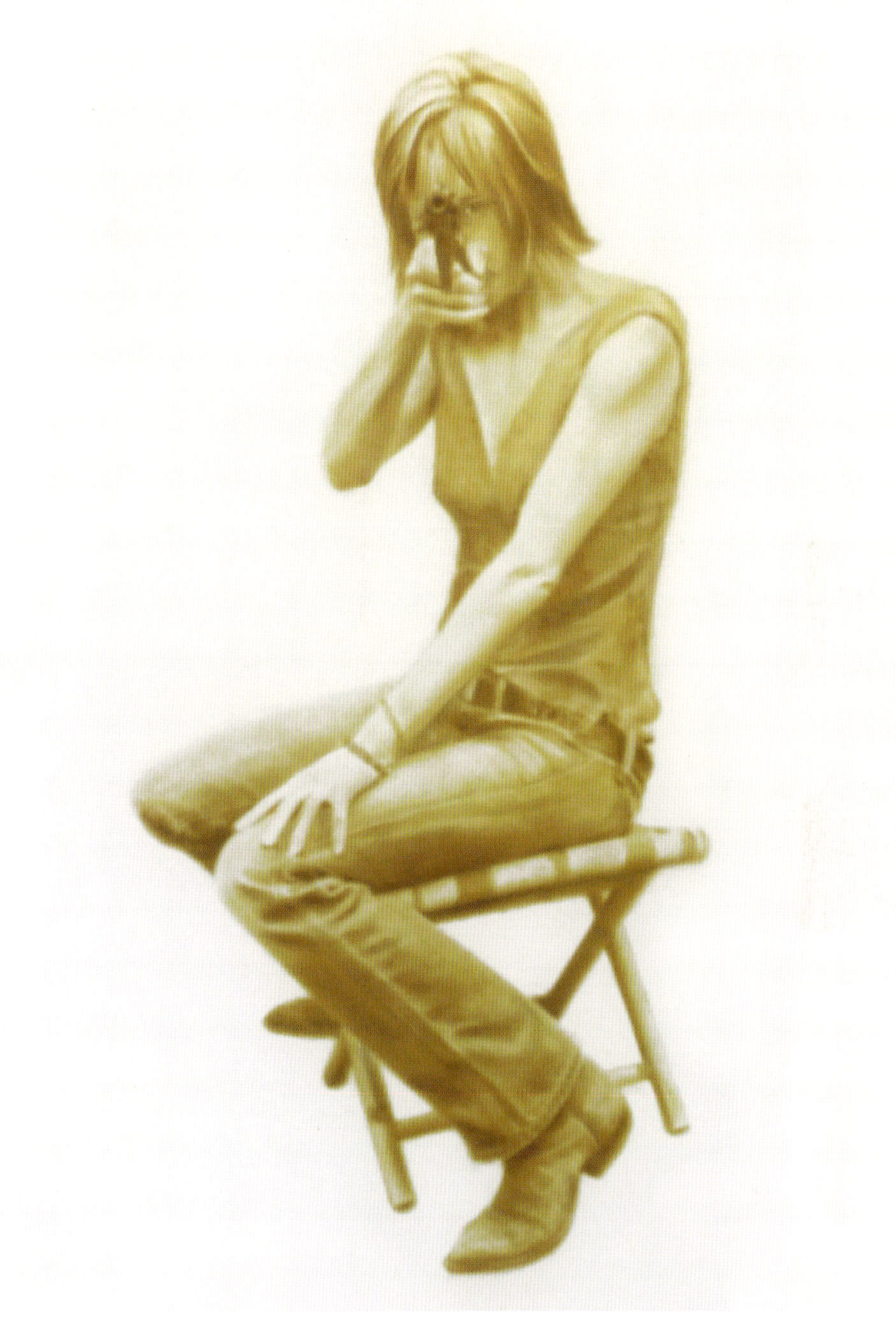

Brigitte Zieger
Women Are Different from Men 16, 2014
drawing with eye shadow and glitter
45¼ × 72½ in.
© Brigitte Zieger

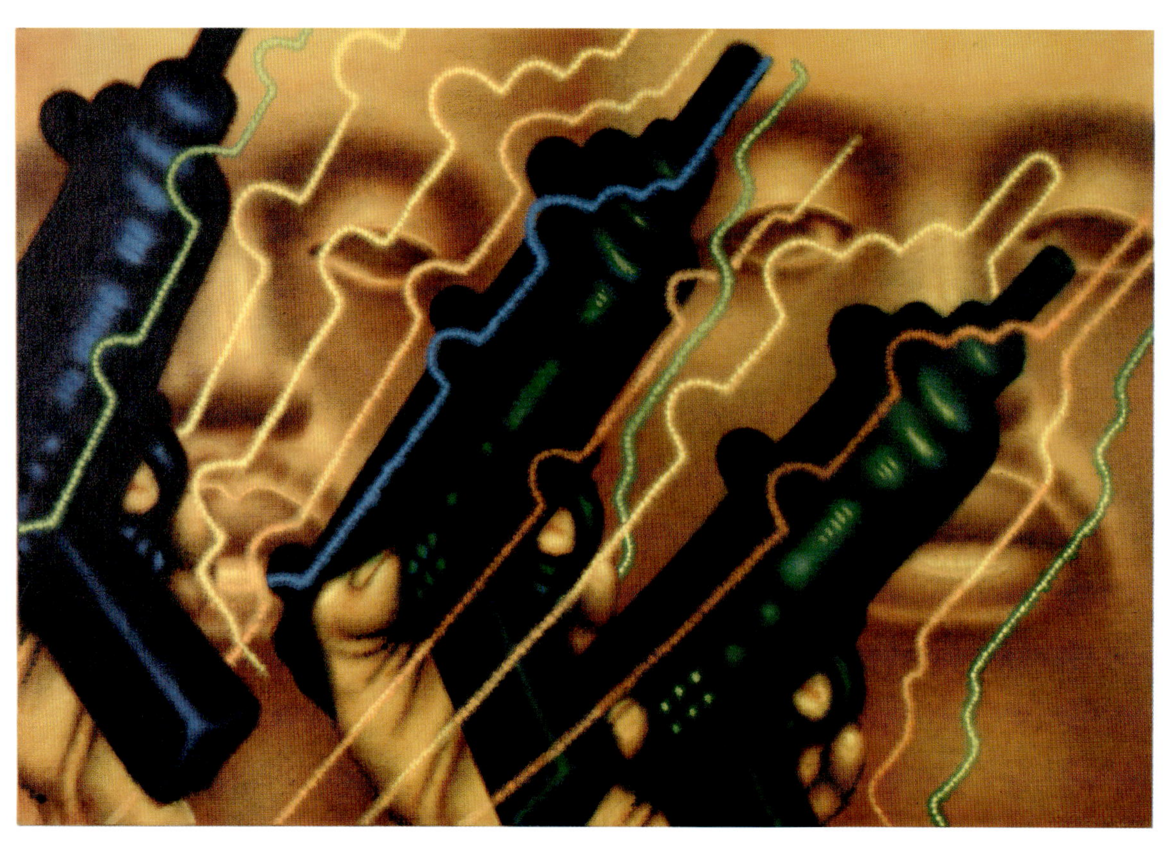

Ed Paschke
Untitled (Uzis), 2004
oil on linen
24 × 36 in.

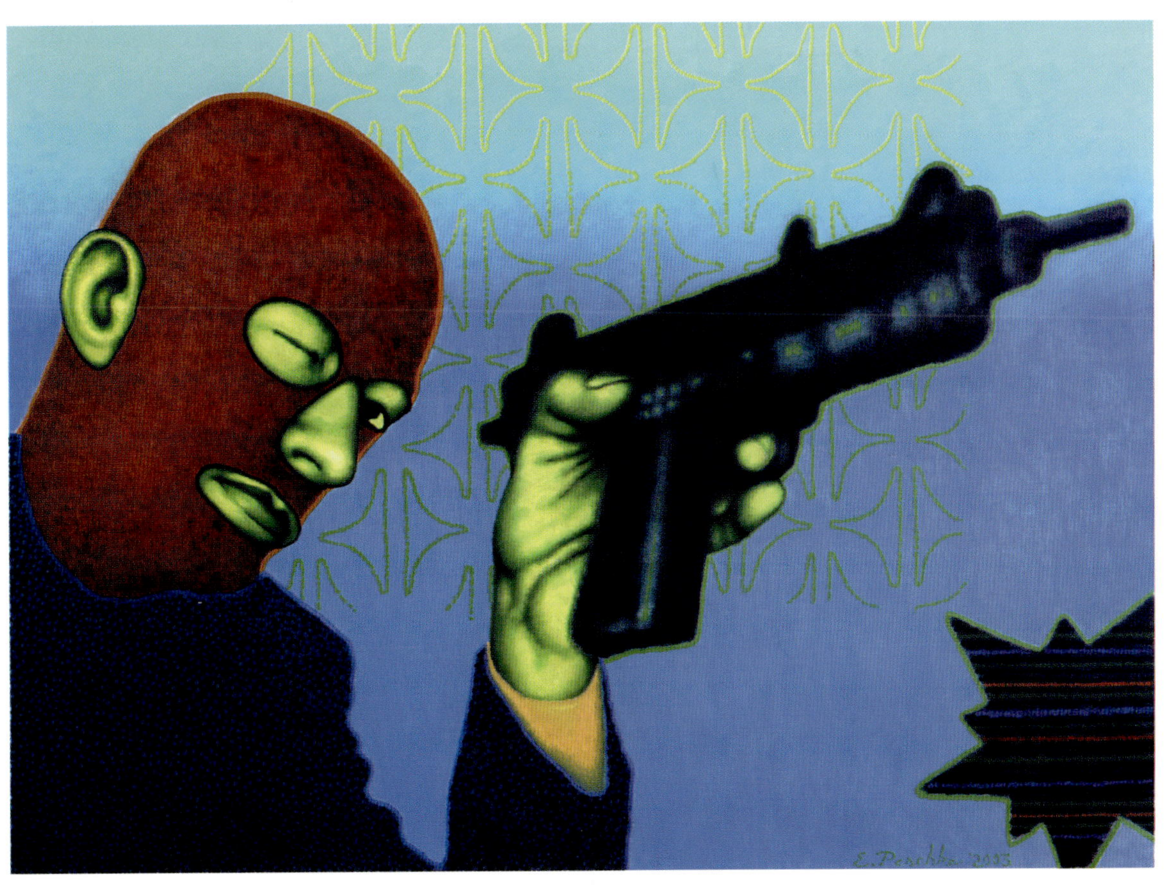

Ed Paschke
Night Sweat, 2003
oil on linen
36 × 50 in.

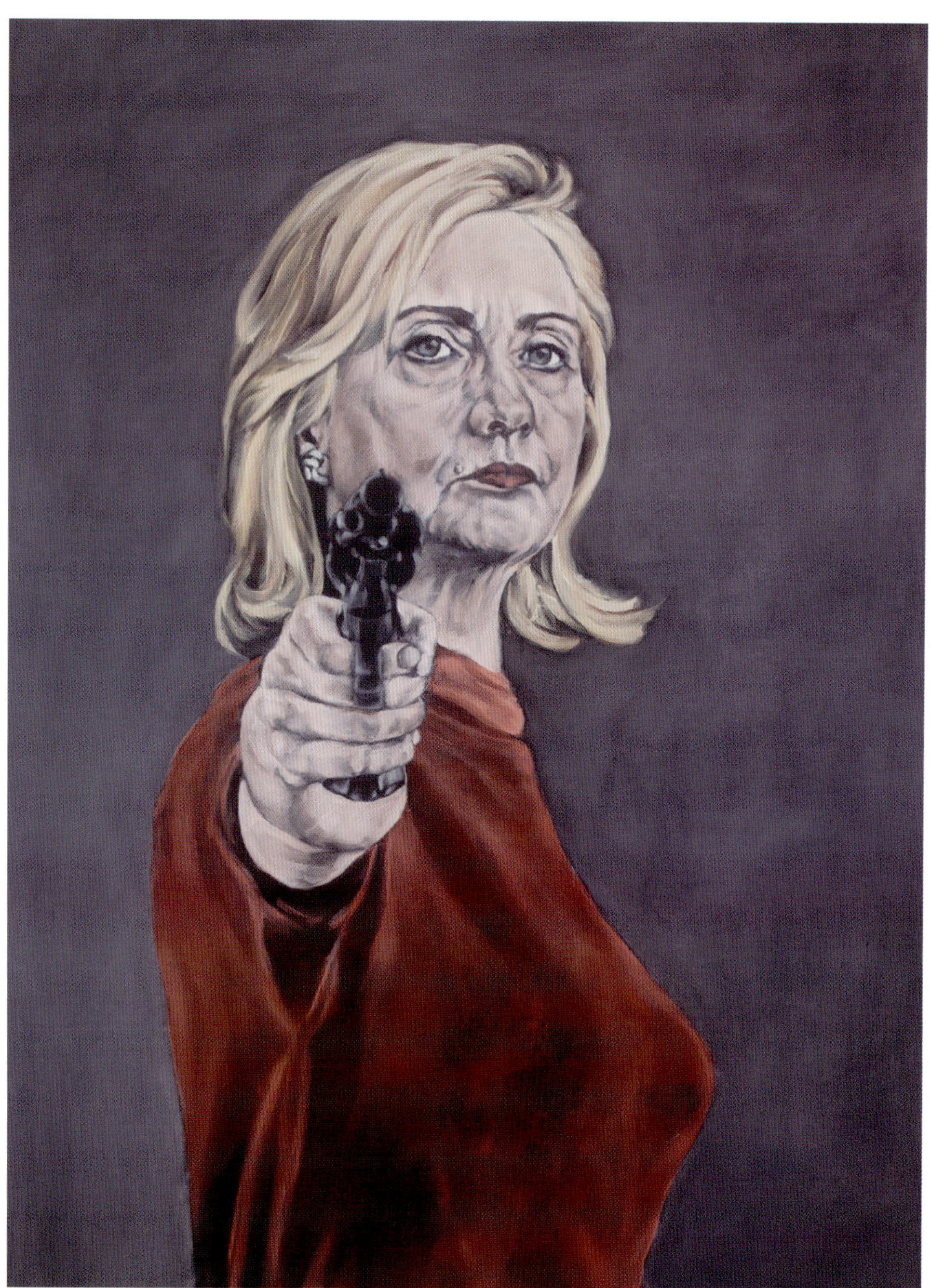

Sarah Sole
Red Gun, 2014
acrylic on canvas
37 × 28 in.
Collection of Ike Sugg and Camille Santry, San Miguel de Allende, Mexico

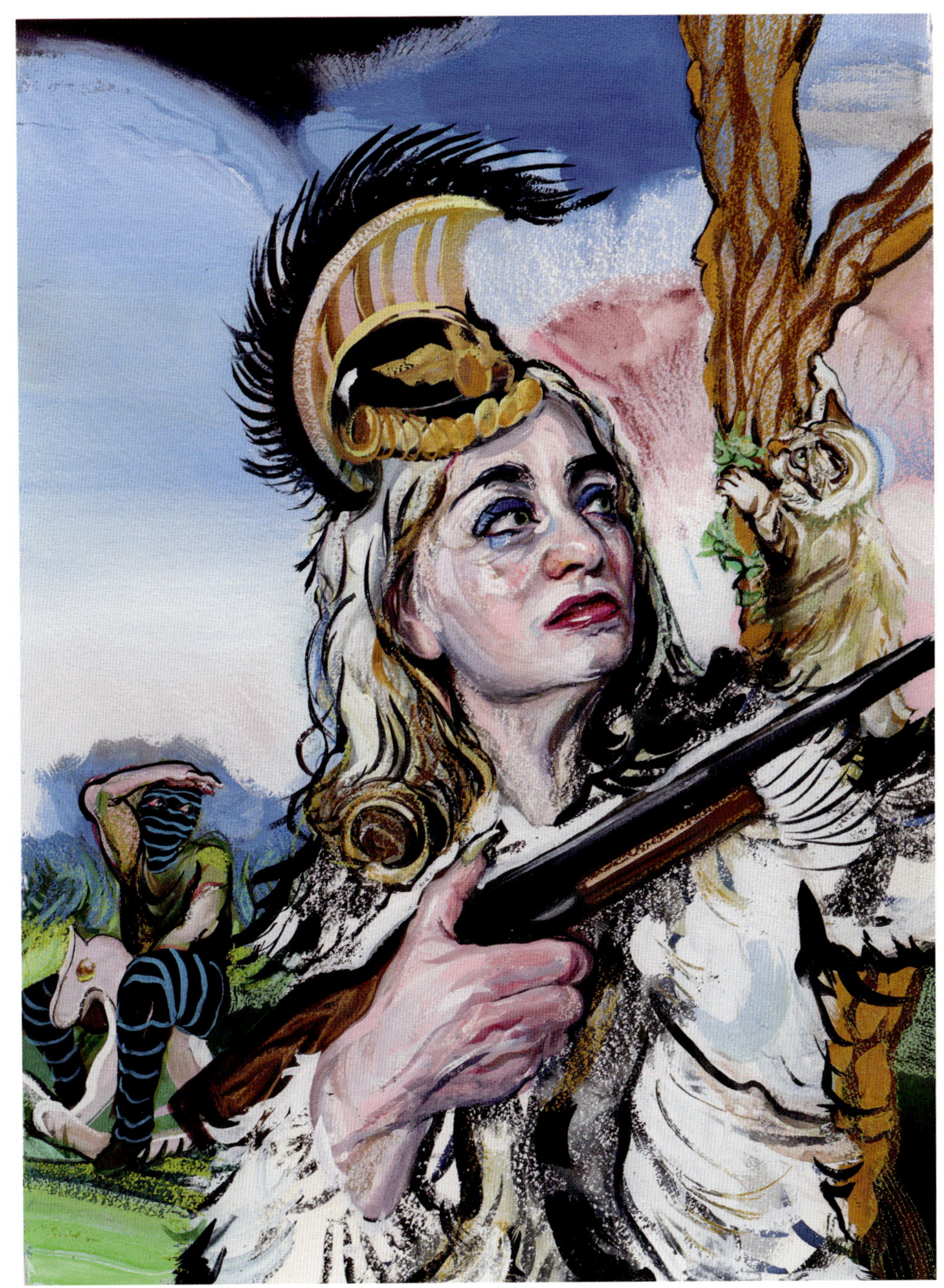

Natalie Frank
The White Cat II, 2019–20
gouache and chalk pastel on paper
34¼ × 26½ × 2 in.
Photo: Farzad Orwang

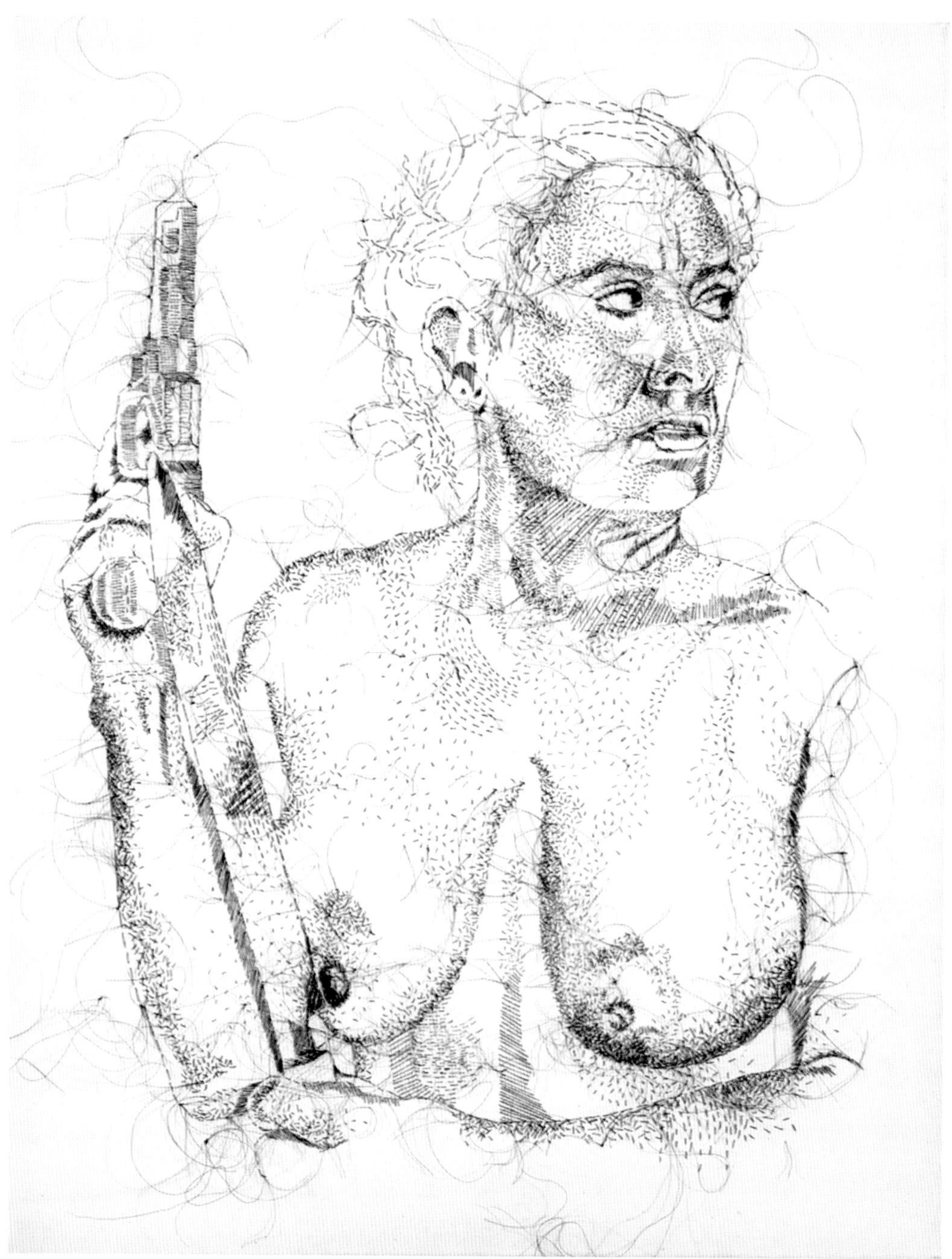

Rosemary Meza-DesPlas
Cry, Die, or Just Make Pies, from Chicks with Guns series, 2013
hand-sewn human hair on canvas
15 × 13 in.
Photo: Harrison Evans

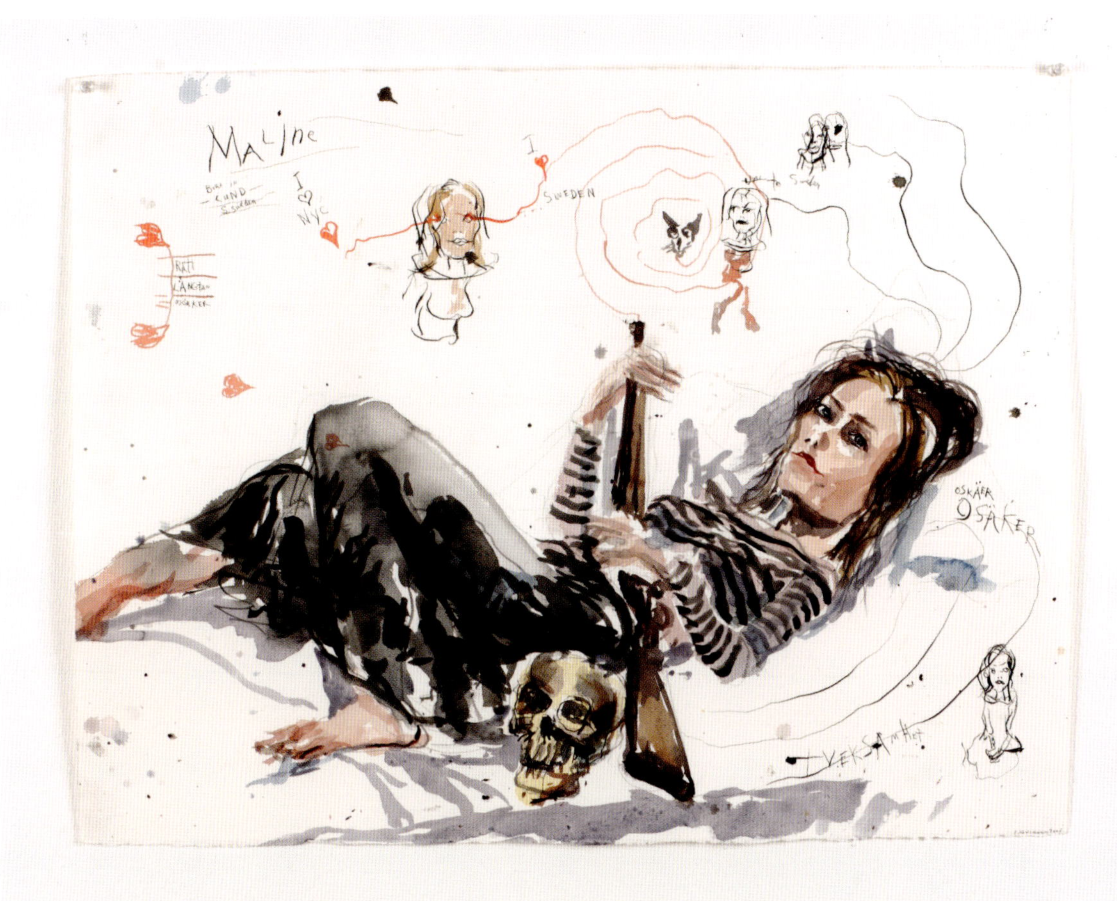

Brad Kahlhamer
Maline, from Urban Prairie Girls series, 2005
watercolor and ink on paper
22 × 29½ in.

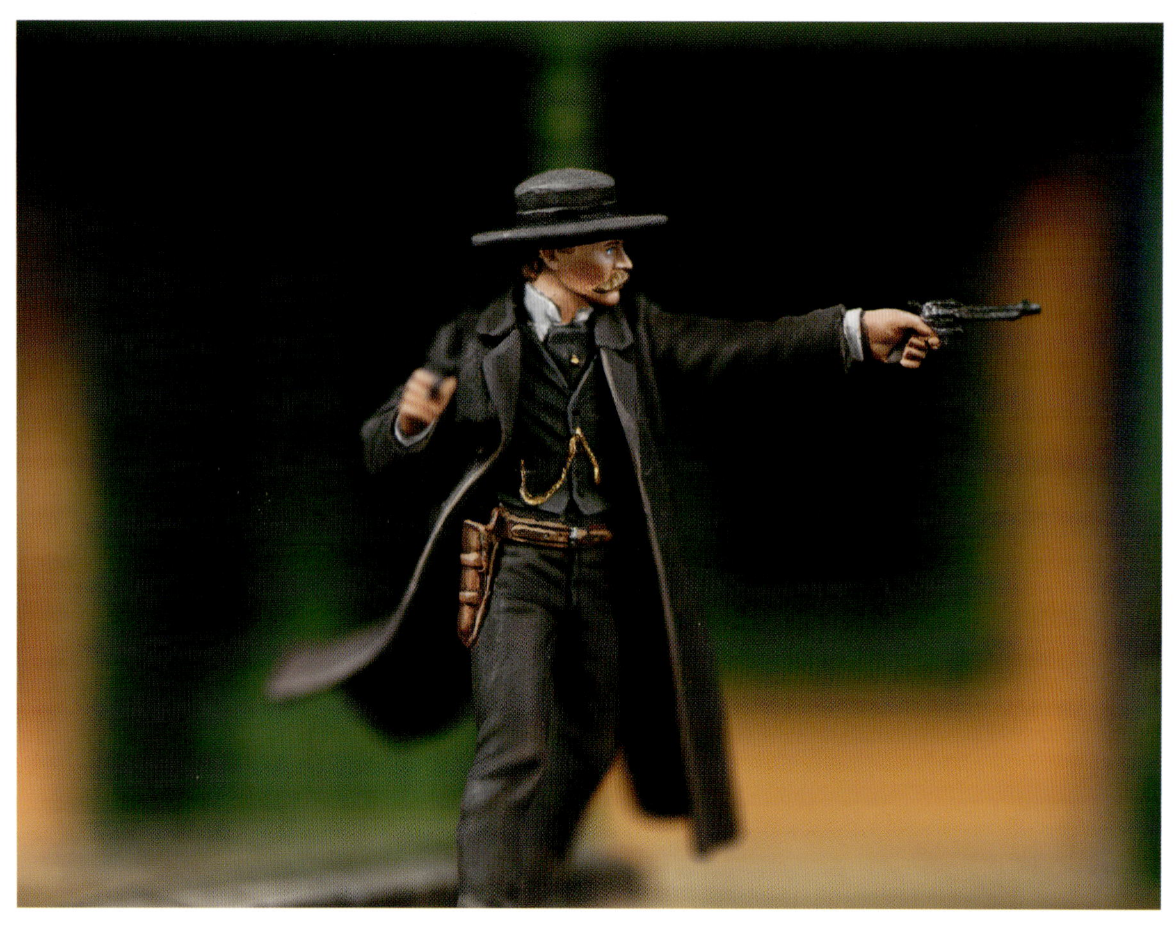

David Levinthal
Untitled, from the History series, 2018
archival pigment print
17 × 22 in.
Photo courtesy of David Levinthal

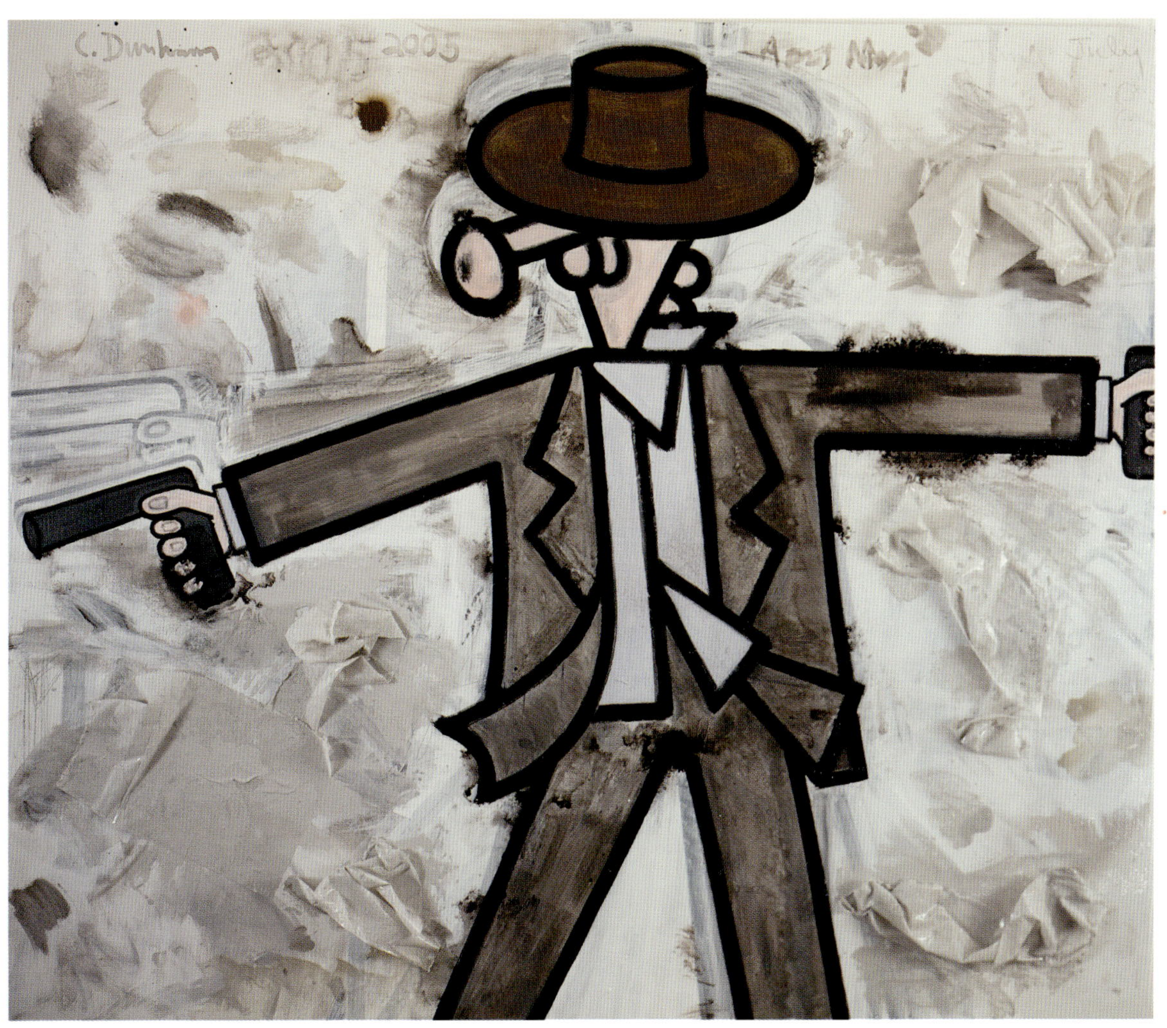

Carroll Dunham
Deadspace (Garbage), 2005
acrylic and polystyrene on canvas
72 × 84 in.

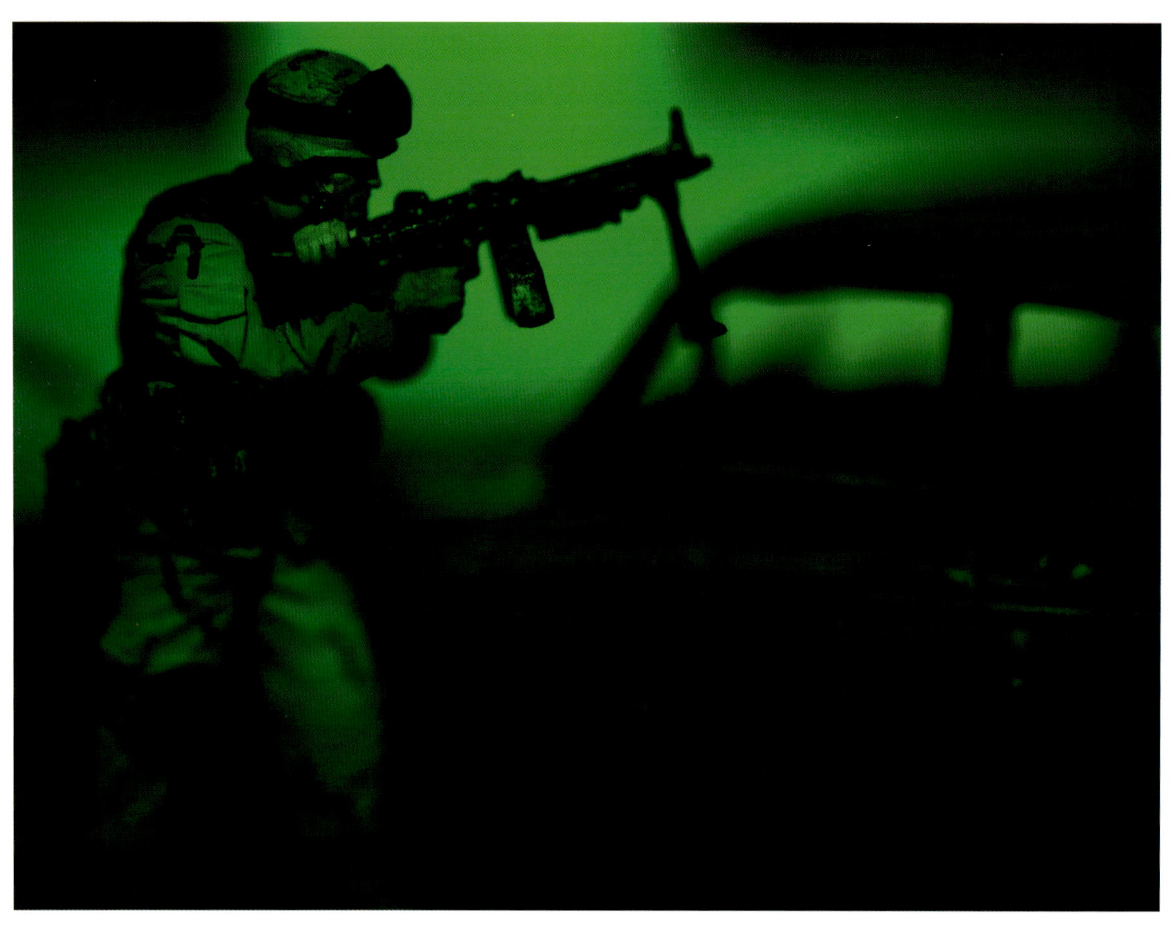

David Levinthal
Untitled, from I.E.D. series, 2018
archival pigment print on polyester film
42½ × 55 in.
Photo courtesy of David Levinthal

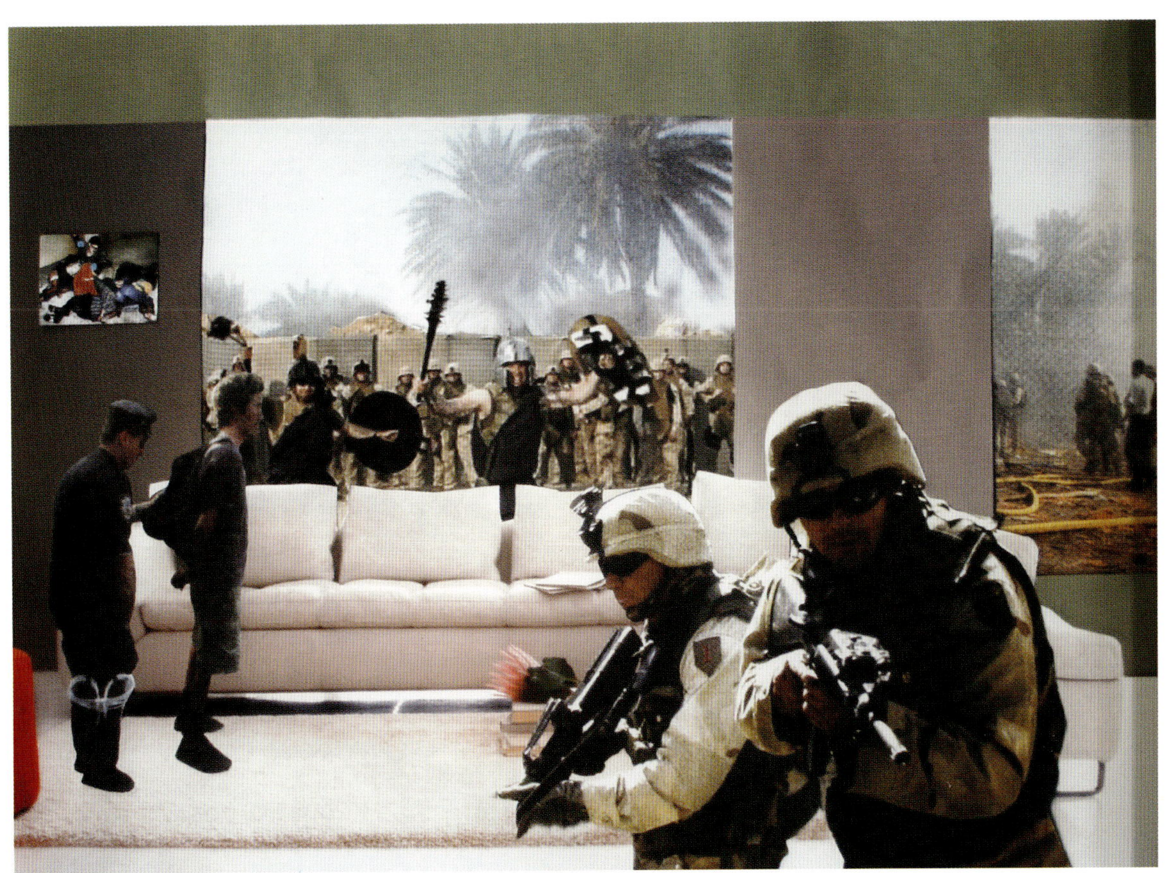

Martha Rosler
Gladiators, from House Beautiful: Bringing the War Home, New Series, 2004
photomontage
20 × 24 in.
© Martha Rosler
Courtesy of the artist and Mitchell-Innes & Nash, New York

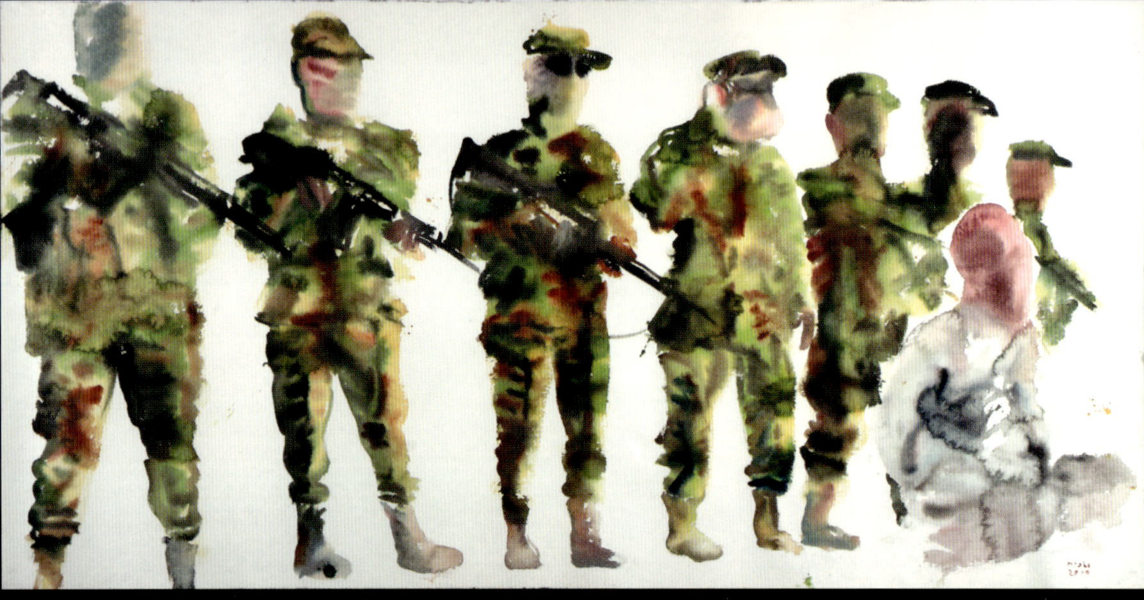

Tawan Wattuya
Isis, 2019
watercolor on paper
38½ × 78¾ in.

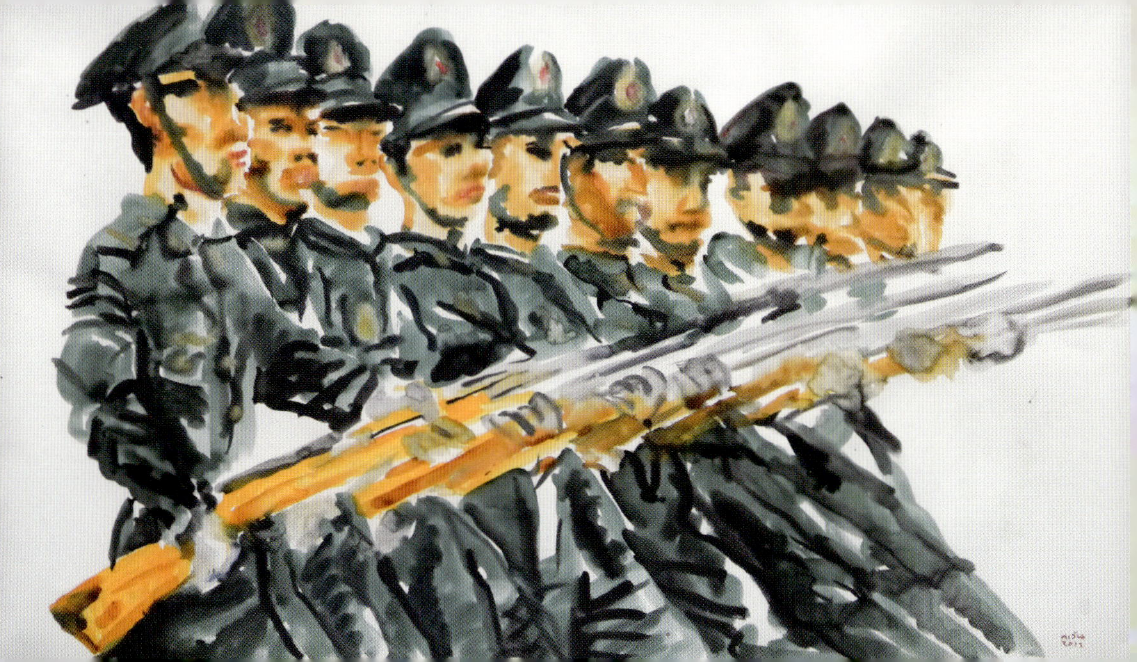

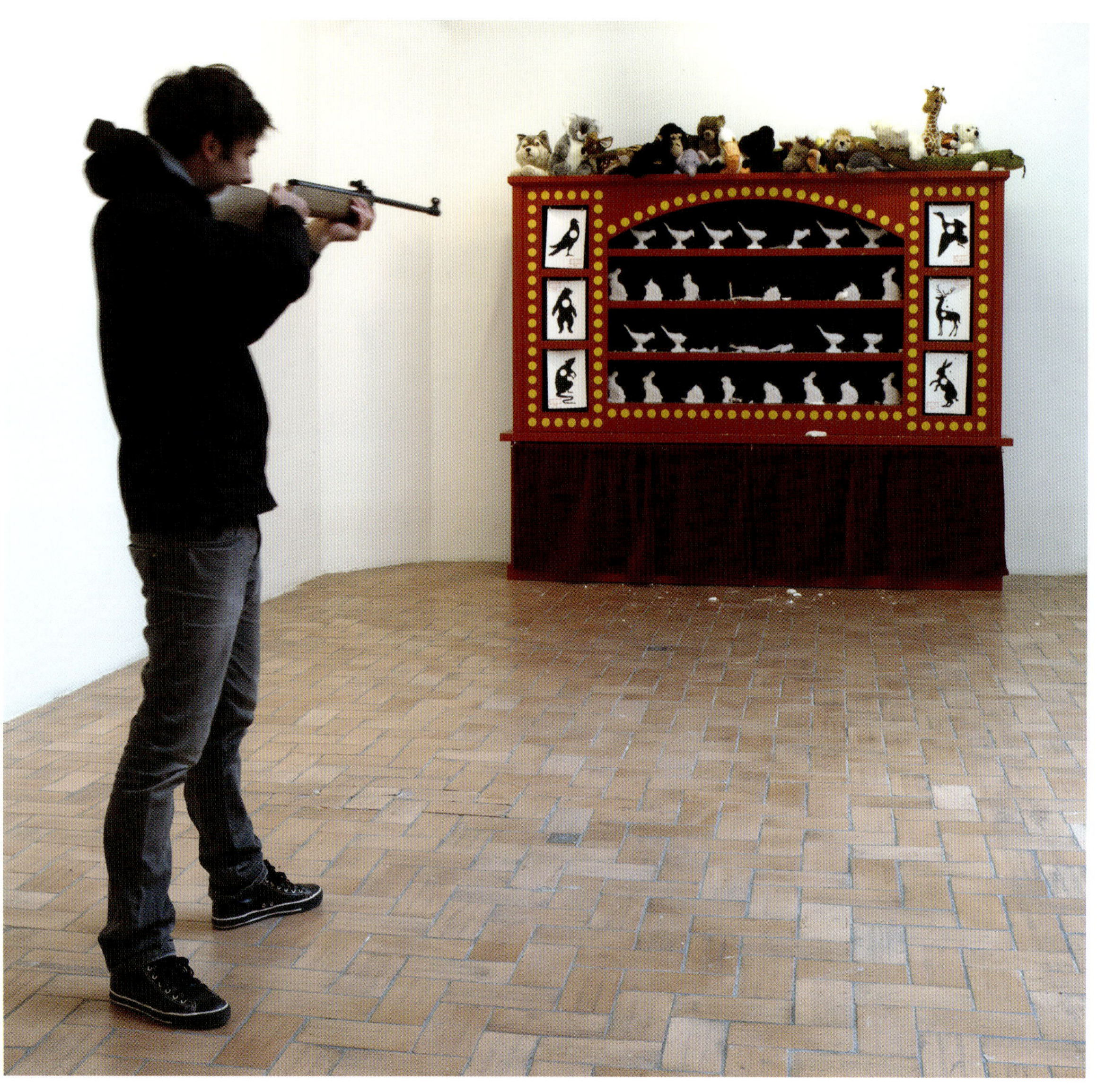

Mark Dion
The Shooting Gallery, 2010
wood cabinet, plush toys, plaster targets (birds and rabbits), velvet curtain, paper targets, air rifle
94½ × 62¼ × 14½ in.
Courtesy of the artist and In Situ-Fabienne Leclerc, Paris
Photo: Marc Domage

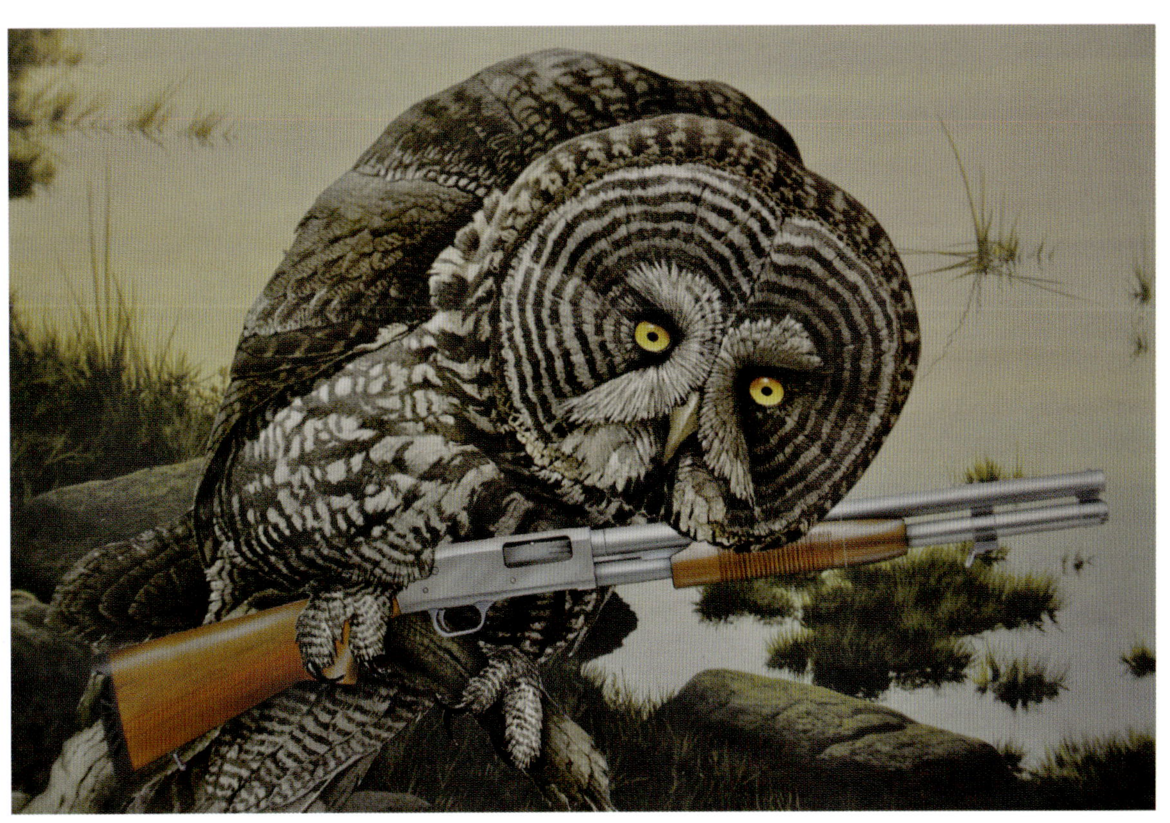

Michael Oatman
Who Me? (Mossberg Shotgun), from the Pornithology series, 2014
collage on paper
10 × 13 in.
Collection of Paul de Jong

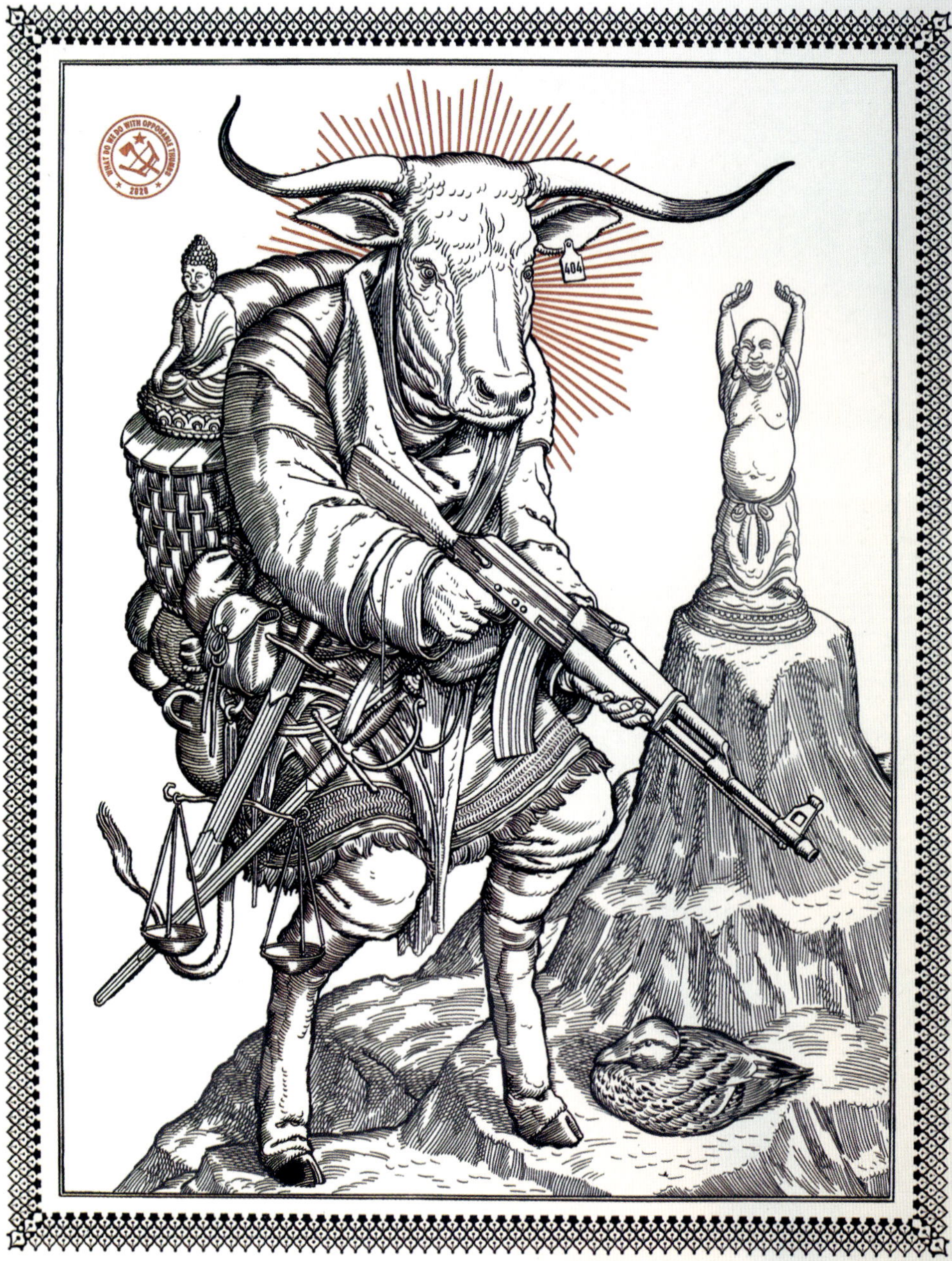

Ravi Zupa
What Do We Do with Opposable Thumbs?, 2020
screenprint and ink on paper
18 × 24 in.

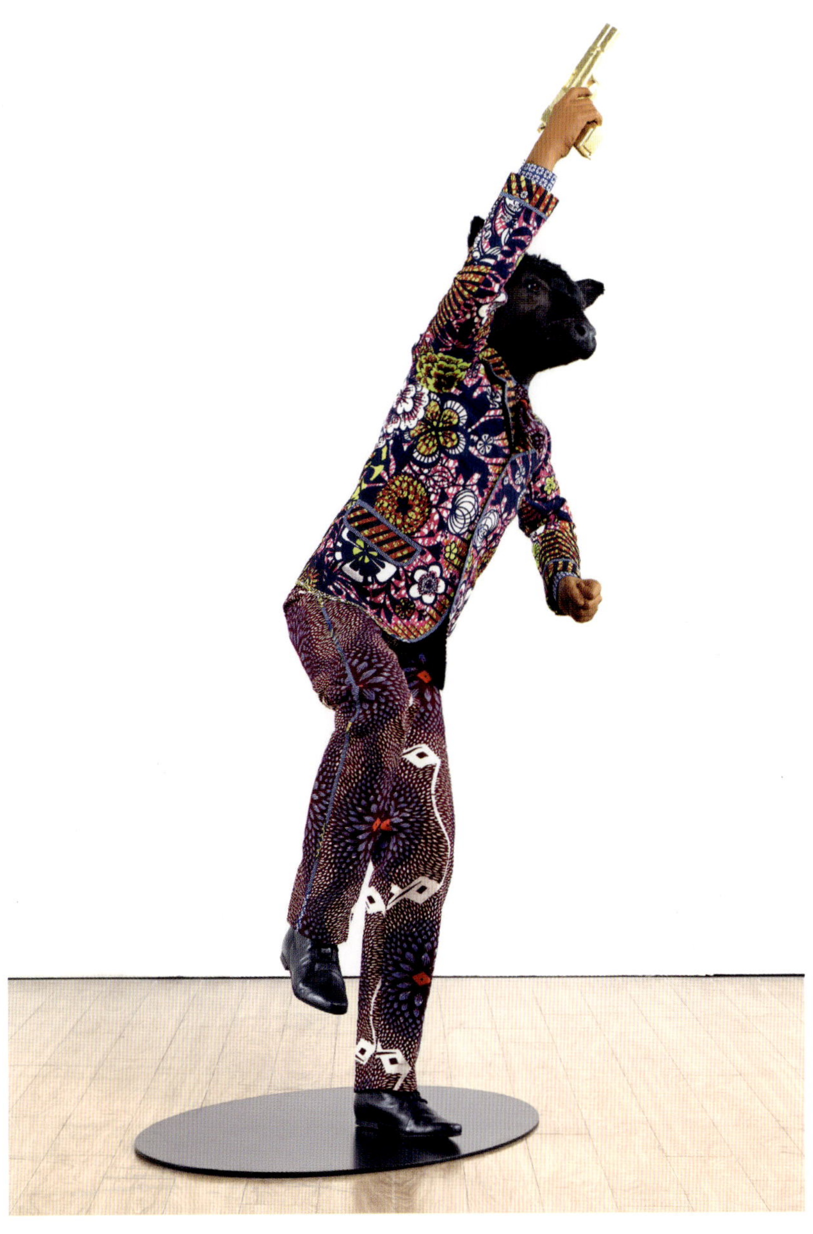

Yinka Shonibare
Revolution Kid (Calf), 2012
mannequin, dutch wax printed cotton, fiberglass, leather, taxidermy calf head, Blackberry, and 24k gold-gilded gun
65 × 25 × 21 in.

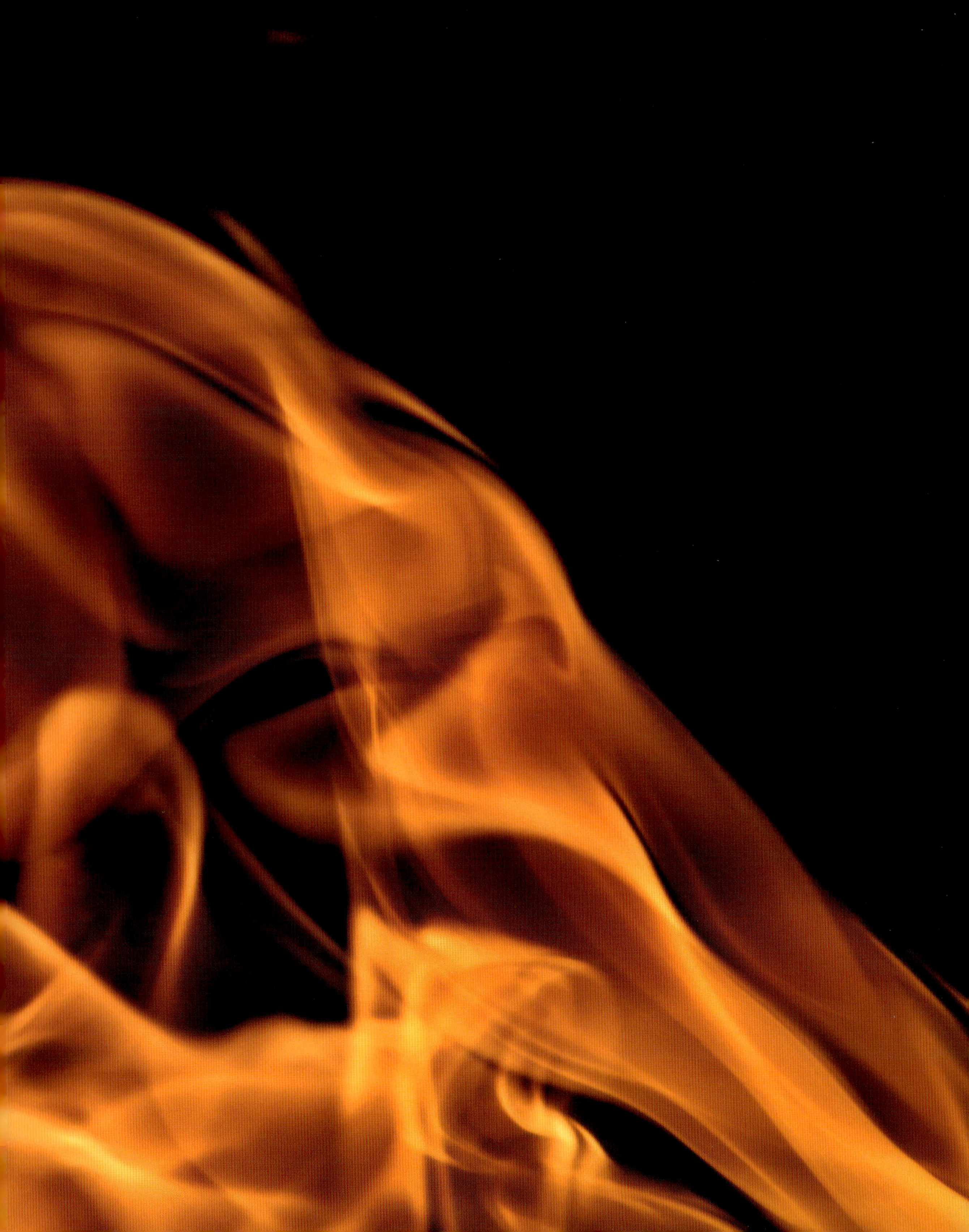

PLAYING WITH FIRE

Images of children with firearms produce a clash of association; between innocence and violence, wonder and horror, youth and death. While children have long used guns for hunting and sport, it is still unnerving to see kids packing heat, especially as depicted by many of these artists, who show tender young shooters as hardened criminals, more squint-eyed than wide-eyed. Part of the unease comes from placing an undeveloped mind behind such a deadly device. The sheer quantity of art addressing minors with firearms highlights how ubiquitous guns have become in our lives, from the cradle to the grave. It is hard to escape the presence of guns, as they permeate playrooms, classrooms, and popular culture.

While toy guns are designed for "make-believe," these colorful arms mingle menace with imaginative fun. Research does not prove that using toy weapons leads to later violence, and the vast majority of kids who play at shooting don't harm others with real guns as adults. Nonetheless, the line between pretend and actual grows thinner when firearms are accessible to minors. In the United States, more than a million children live with unlocked guns in their homes, and most accidental shooting deaths of youth occur while playing with a gun in the absence of parents. As witnessed time and again, a child with a firearm can be a recipe for tragedy.

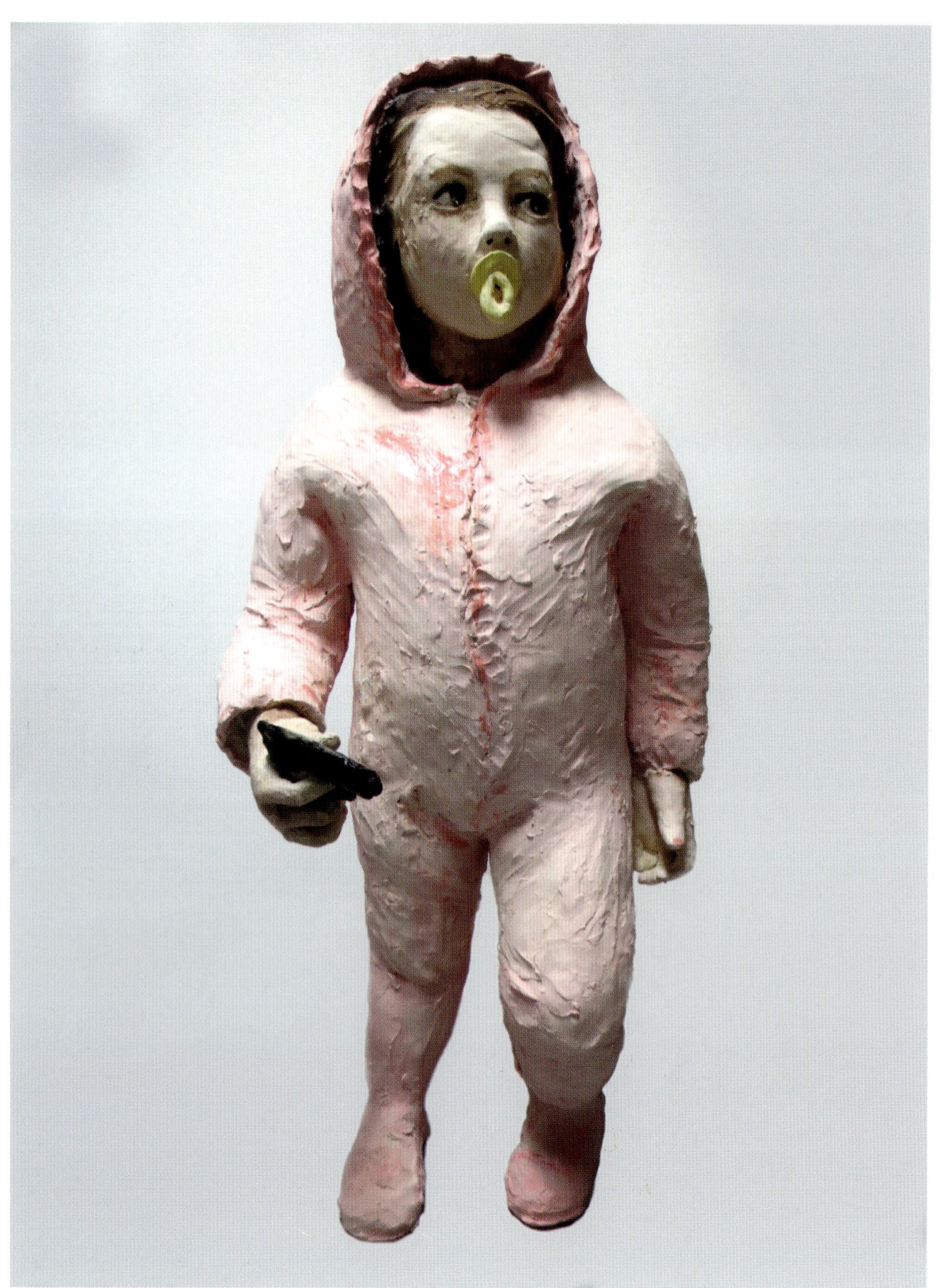

Claudia Alvarez
El Chupon II, 2014
glazed stoneware
35 × 17 × 14½ in.
Photo: Claudia Alvarez

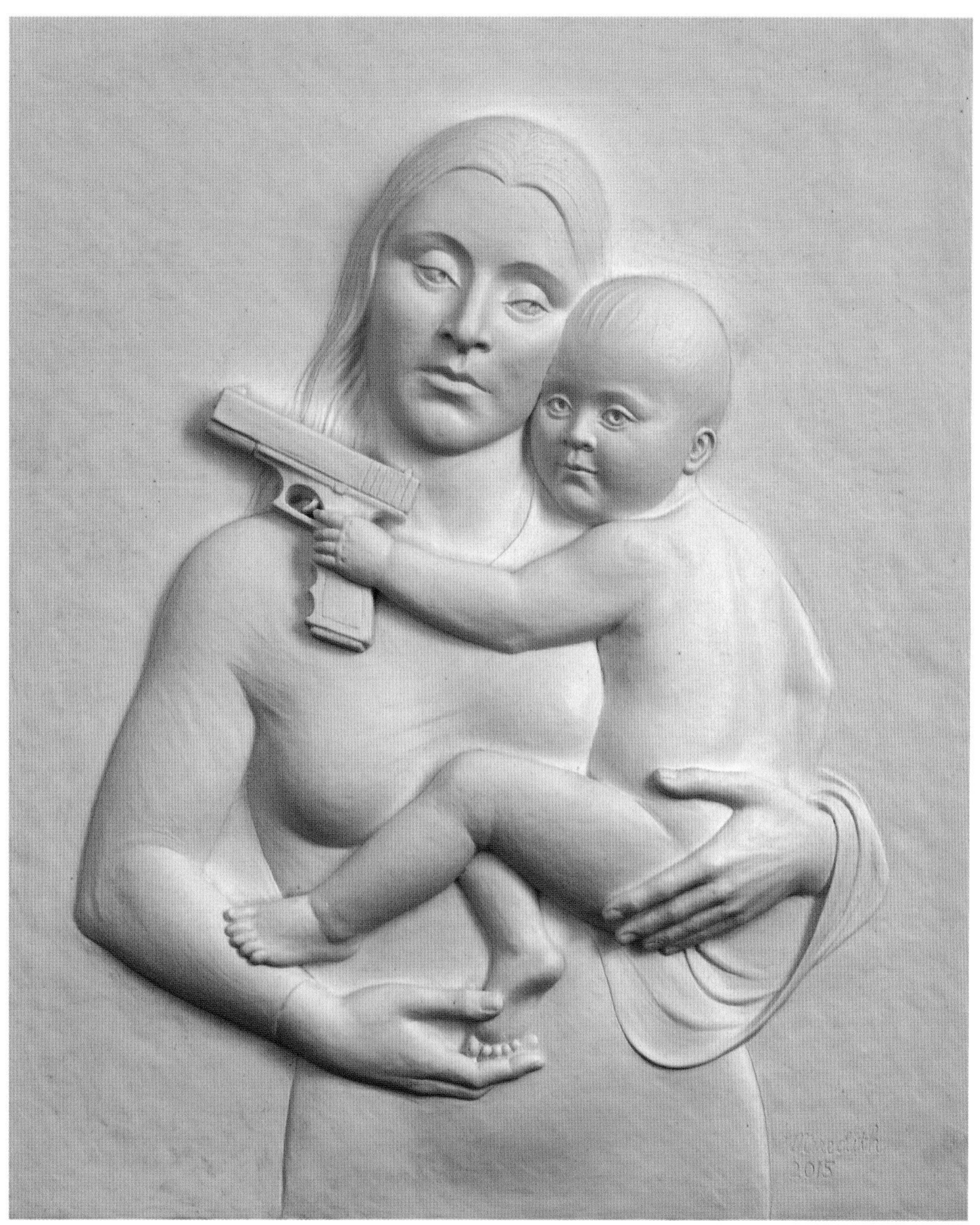

Meredith Bergmann
Mother and Child with a Glock, 2015
bonded marble
22 × 18 × 2 in.
Photo: Michael Bergmann

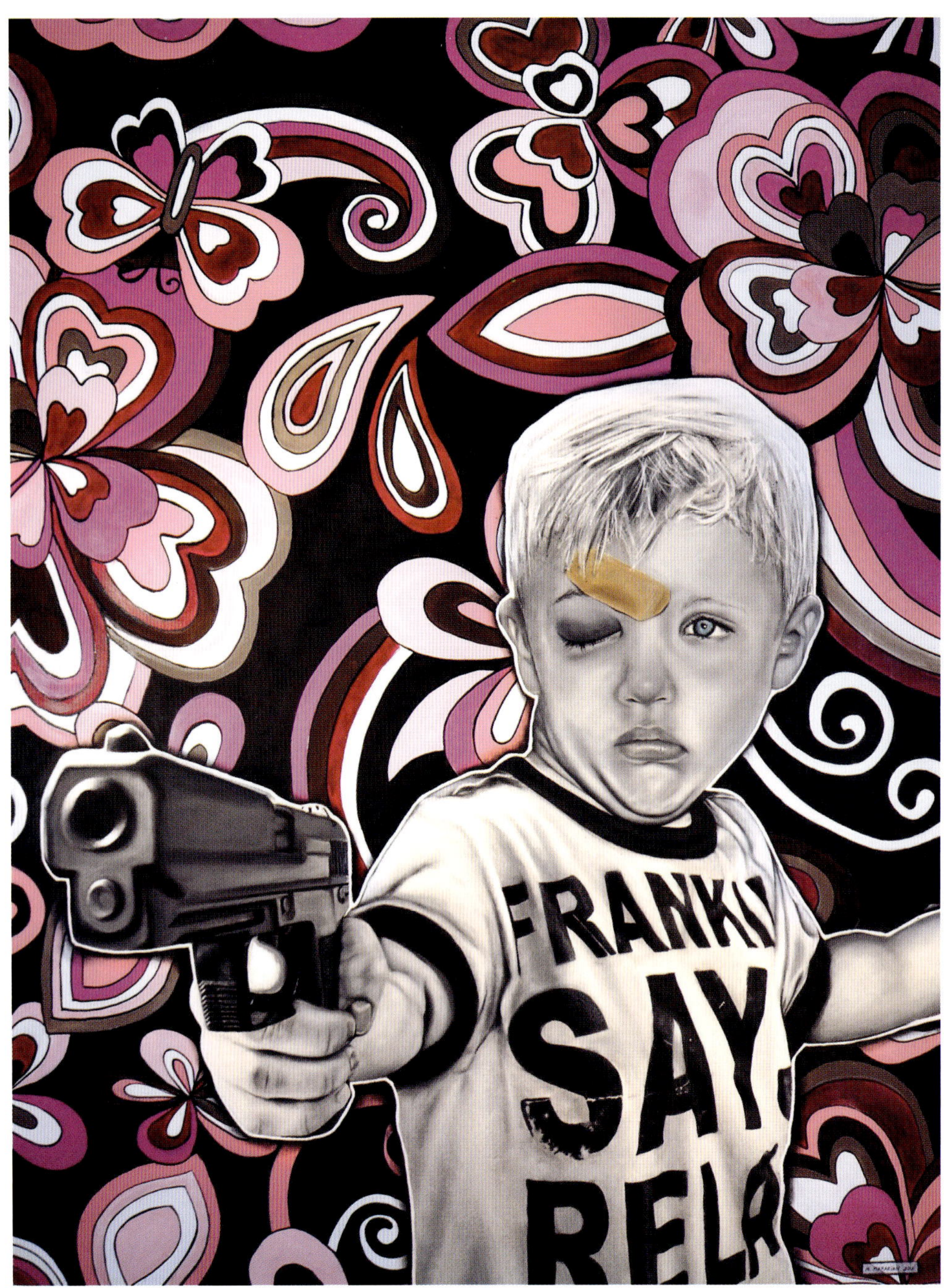

Michael Mararian
Dawn of the Bullied, 2013
acrylic on paper
40 × 60 in.

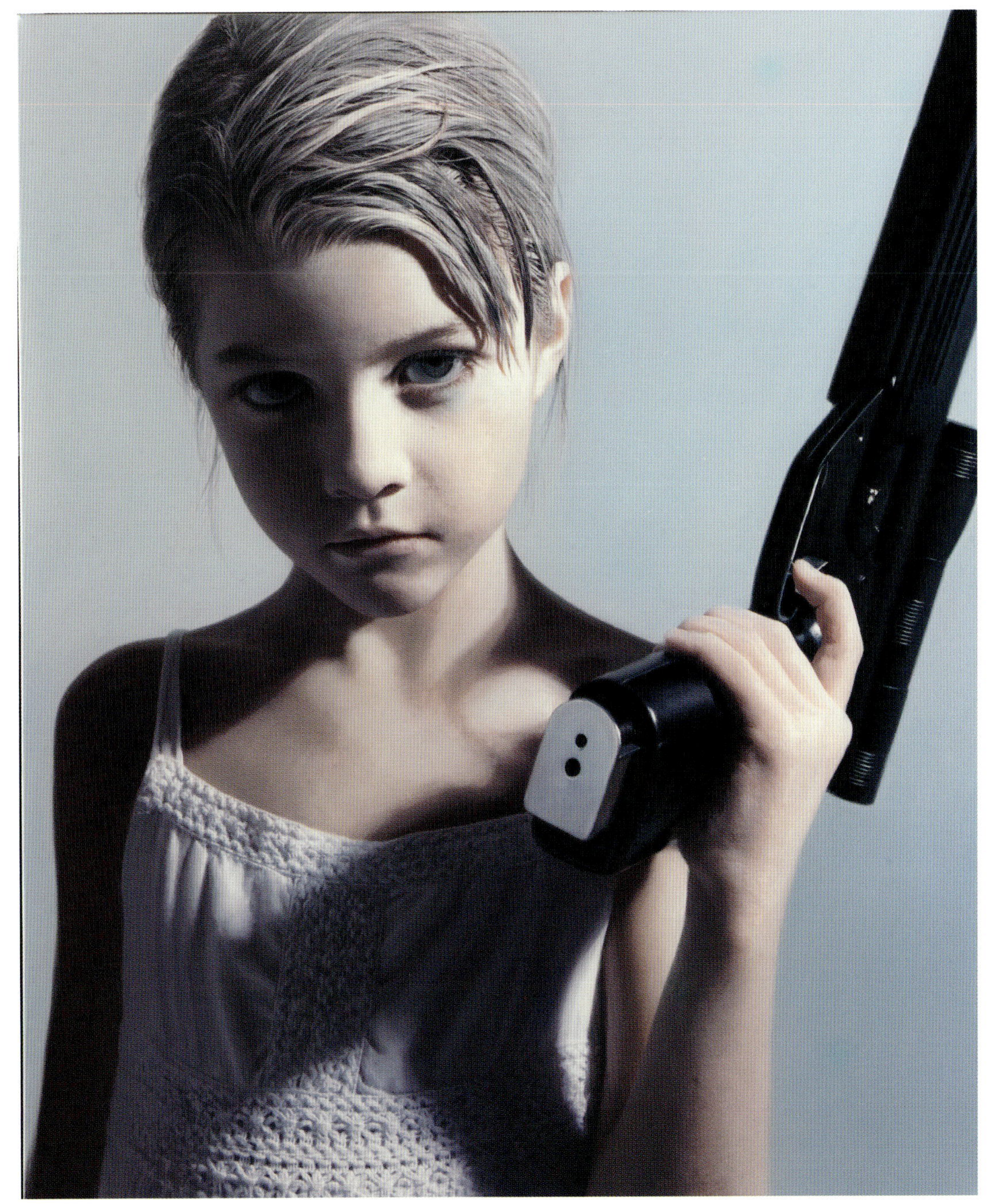

Gottfried Helnwein
Jana, 2011
oil and acrylic on canvas
48 × 39¾ in.

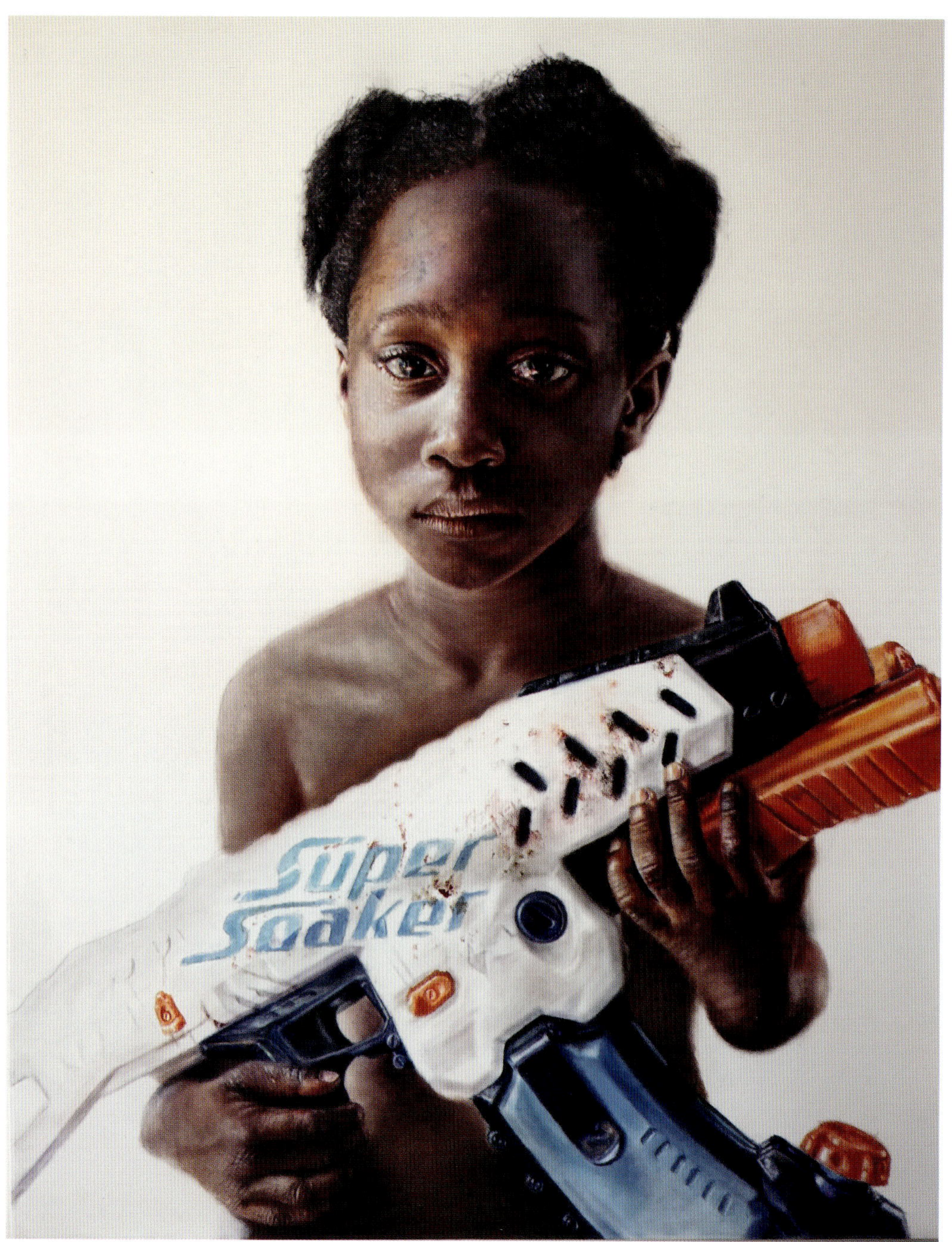

Johan Andersson
Super Soaker from Toy Guns series, 2016
oil on canvas
56 × 48 in.
Photo: Johan Andersson

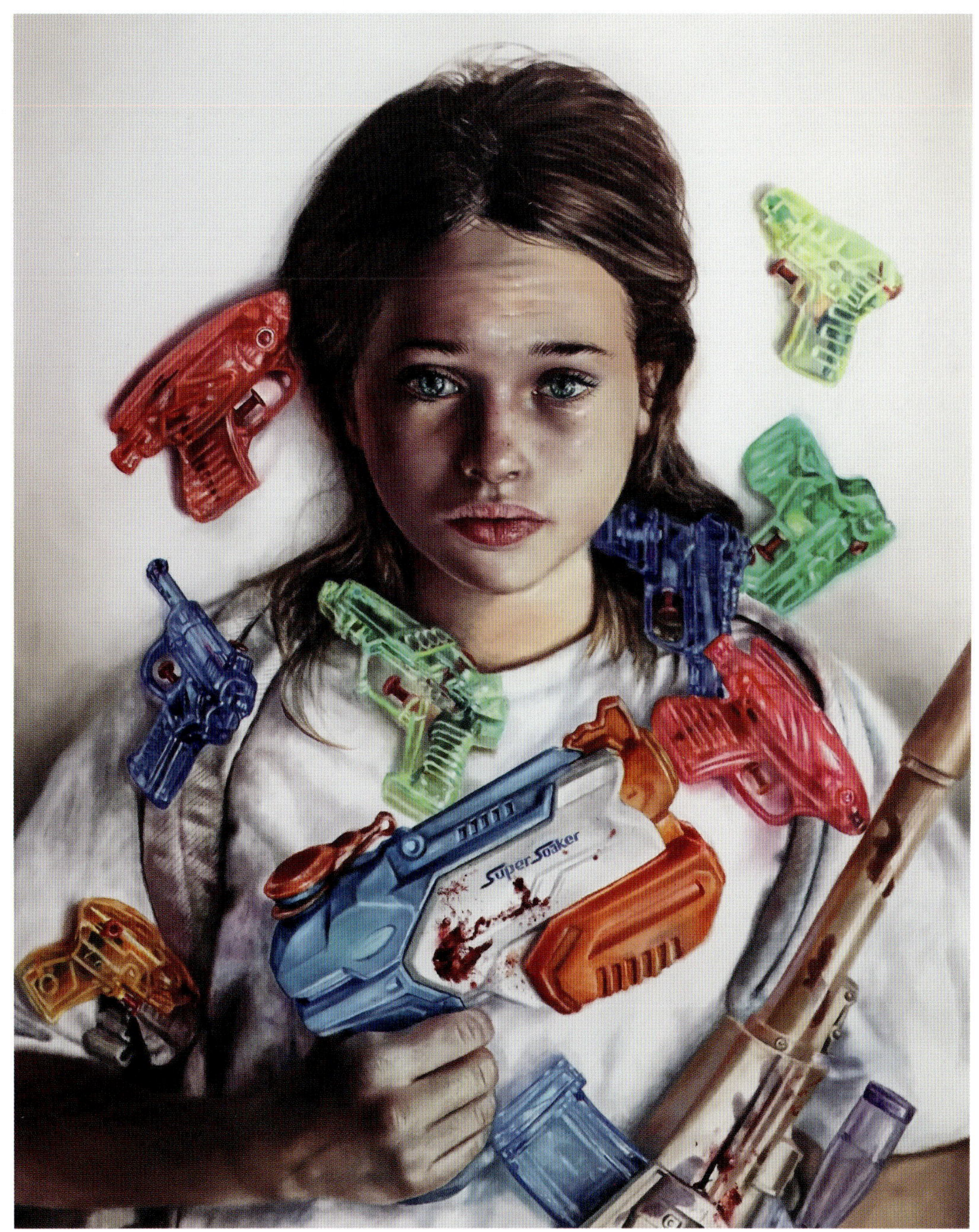

Johan Andersson
Halo, from Toy Guns series, 2017
oil on canvas
52 × 48 in.
Photo: Johan Andersson

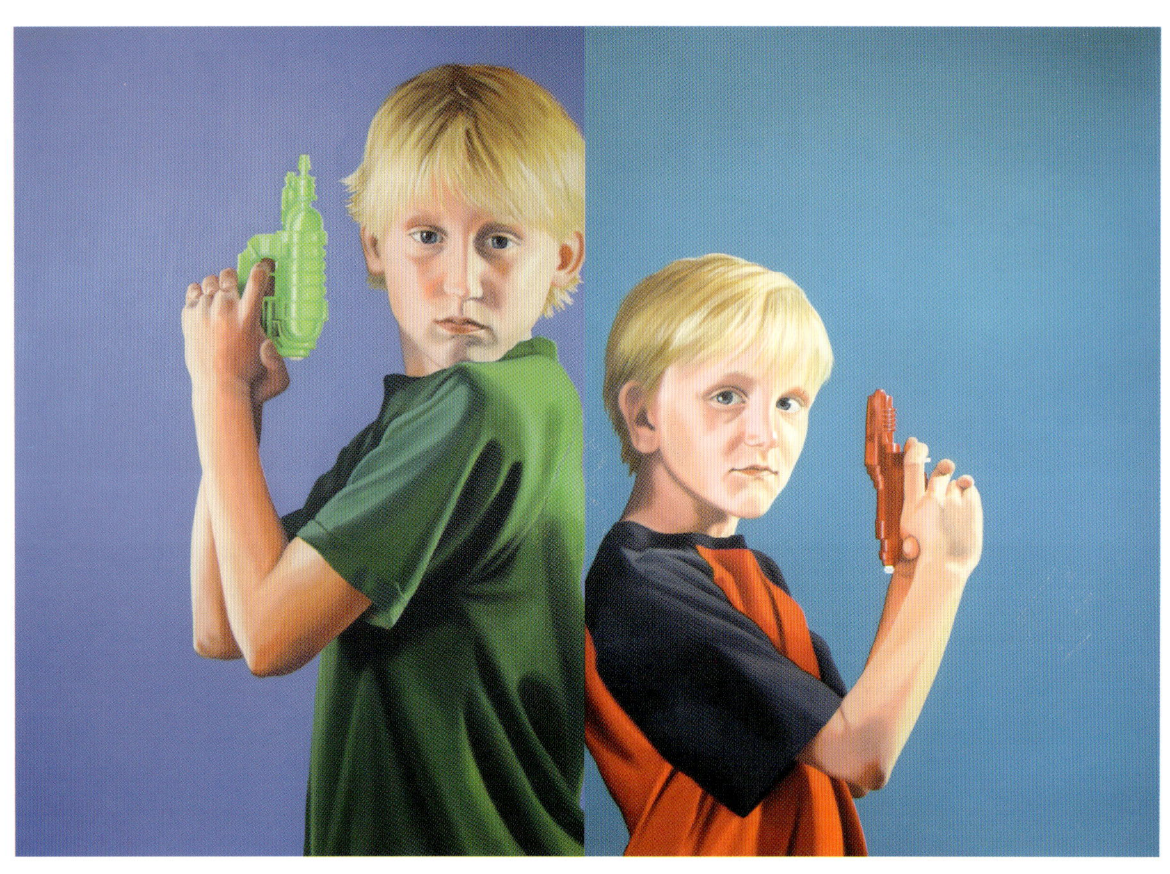

Shannon Cannings
Alex & Joey, 2013
oil on canvas
56 × 81 in.

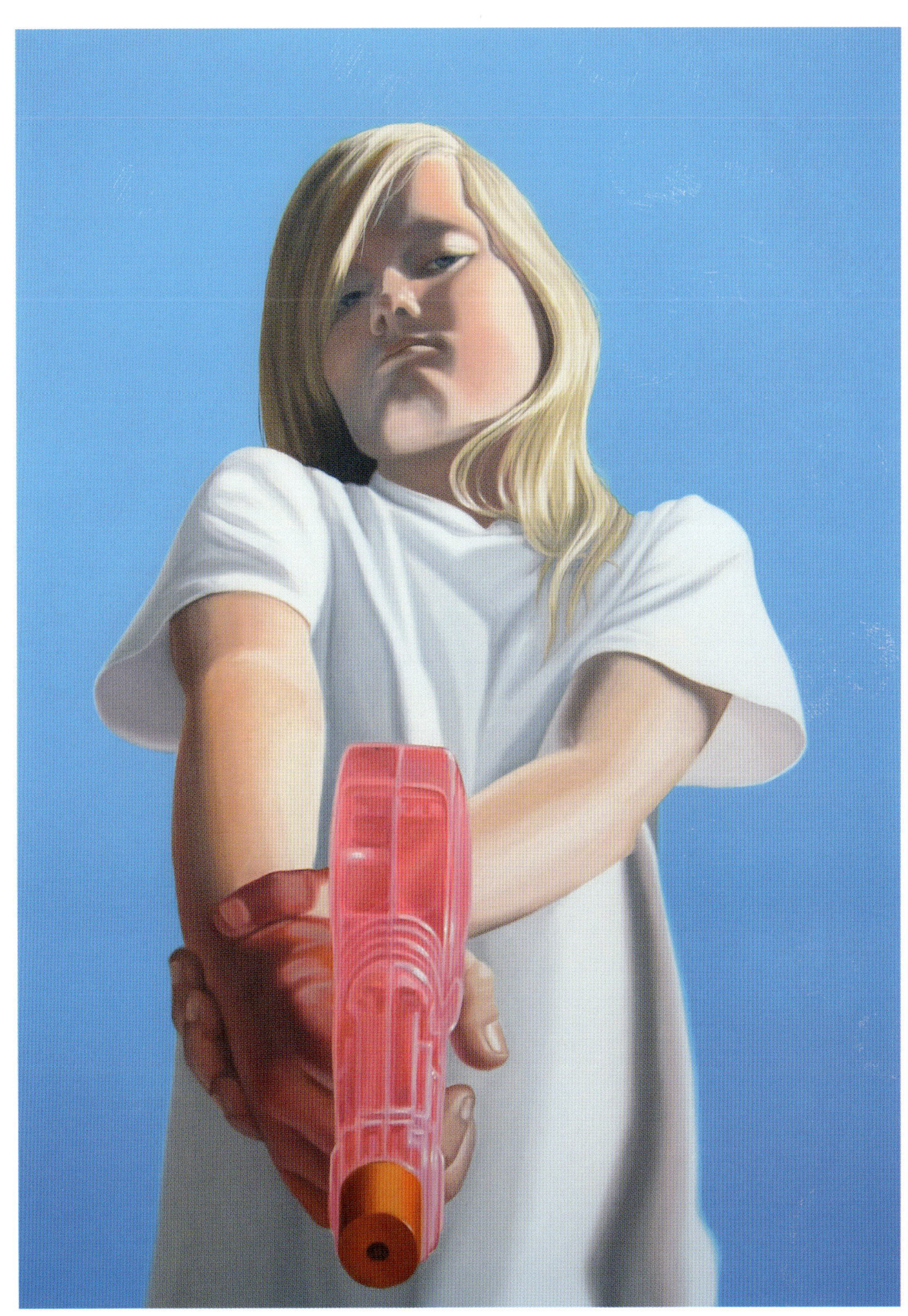

Shannon Cannings
Angel, 2013
oil on canvas
56 × 40 in.

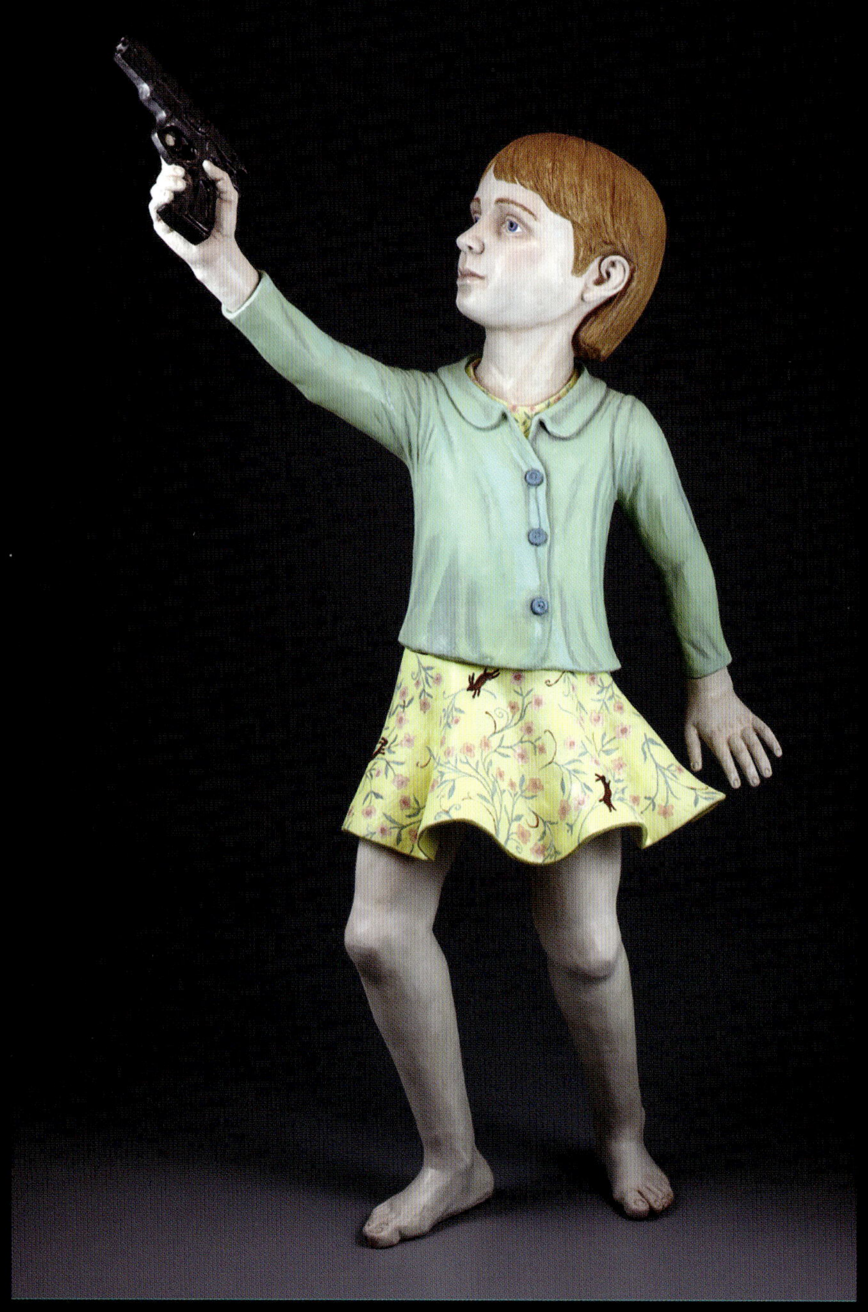

Cynthia Consentino
Alice-Girl with Gun, 2009
stoneware, mixed media

Mueranze hijos de Puta!!!

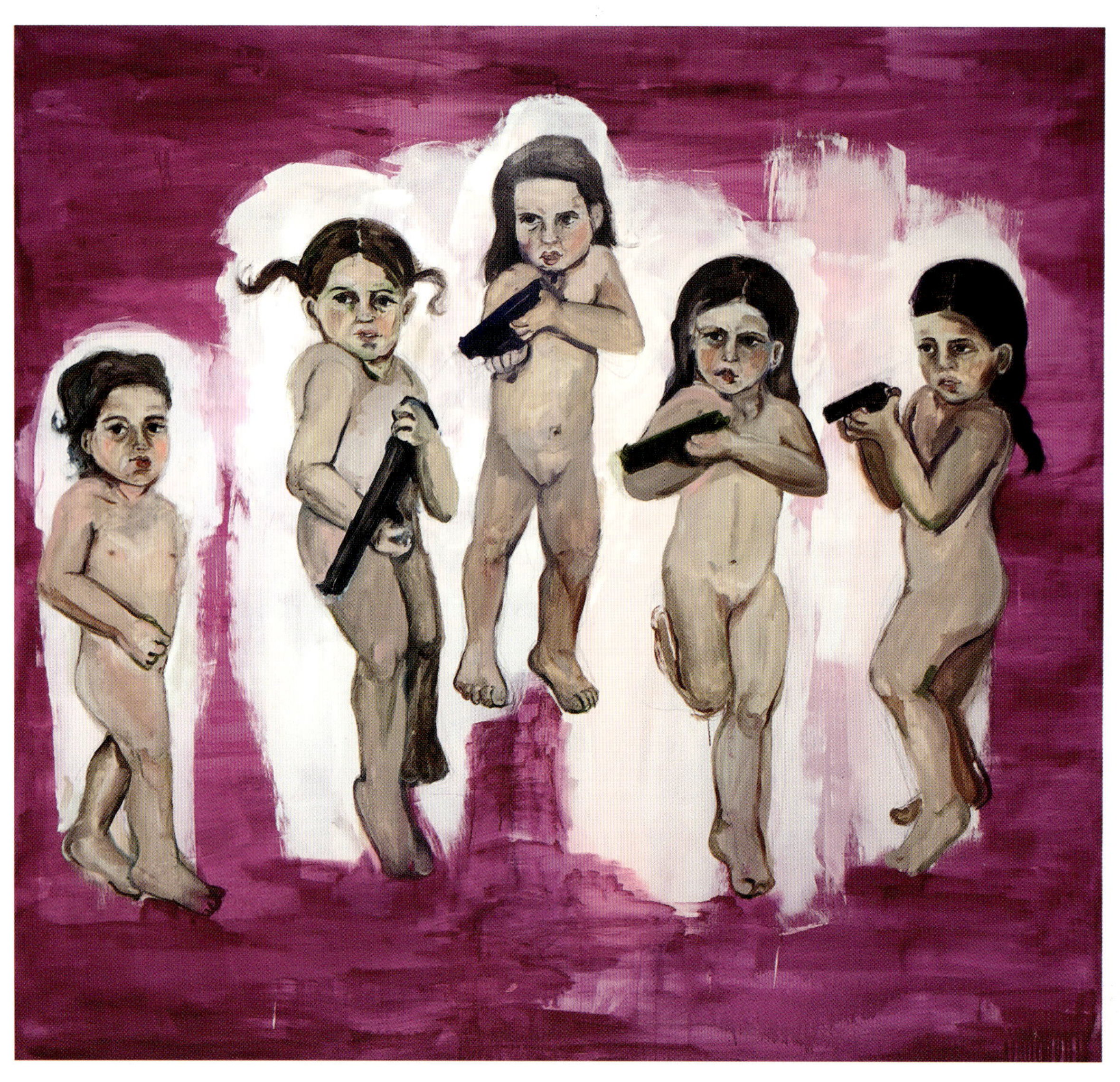

Claudia Alvarez
Chicas Pistoleras, 2012
oil on canvas
65 × 72 in.
Photo: Claudia Alvarez

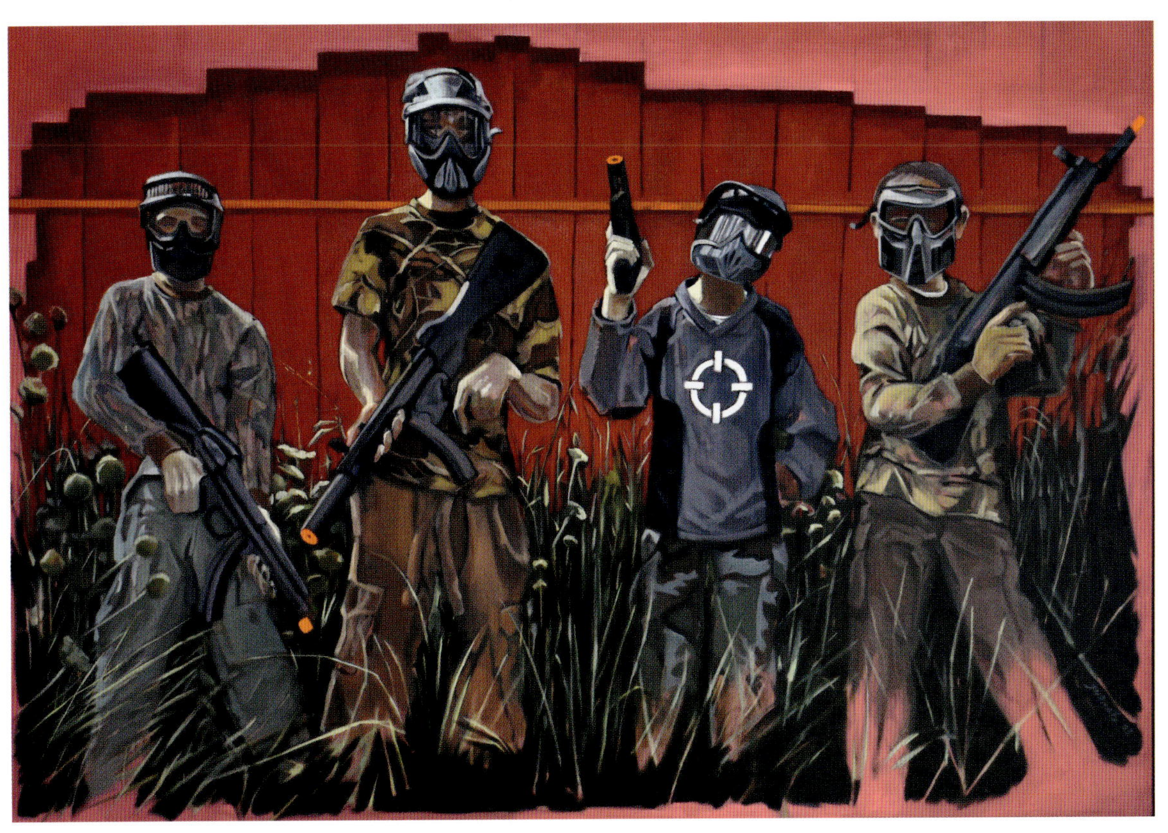

Linda Guenste
War Games, 2013
oil on canvas
48 × 60 in.

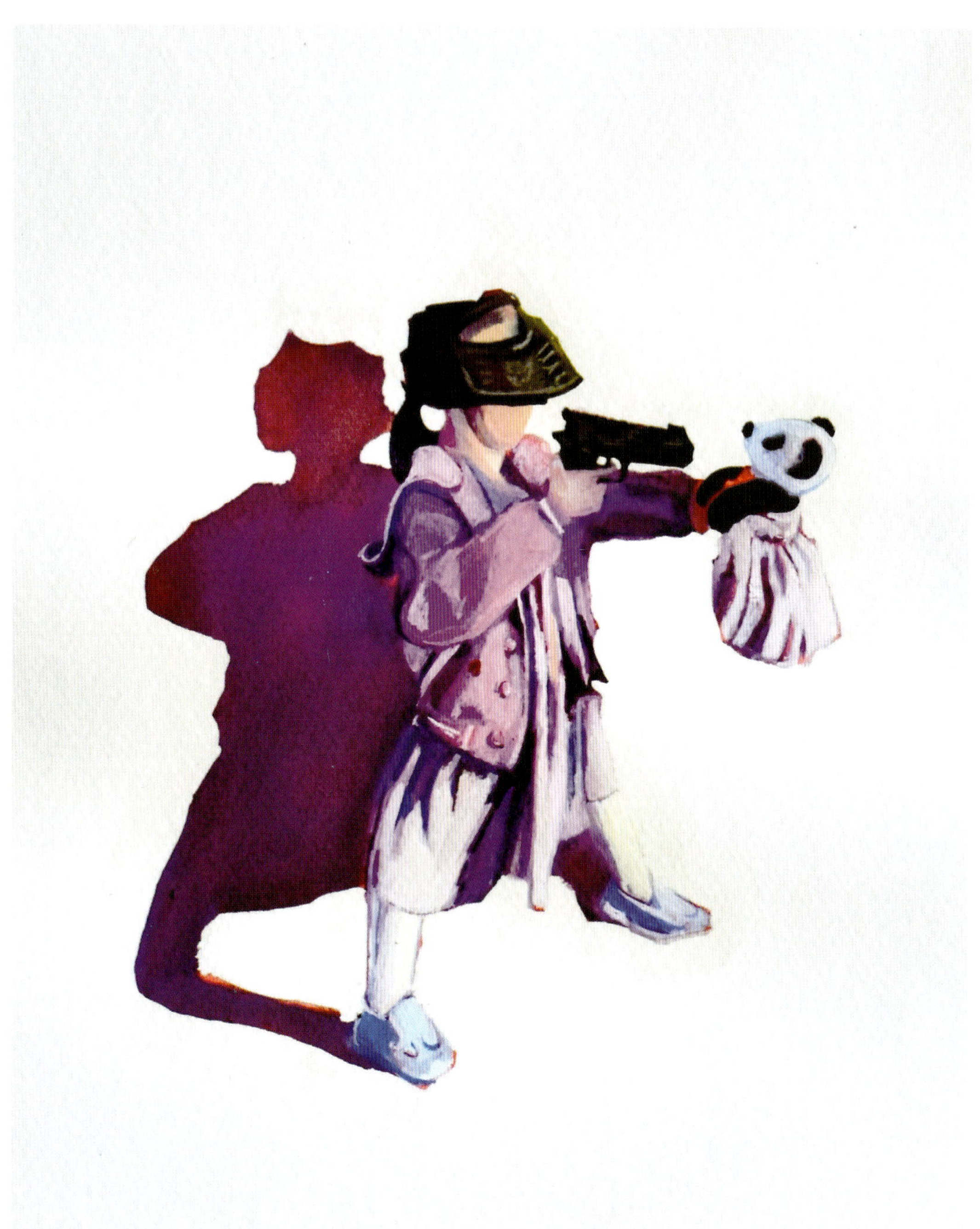

Linda Guenste
Fun with Toys, 2005
mixed media on paper
31 × 39 in.

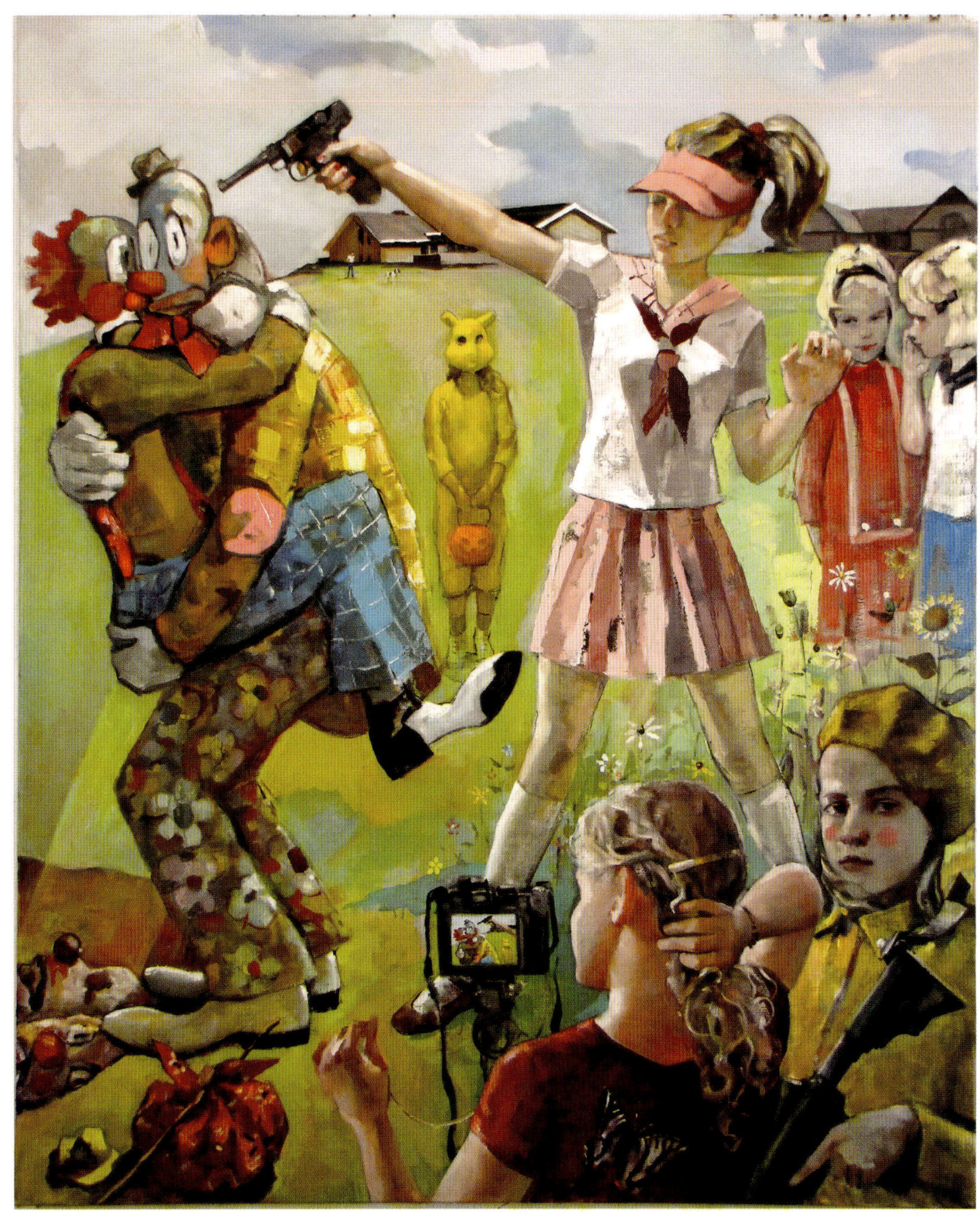

Mike Cockrill
Gossip Girls, 2010
oil on canvas
62 × 50 in.

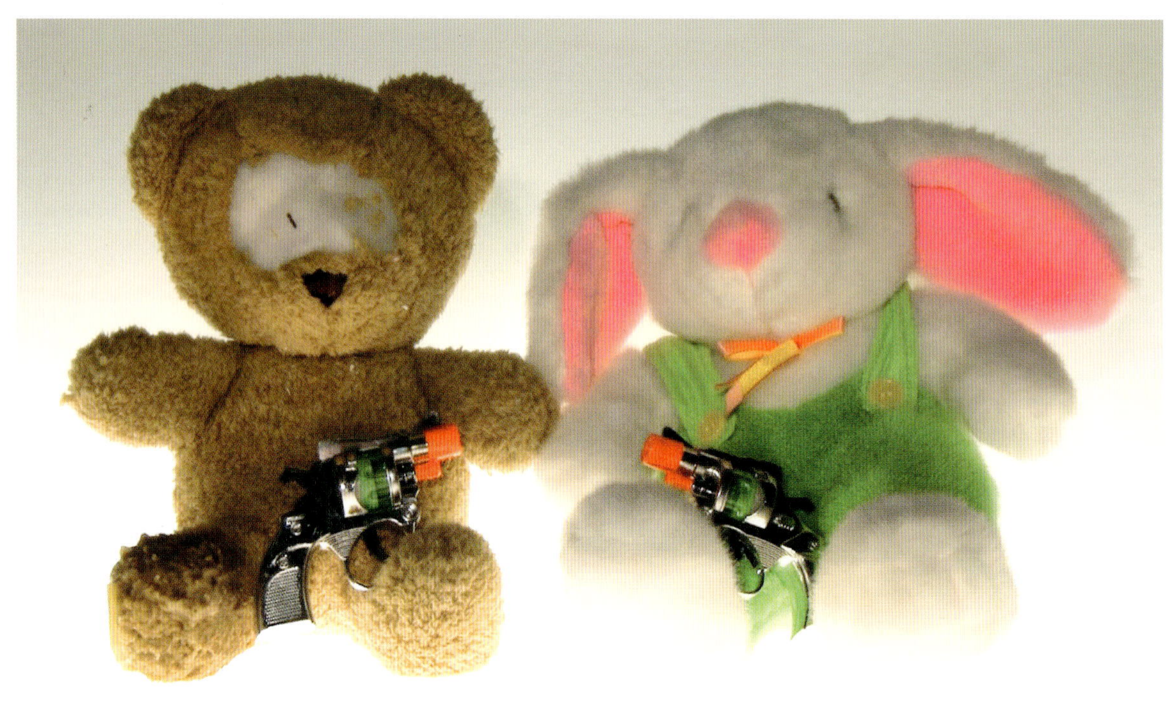

Claire Lieberman
Bunny & Bear, 2010
C-print face mounted to acrylic
7 × 12 × 1 in.

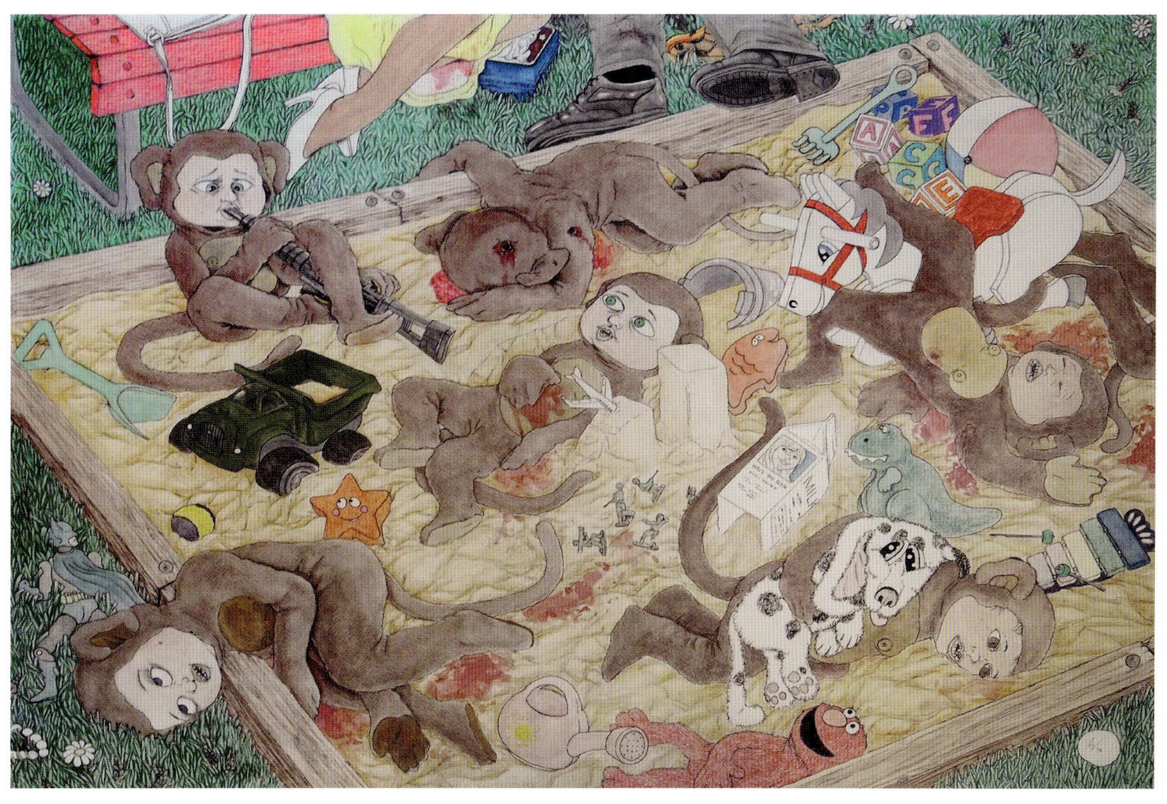

Joachim West
Boys Will Be Boys, 2014
mixed media on paper
31 × 39 in.

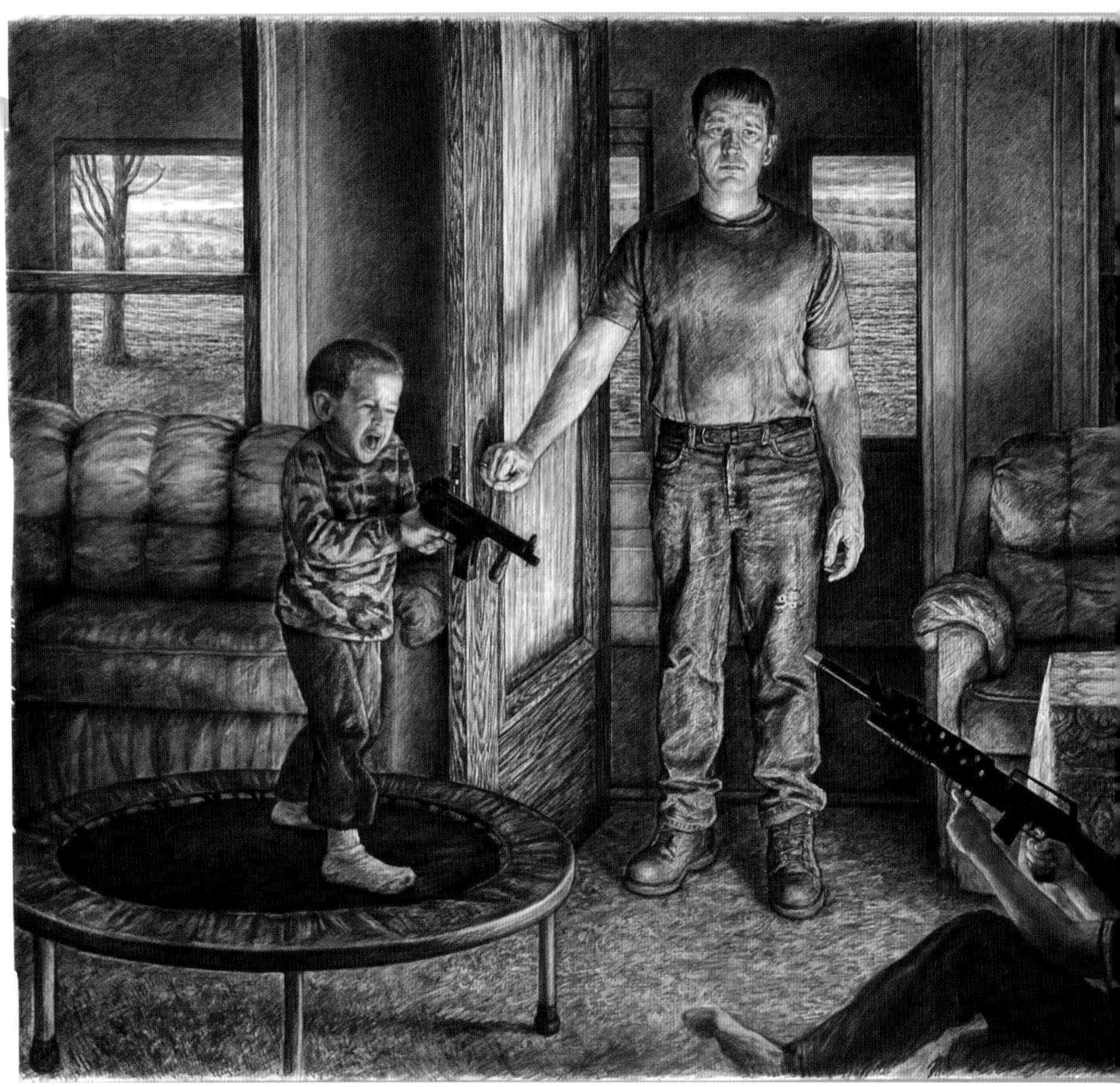

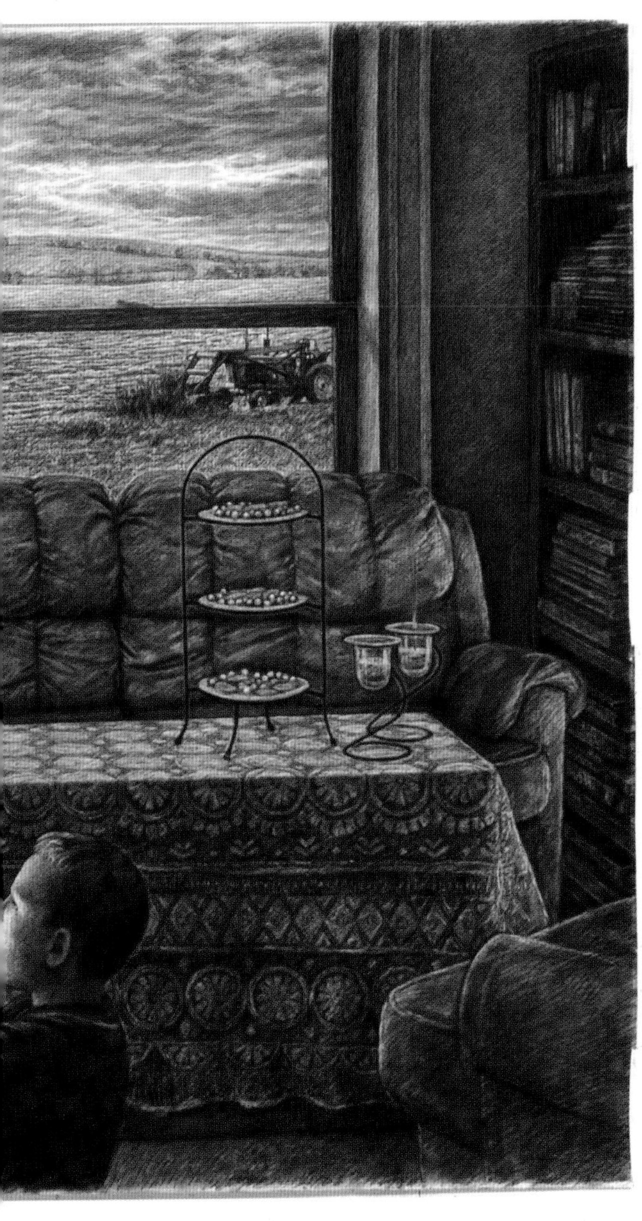

Edgar Jerins
Christmas Day, Yutan, Nebraska, 2014
charcoal on paper
60 × 103 in.

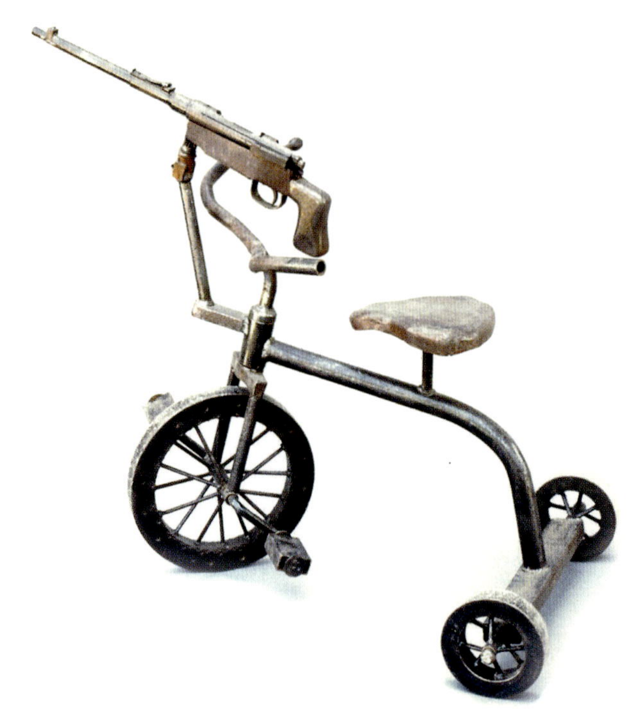

Ed Wilson
Child's Play, 1994
steel
25 × 47 × 21 in.

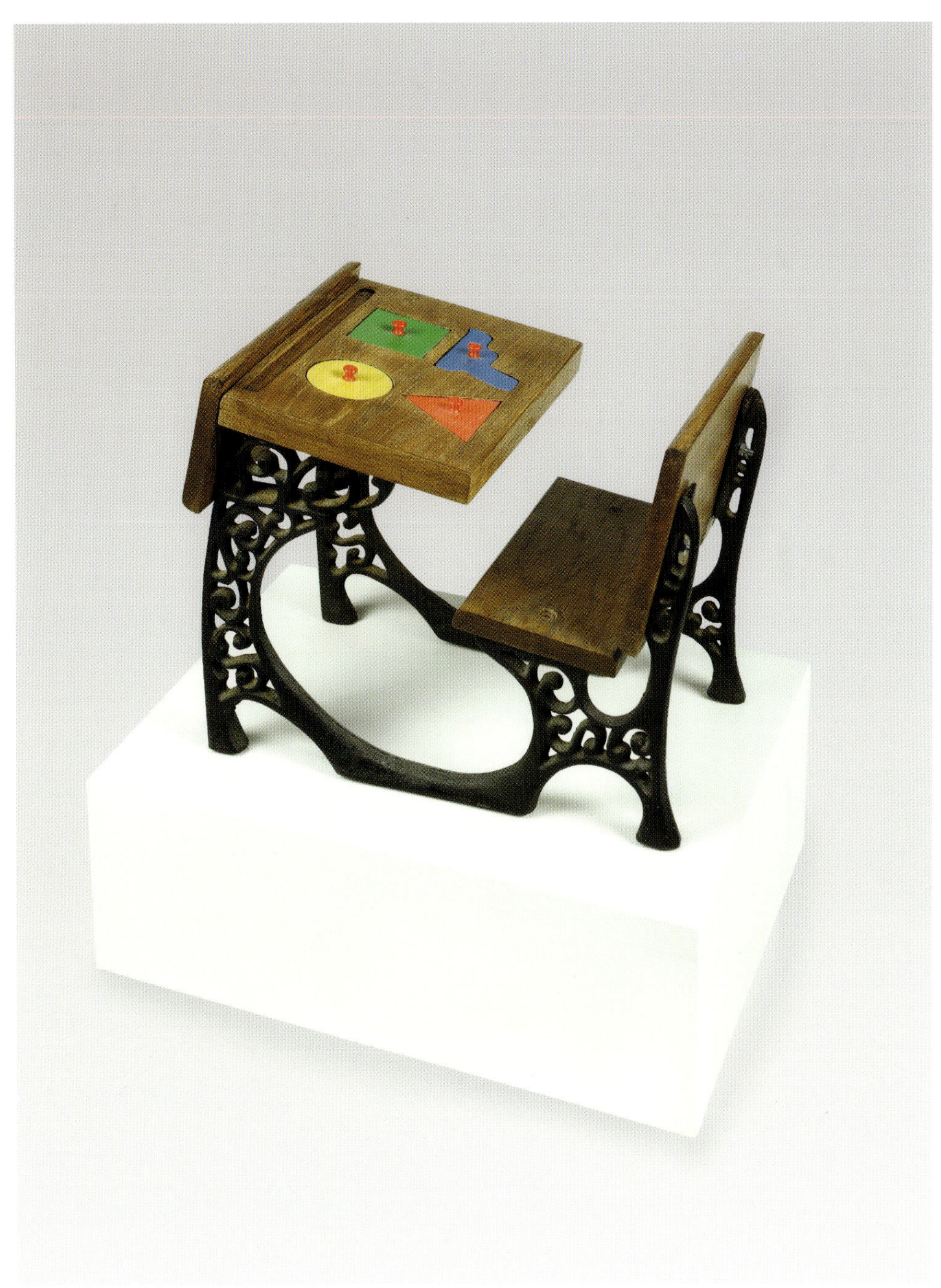

Ben Turnbull
Learning Early, 2008
altered school desk
11¾ × 7¾ × 9½ in.

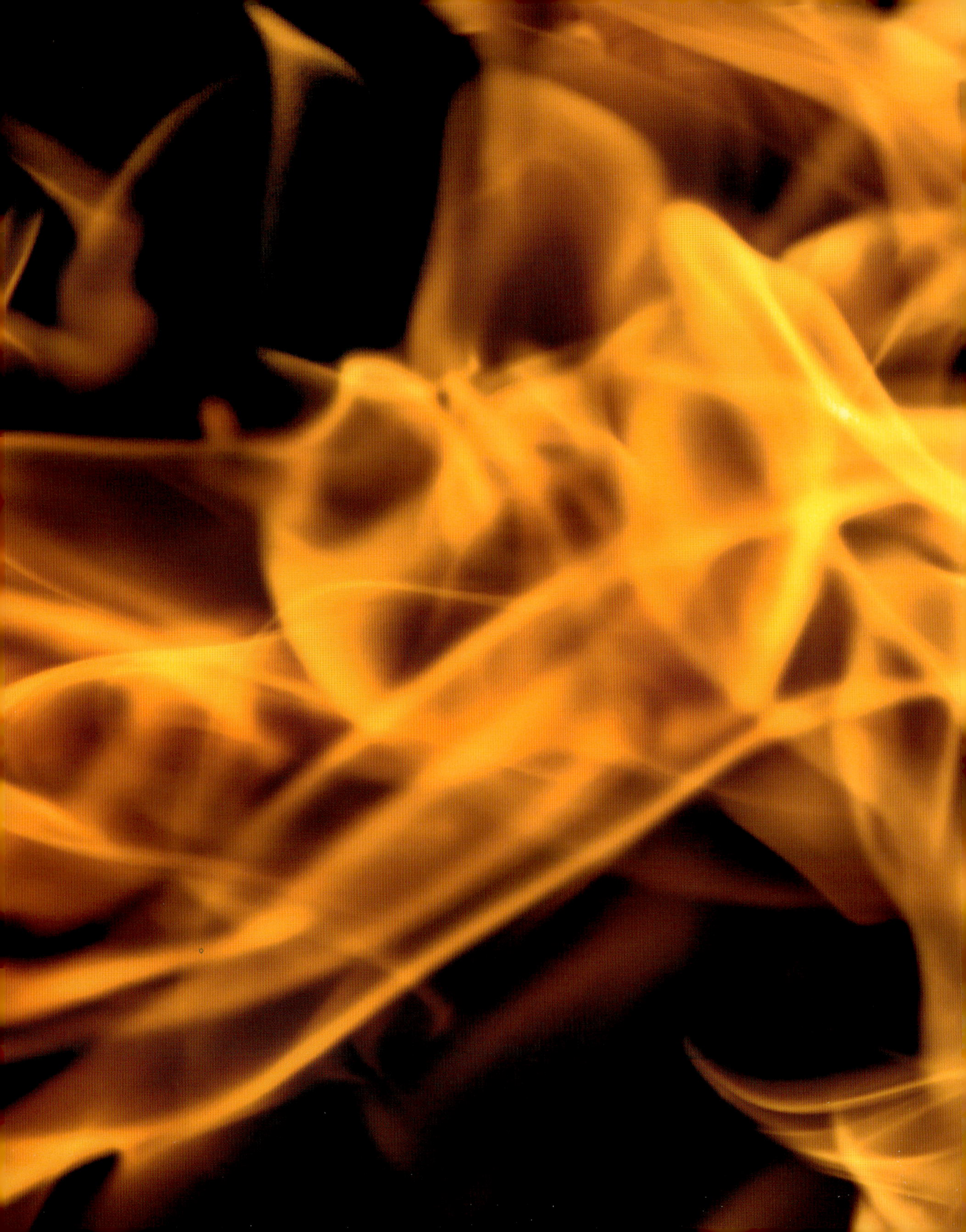

KILLER PORTRAITS

A portrait imparts the likeness of a subject, rendering one's distinctive appearance and traits. These portrayals, which typically highlight the face, often probe beneath the surface to capture a sitter's unique character. The works in this section can be seen as a subset of portraiture; the firearm portrait. Accordingly, guns are treated as a personage, with the weapon standing in for a shooter or crime. Like famous figures, many guns have gained celebrity status, known by mononyms such as "Uzi" or nicknames such as "Tommy." Through an array of gun portraits, we are here brought face to face, nose to muzzle, with the imposing tool. Going beyond mere description, artists penetrate the subject's hard exterior to find its deeper nature.

Such object portraits converge with the genre of still life. While depicting inanimate things, they also imbue them with agency and palpable presence, hinting at the fetishism oft aligned with guns. More specifically, these representations fit the tradition of memento mori or vanitas still lifes, which remind viewers of the fleeting frailty of human existence. Artistic memento mori, translated as "remember you must die," feature skulls, hourglasses, old fruit, or snuffed candles to symbolize age and the passage of time. As objects associated with death, guns perfectly embody this message of mortality, which is further enhanced in these contemporary works by the inclusion of flowers, flesh, and bones.

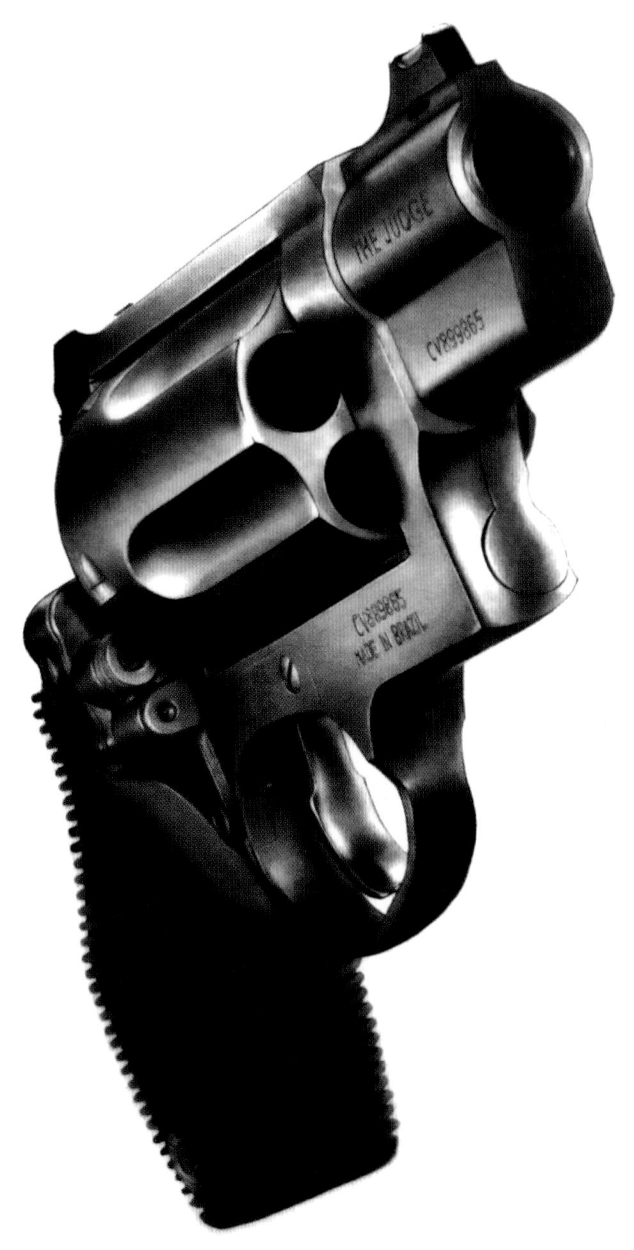

Robert Longo
Study for The Judge, 40 caliber, 2012
ink and charcoal on vellum
21 × 15 in.
Courtesy of the artist and Metro Pictures, New York

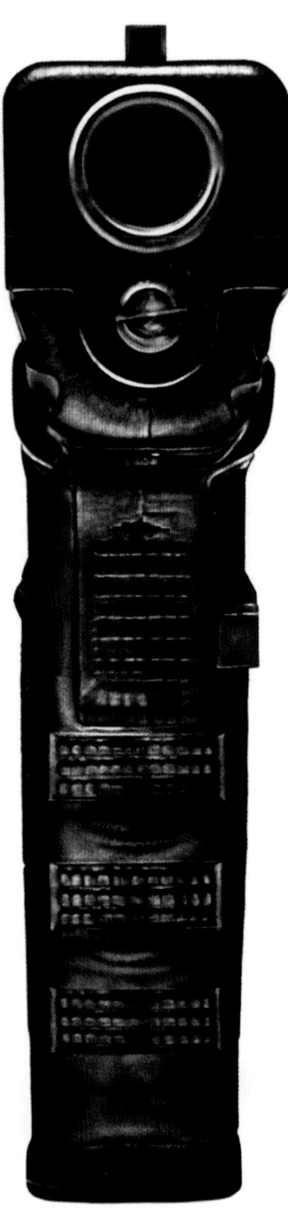

Robert Longo
Untitled (New Glock), 2013
graphite and charcoal on mounted paper
96 × 48 in.
Courtesy of the artist and Metro Pictures, New York

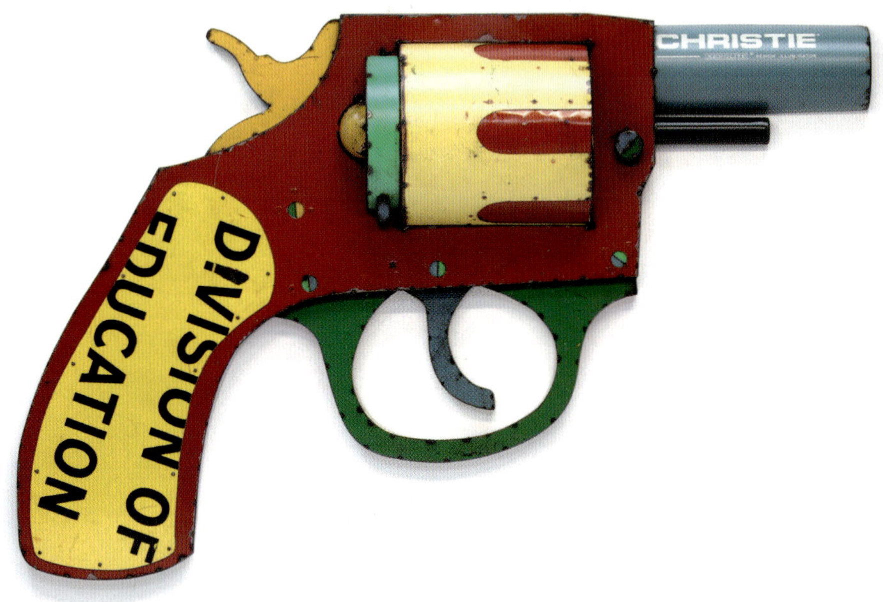

David Buckingham
Sirhan Sirhan II, 2011
cut and found welded metal
41 × 65 × 7 in.
Photo: Gilbert Ortiz

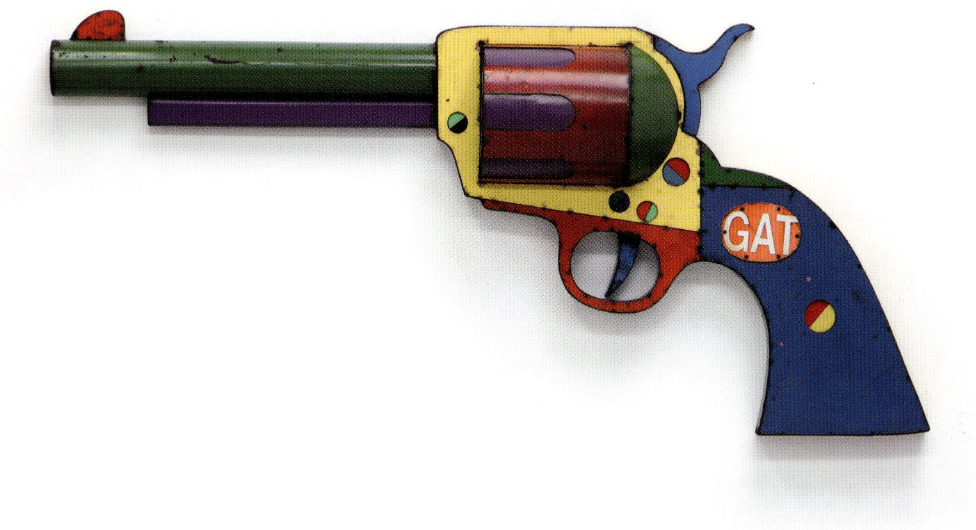

David Buckingham
Butch Cassidy III, 2015
cut and found welded metal
23 × 50 × 5 in.
Photo: Gilbert Ortiz

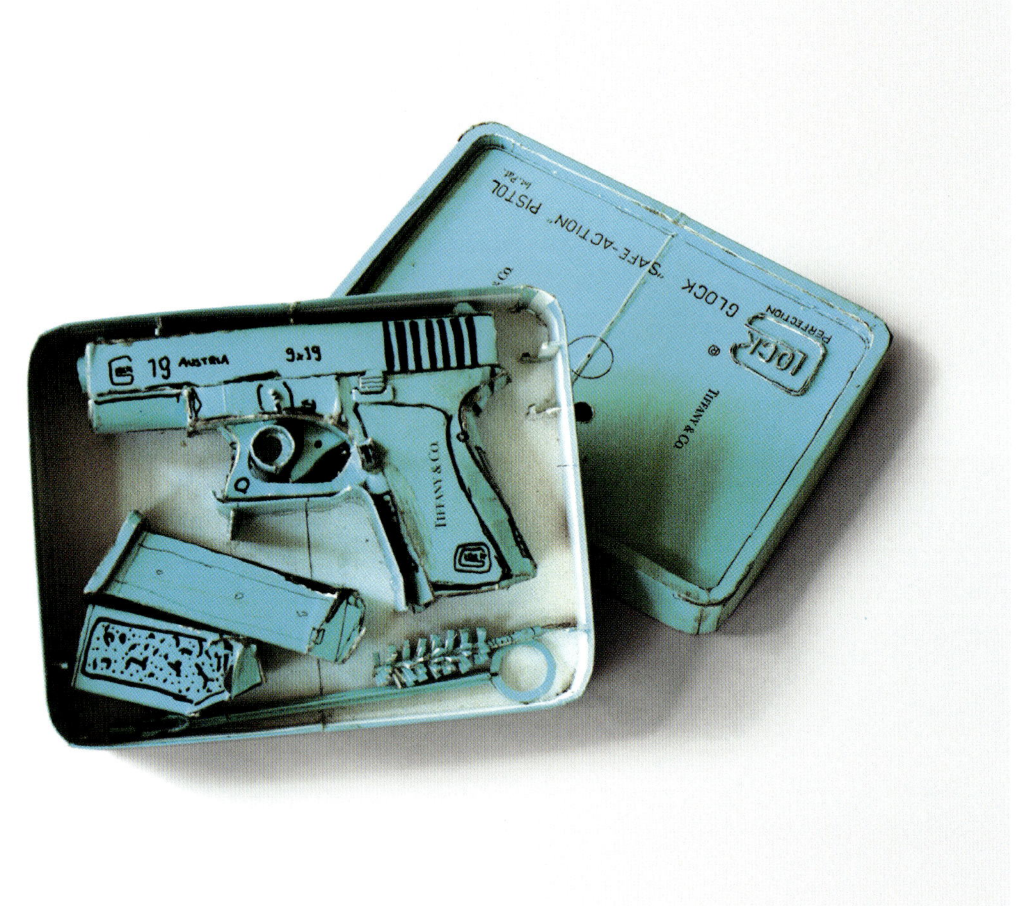

Tom Sachs
Tiffany Glock Model 19, 1995
cardboard, ink, thermal adhesive
2½ × 6½ × 9 in.
(S/N: 1995 42)

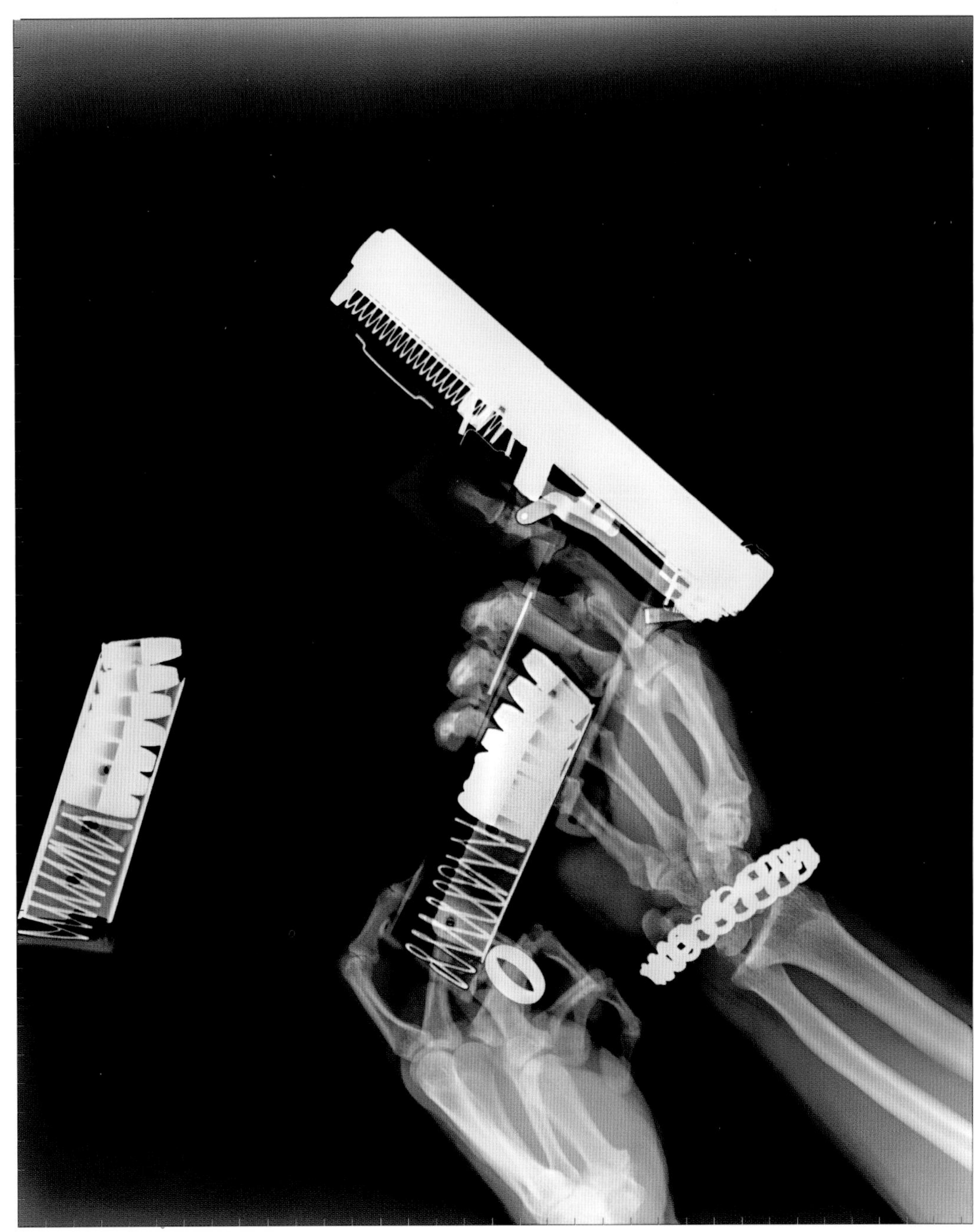

Steve Miller
Glock, 2007
Iris print
19½ × 16 in.
Courtesy of Laumont Editions

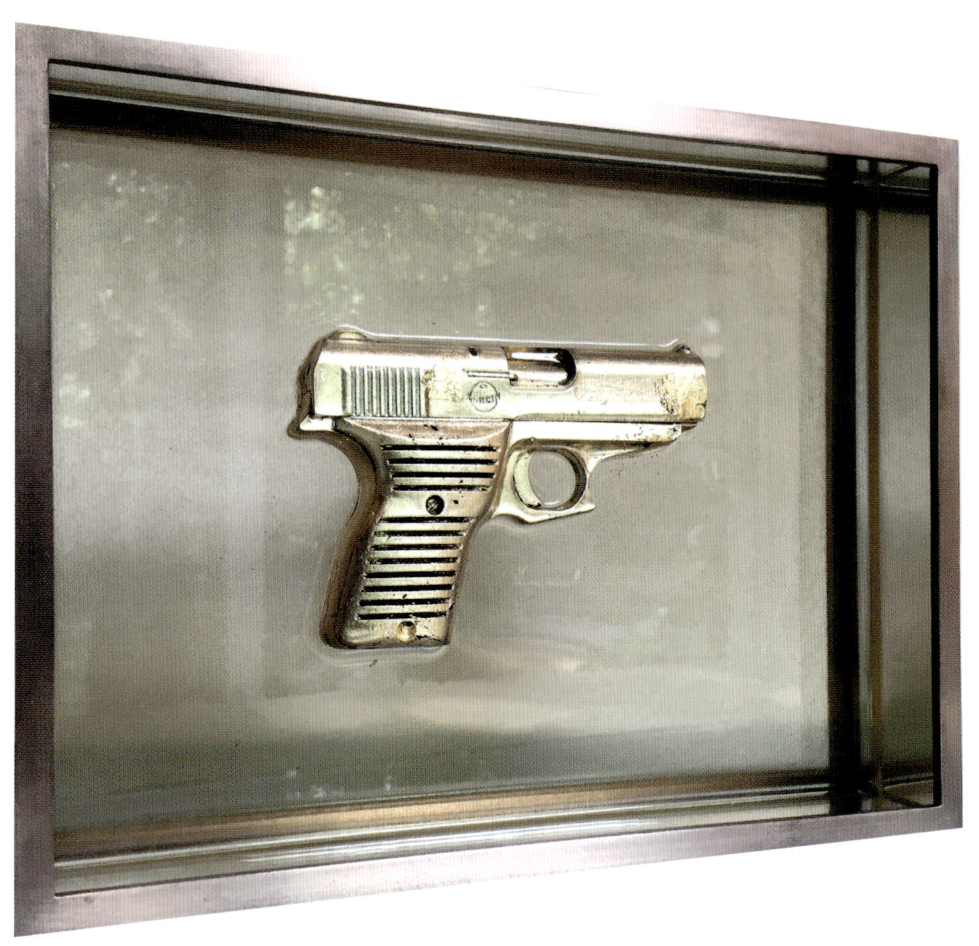

Peter Diepenbrock
American Obsession, 2016
silicone bronze, epoxy resin, handgun, metallic leaf, mirror
10½ × 14 × 3 in.

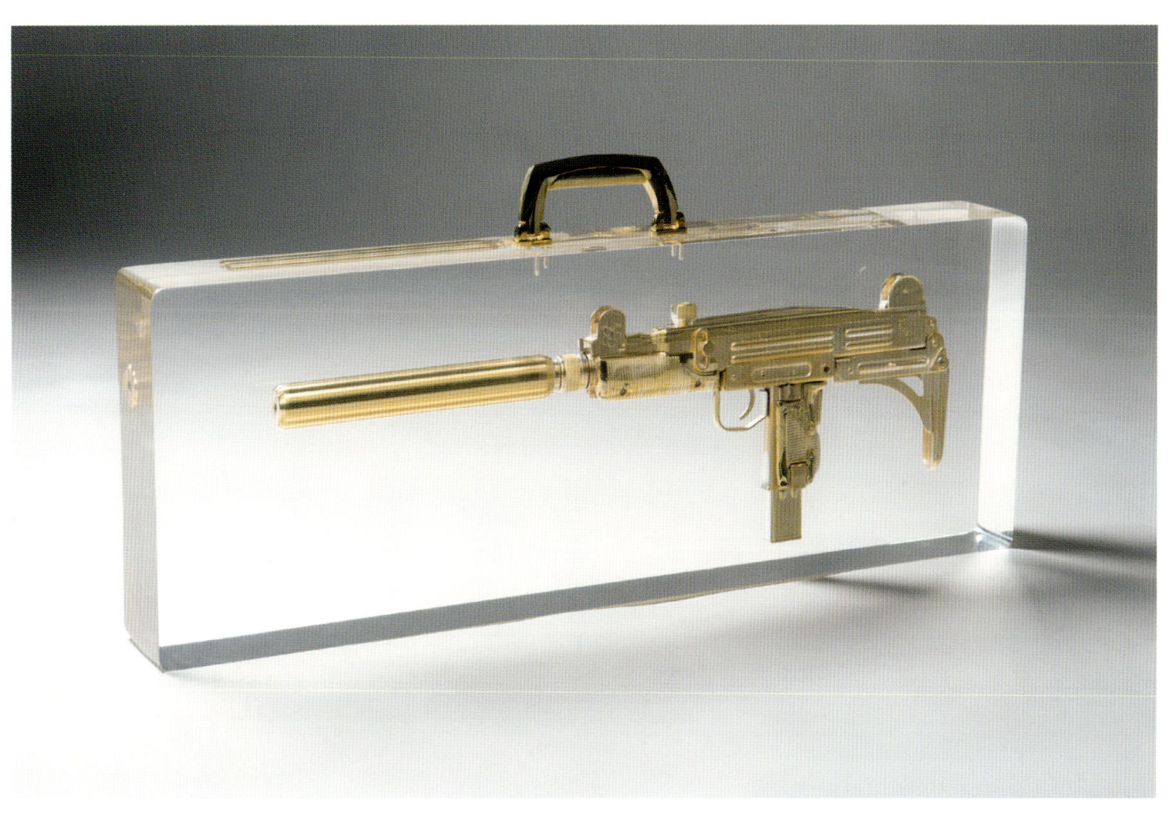

Ted Noten
Uzi Mon Amour, 2009
Uzi 24K gold-plated cast in acrylic, brass handle, engraved poem
12 × 32½ × 3¾ in.
Photo: Ted Noten

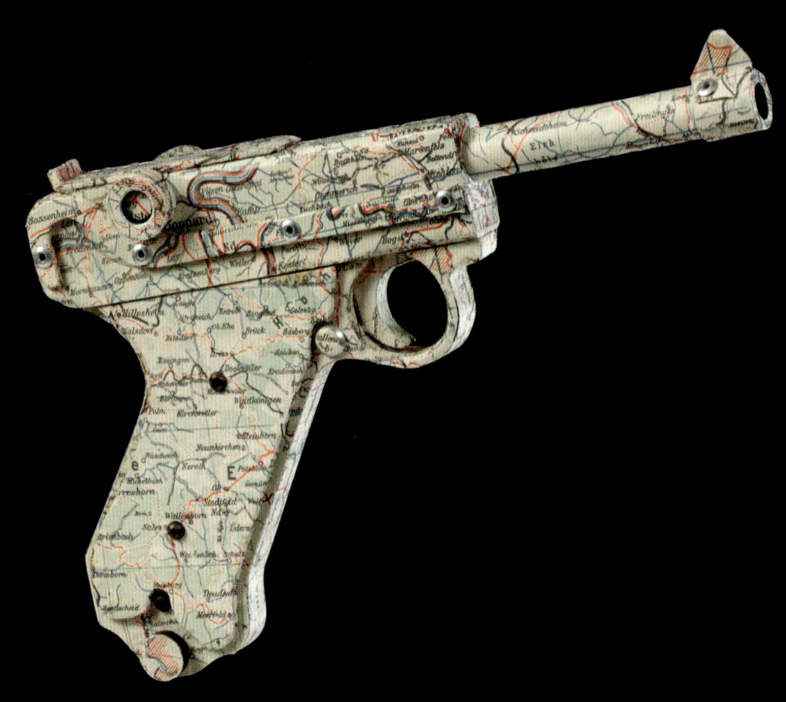

Ken Kalman
German Lugar, from Topicals series, 2012
aluminum sheet and rods, rivets, screws, and paper
6 × 9 × 1 in.

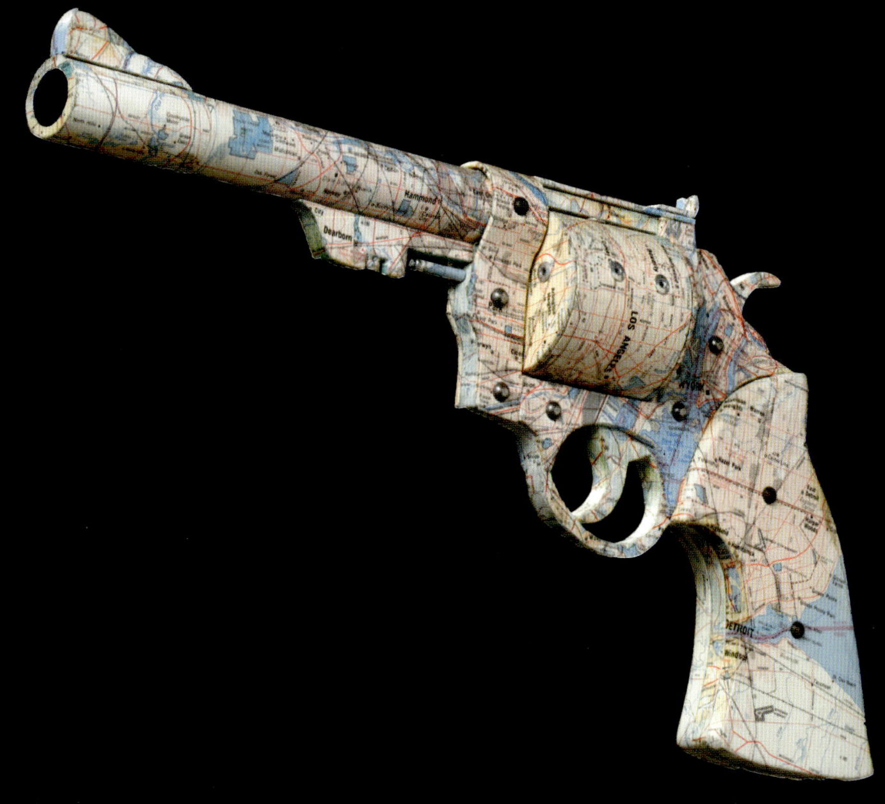

Ken Kalman
Magnum from Topicals series, 2012
aluminum sheet and rods, rivets, screws, and paper
7 × 13½ × 2 in.

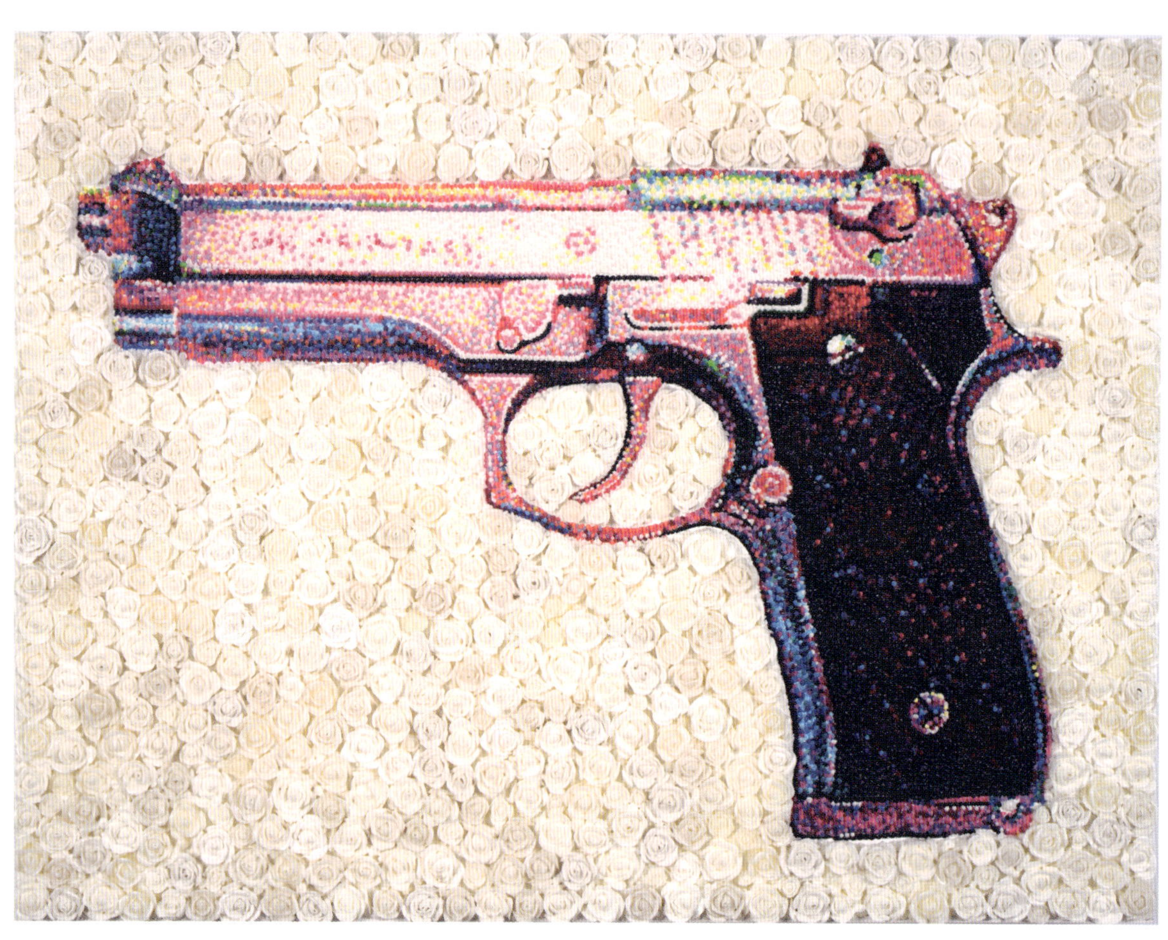

Lisa Alonzo
The Gun in Roses 2.0, 2013
acrylic paint and gel medium on panel
18 × 24 × 2 in.
Collection of Claire Oliver Gallery
Photo: Ian Rubinstein

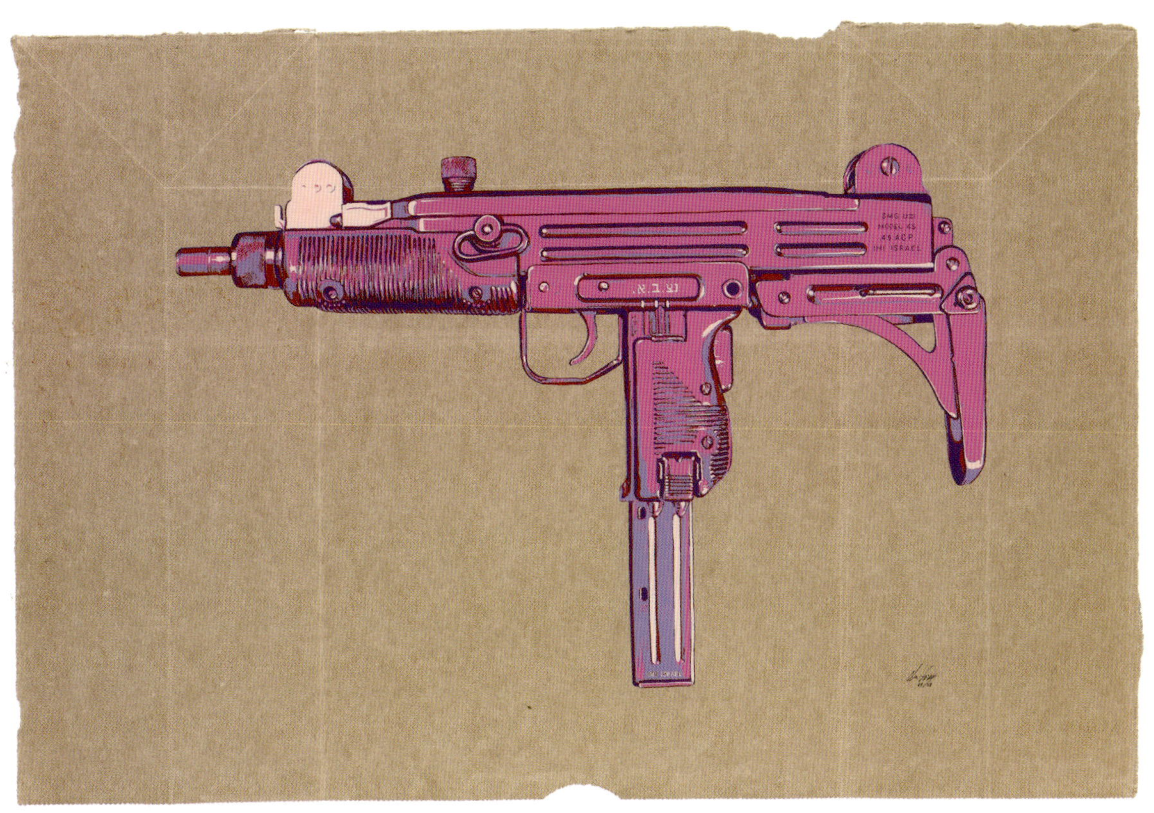

Chris Crites
Uzi, 2008
acrylic on paper bag
25½ × 17 in.

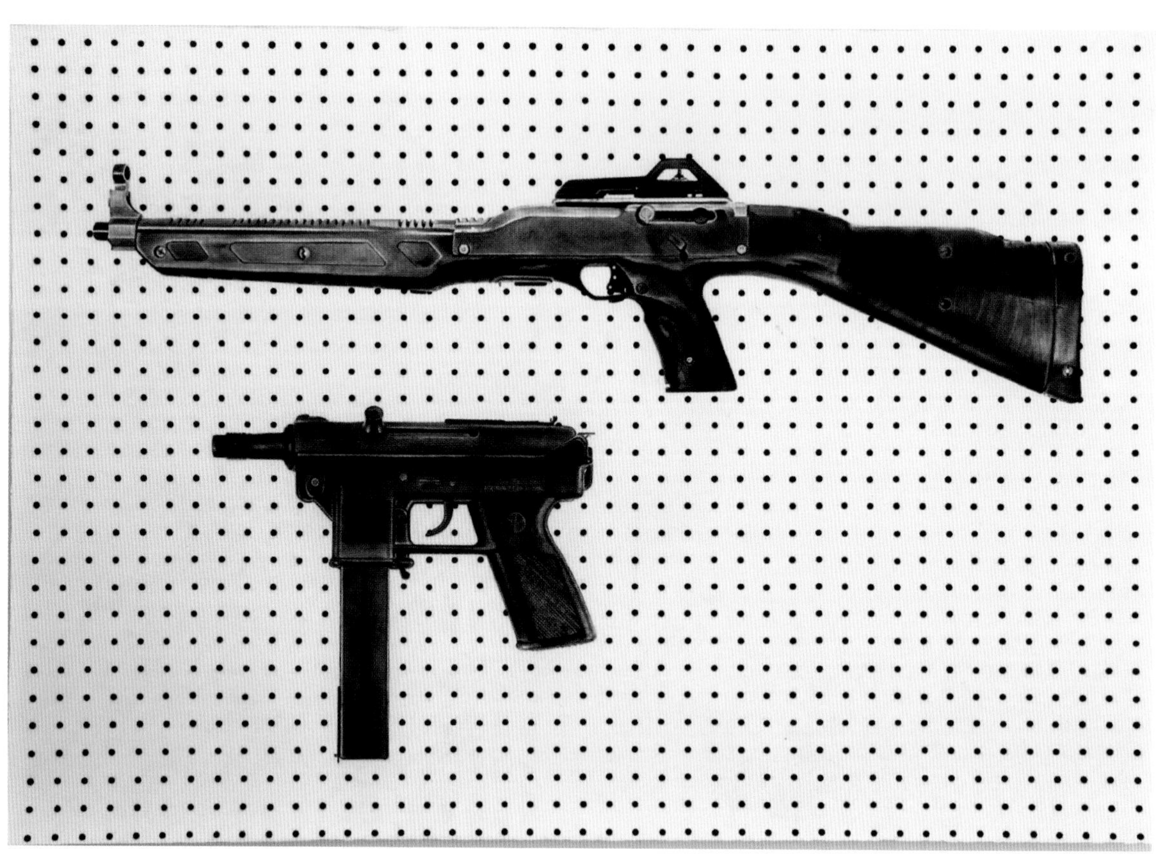

Linda Bond
Guns in America: Columbine (1999), 2016
gunpowder and graphite on paper
30 × 44 in.
Photo: Richard Brotman

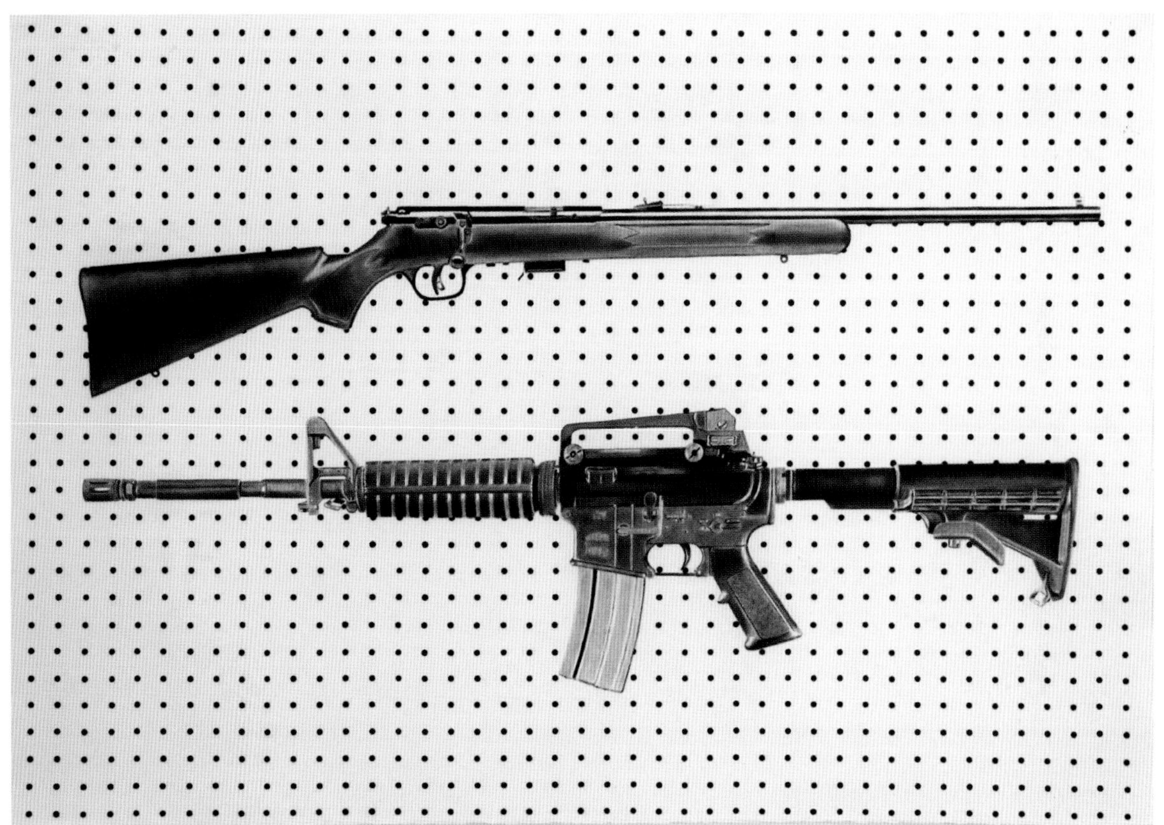

Linda Bond
Guns in America: Sandy Hook (2012), 2016
gunpowder and graphite on paper
30 × 44 in.
Photo: Richard Brotman

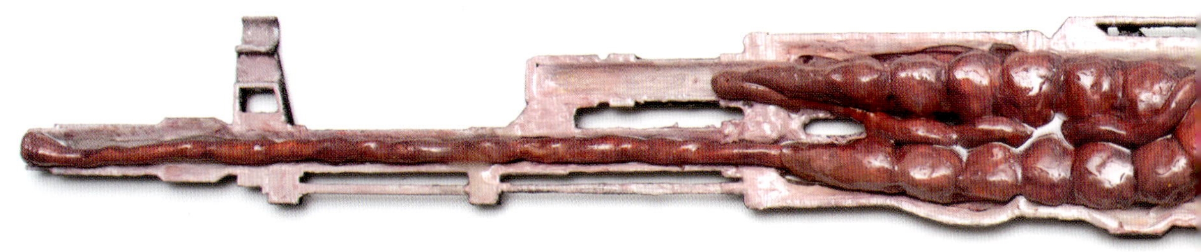

Noah Scanlin
Anatomy of War: AK-47 I, 2015
polymer clay, polymer resin, acrylic, enamel, epoxy
39 × 11 × 2 in.

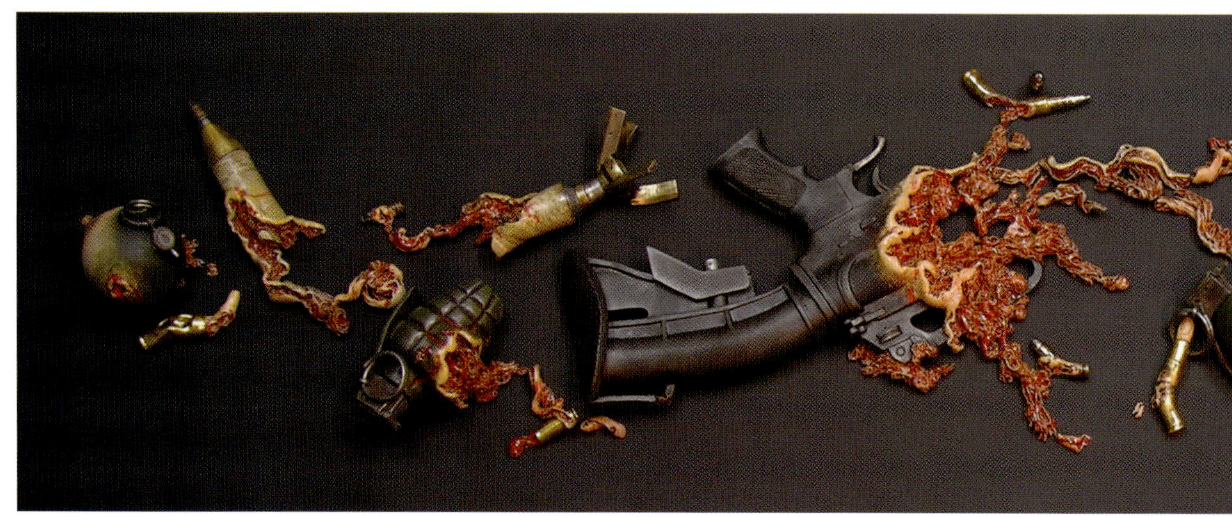

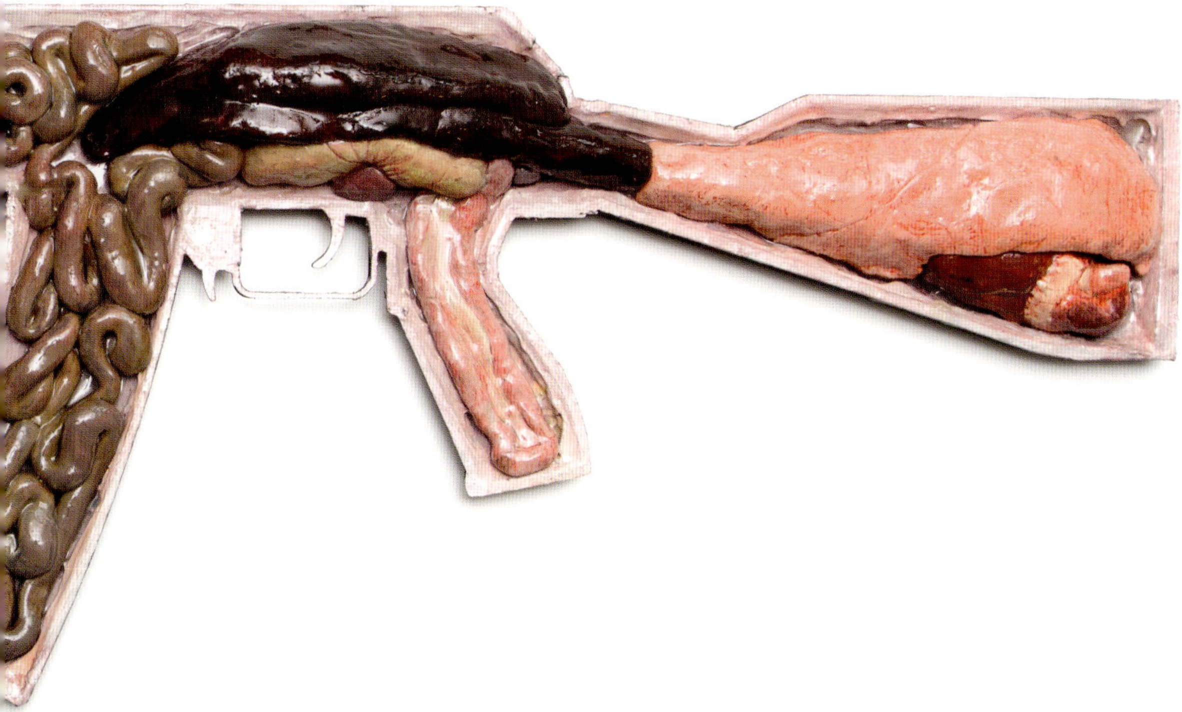

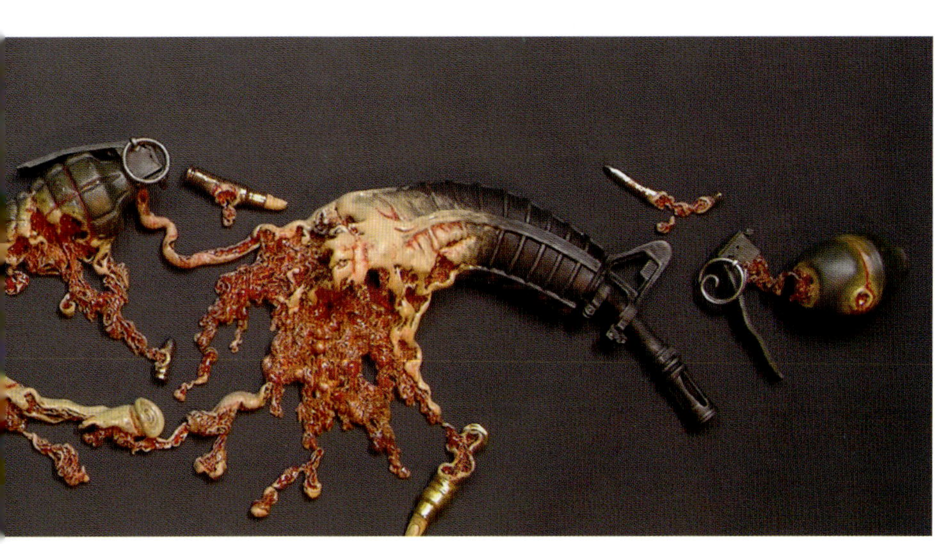

Johnson Tsang
Karma III-Battlefield, 2005
glazed stoneware
24 × 78¾ × 3¼ in.
Photo: Johnson Tsang

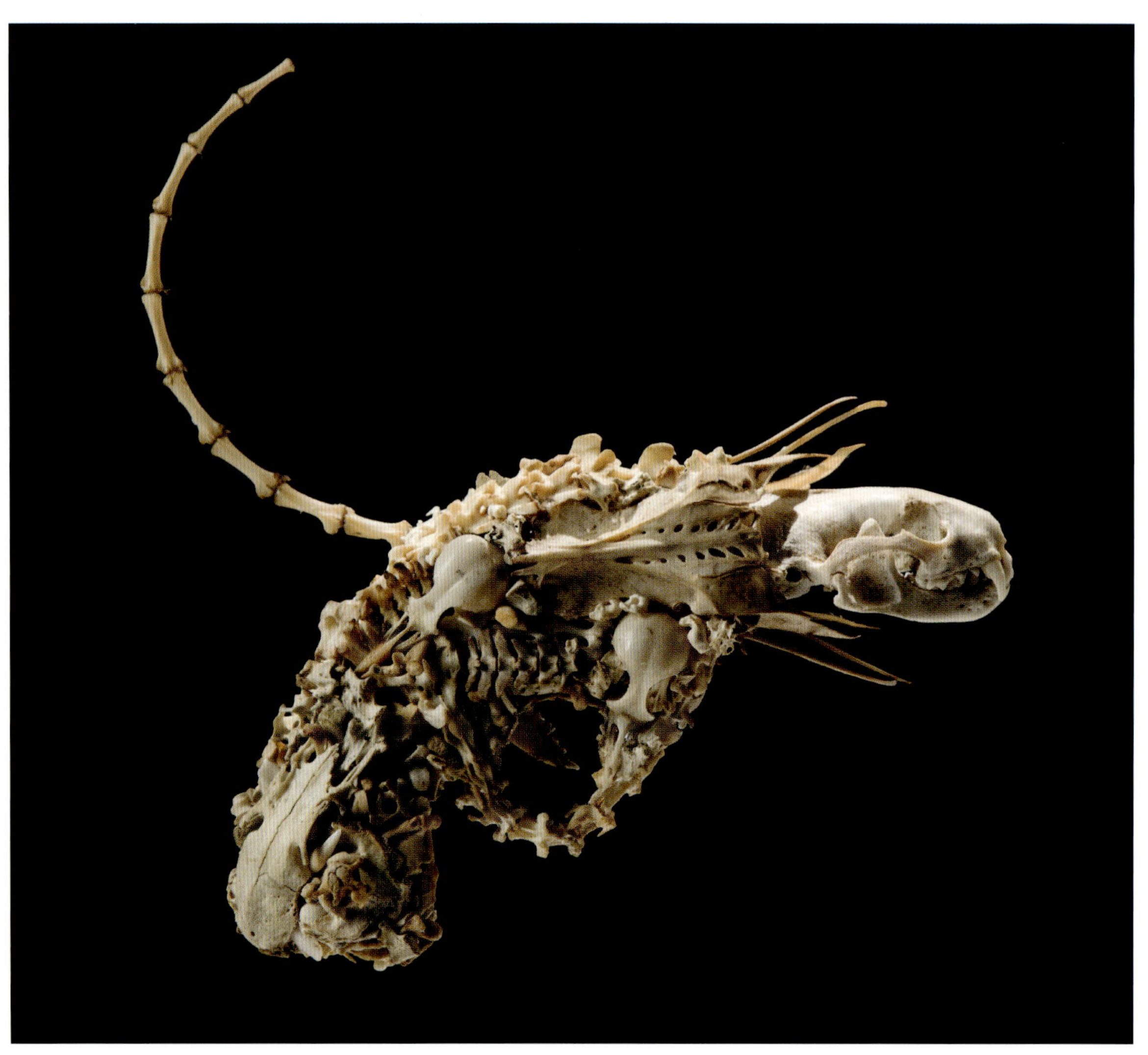

Bruce Mahalski
Ferret-Barreled Dueling Pistol, 2014
bone, wire
8¼ × 8¼ in.

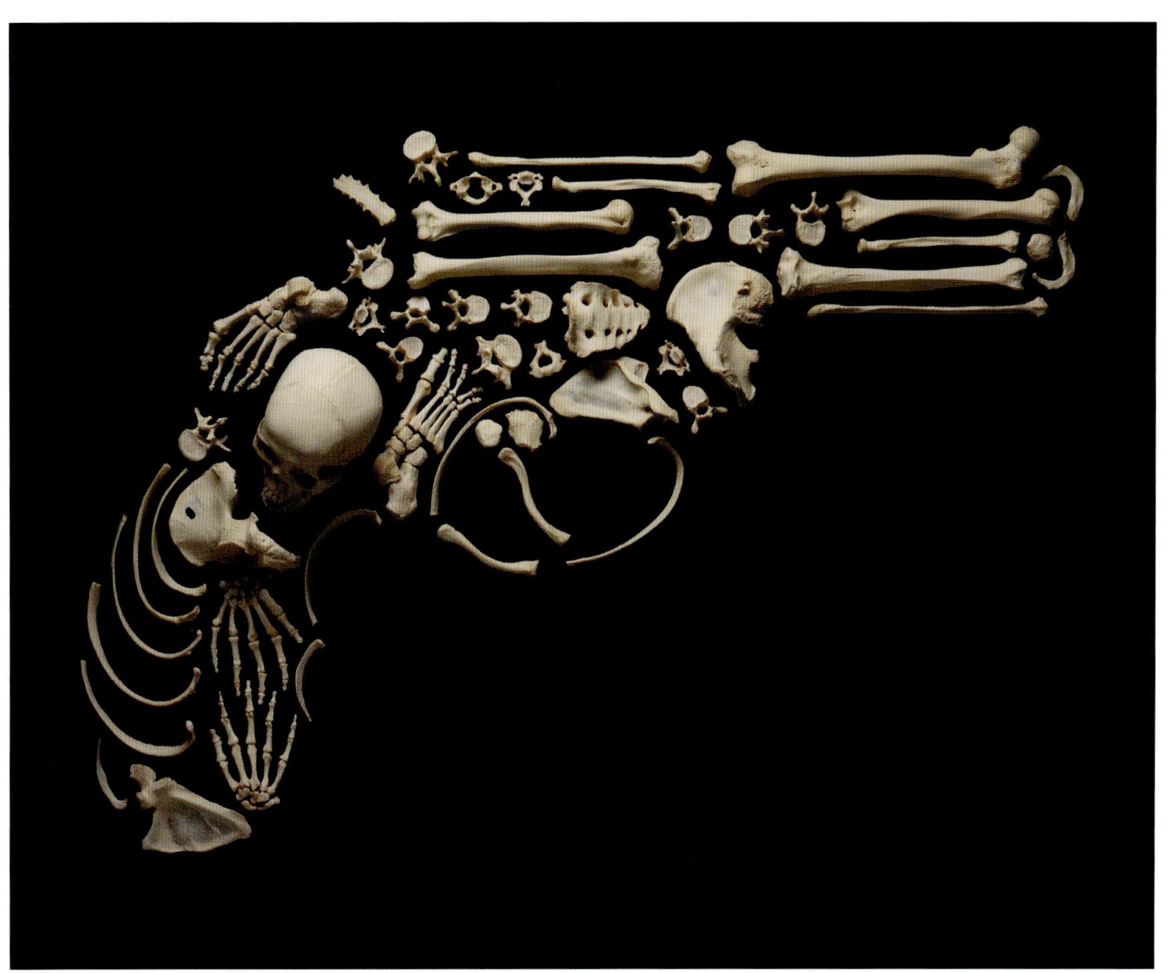

Francois Robert
Gun, from Stop the Violence series, 2008
archival digital print
12 × 16 × 2 in.

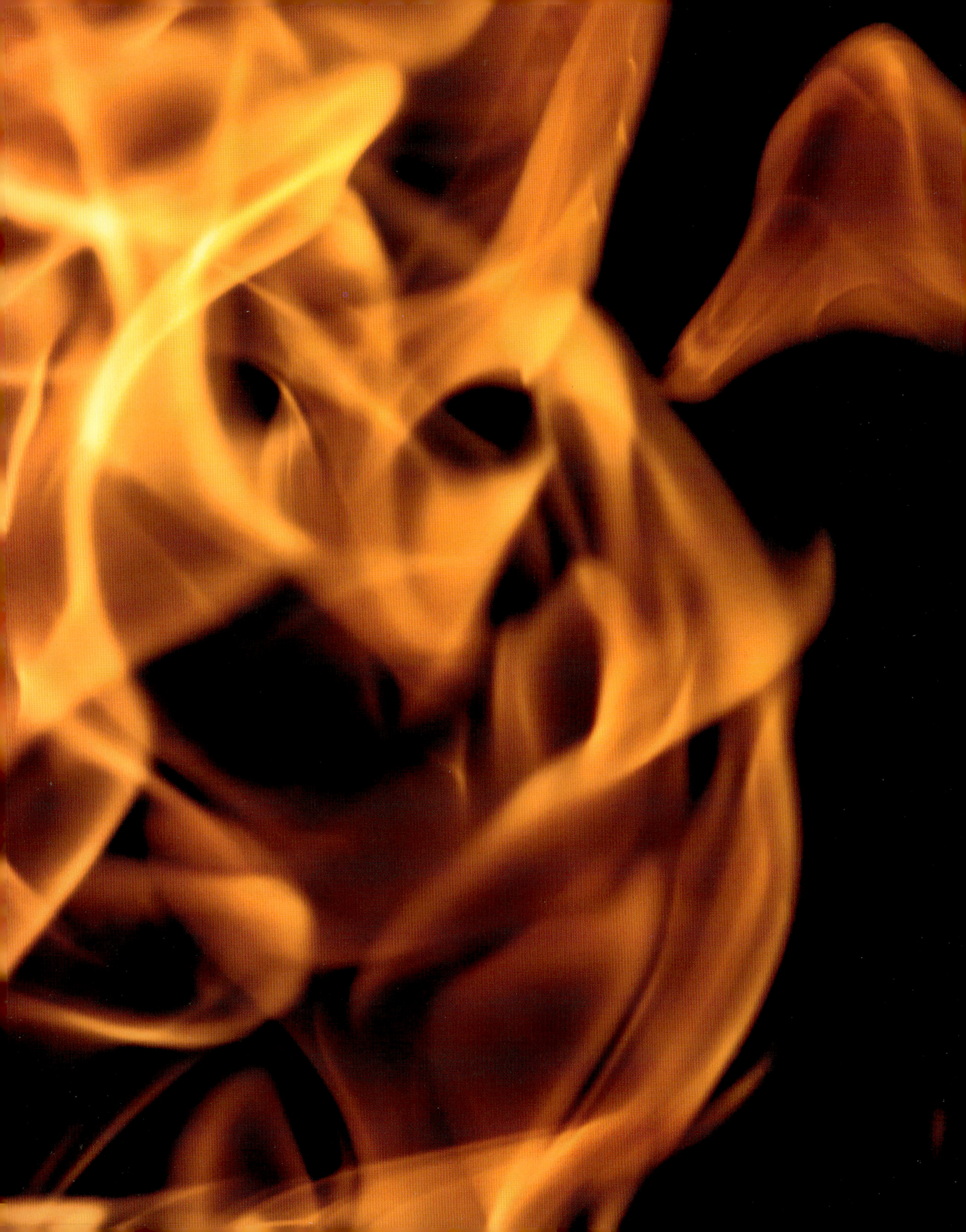

DISARMED FIREARMS

The engineering of guns is so remarkably sound that they can withstand almost every attempt to destroy them. Designed to contain an explosion, a firearm is nearly invincible; it is hard to kill a gun. Ironically, fire is the nemesis of firearms, since their metal parts can be melted and forged anew. This is the principle behind the well-known phrase "turning swords to plowshares." The saying stems from an Old Testament verse, "They shall beat their swords into plowshares, and their spears into pruning hooks." Throughout history there have been variations on this process of repurposing weapons for peaceful and creative ends.

Within contemporary culture, guns can be decommissioned through buyback and recycling programs run by police and other agencies that offer incentives for surrendered weapons. Such deactivated firearms are altered to no longer discharge projectiles, a condition meant to be permanent. Gun disposal programs have also provided rich fodder for artists' works and exhibitions. With the skill set and vision to handle these perilous instruments, artists have devised new ways to render them physically and metaphorically impotent. The creatively neutered guns in this section have been crushed, bound, shot at, fractured, and thorn covered. Guns have also been rendered harmless through the use of fragile or benign materials such as glass, porcelain, paper, and sugar. In the intrepid efforts of artists to disarm firearms, guns may have finally met their match.

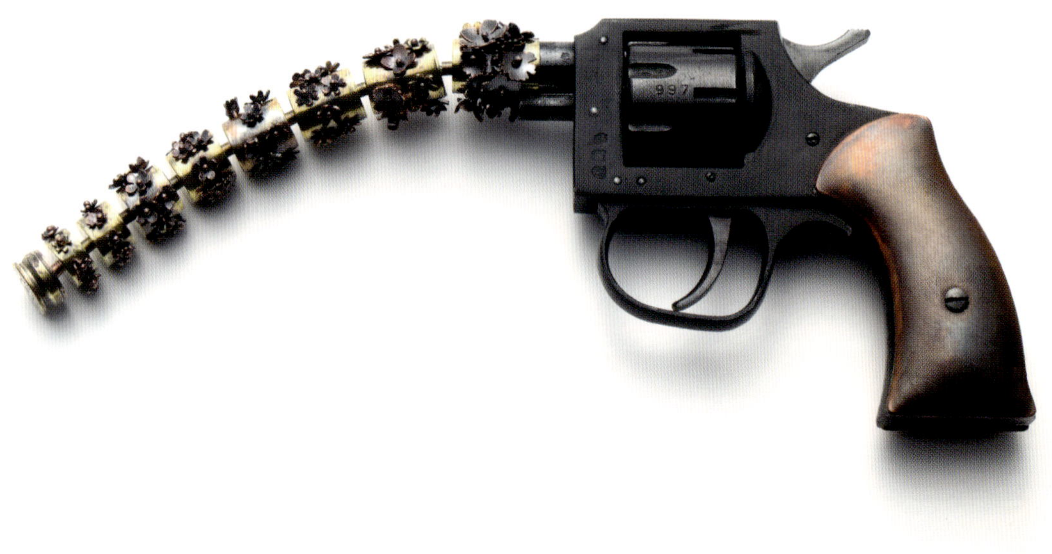

Liz Clark
Projectile Disfunction, 2015
brass, copper, steel
4 × 10 × 2½ in.

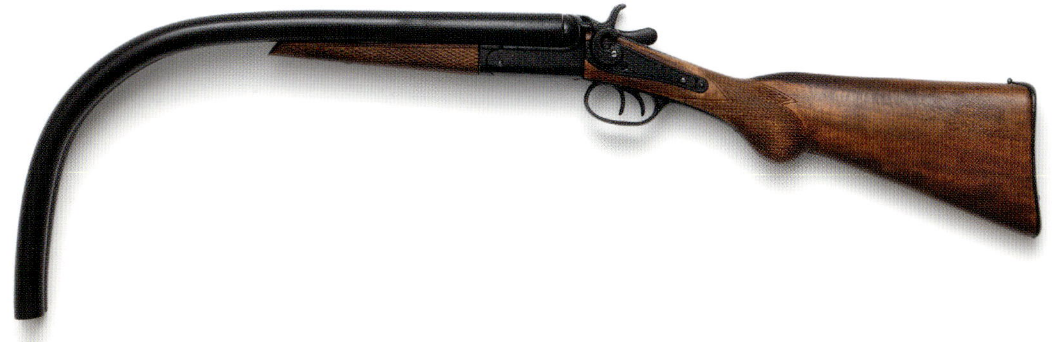

Mark Dion
On the Topic of Hunting, 2015
double-barreled stage shotgun, wood, steel, tubing
9¾ × 35½ × 2 in.
(Edition of 7, 2 APs)
Neue Berliner Kunstverein
Courtesy of the artist and Tanya Bonakdar Gallery, New York / Los Angeles

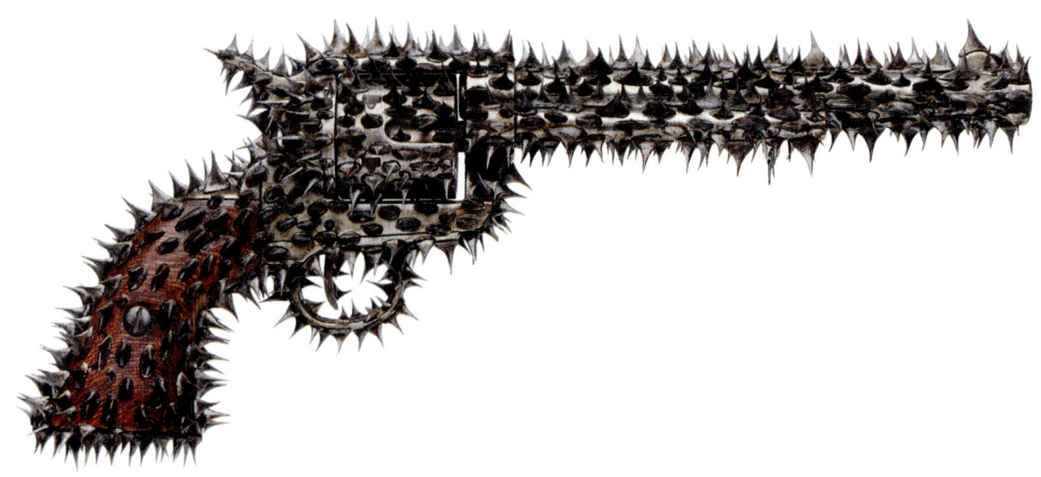

Nancy Fouts
Peacemaker, 2012
pistol, rose thorns
5½ × 13½ × 2½ in.

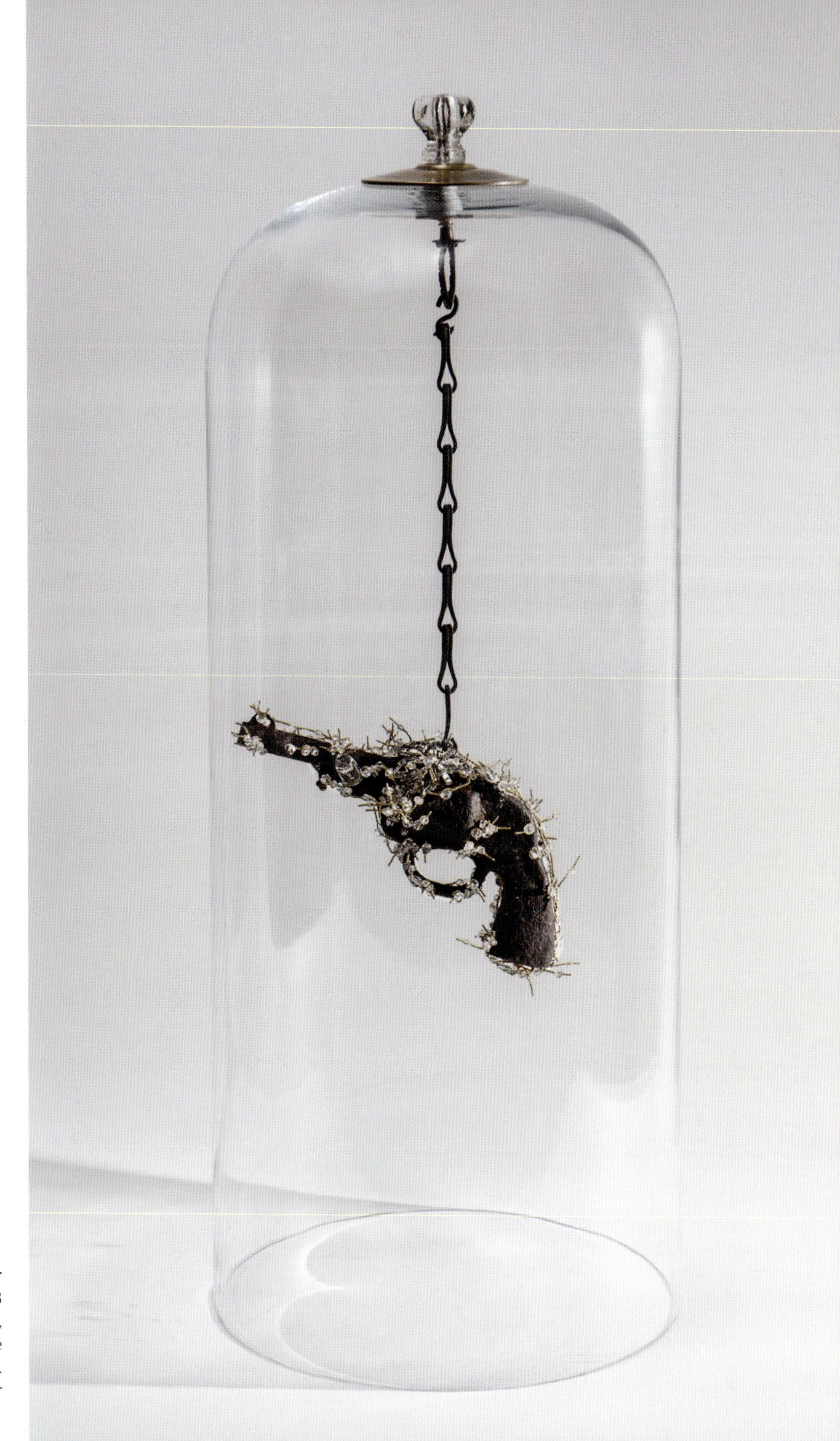

Karin Broker
A Pretty Gun, 2018
crystals, wire, steel,
glass dome
25½ × 9½ × 9½ in.
Photo: Paul Hester

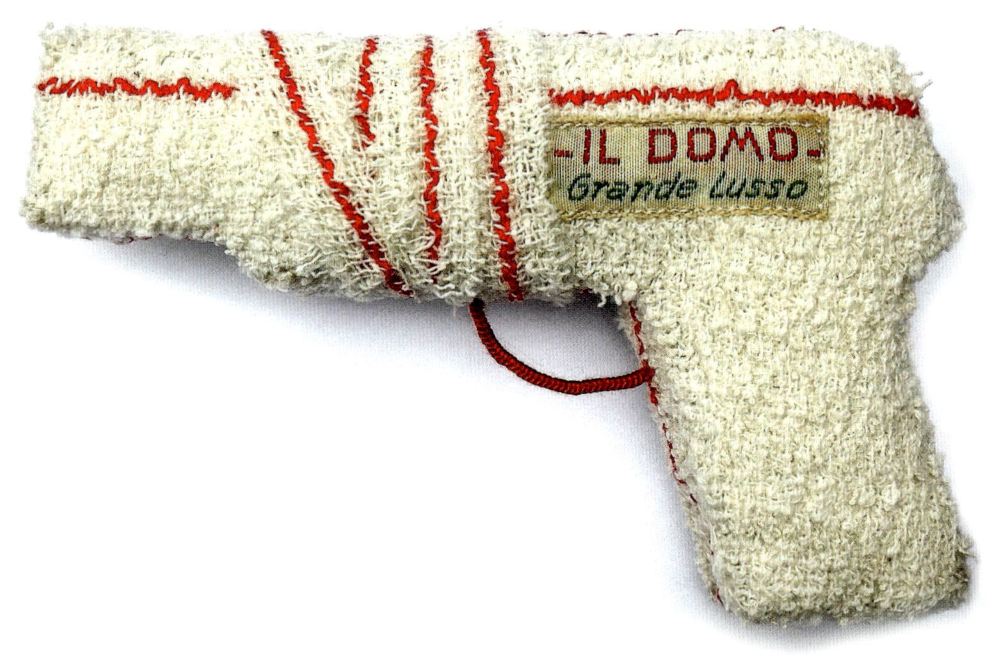

Cécile Bertrand
Il Domo, 2016
medical bandages
length 8 in.
Photo: Cécile Bertrand

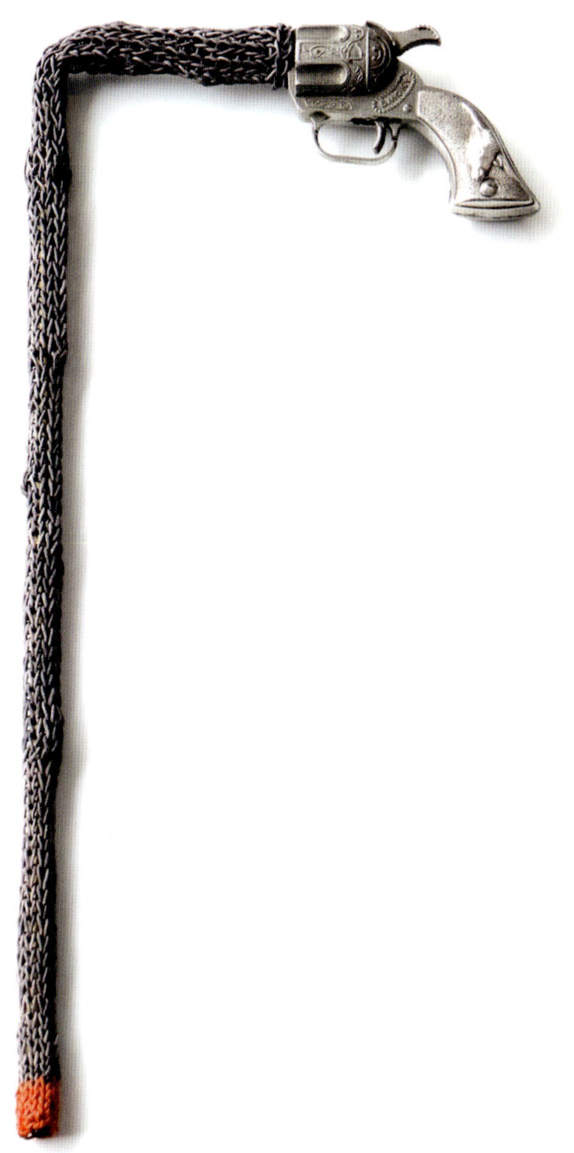

Brooke Marks-Swanson
Family Heirloom, 2015
1950 SMOKEY cap gun, Hubley Manufacturer; brass; hand-knit leather
13½ × 6 × 1 in.

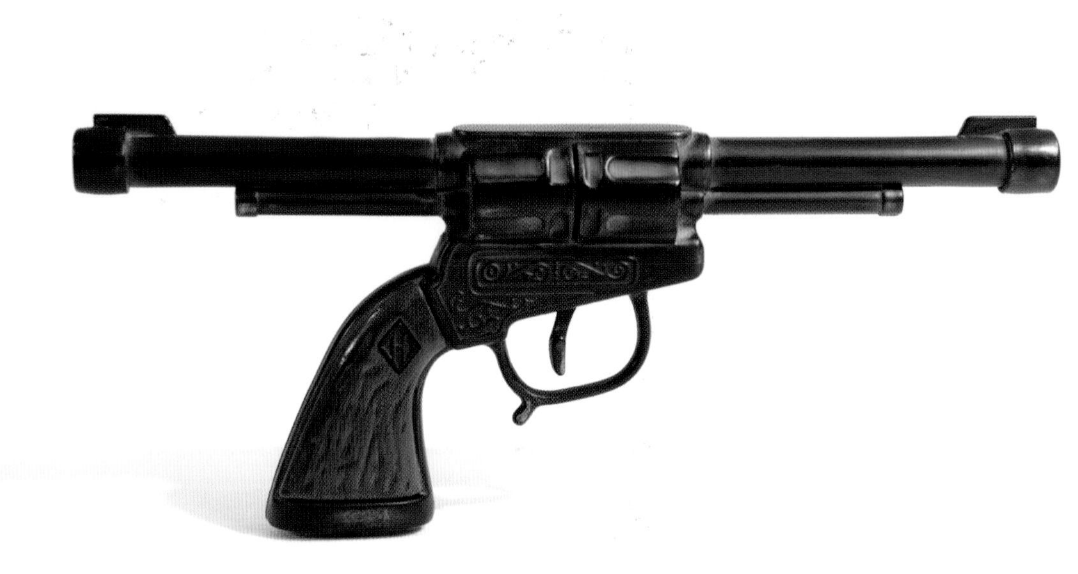

Seyo Cizmic
Civil War Gun, 2006
redesigned replica pistol
4 × 10 × 1 in.

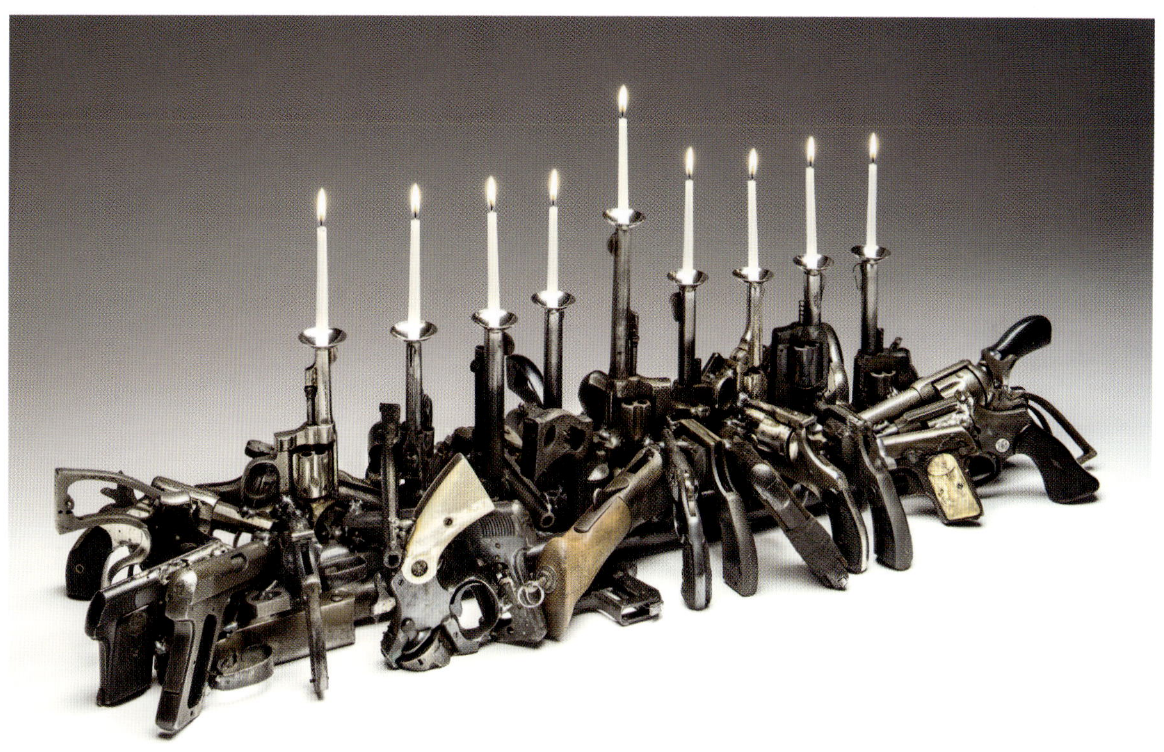

Boris Bally
Loaded Menorah, 2016
altered handguns, gun barrels, and components, 925 silver;
weapons courtesy of Good4Guns Anti-violence Coalition, Pittsburgh, PA
11¾ × 15 × 40 in.
Photo: Aaron Usher Photography

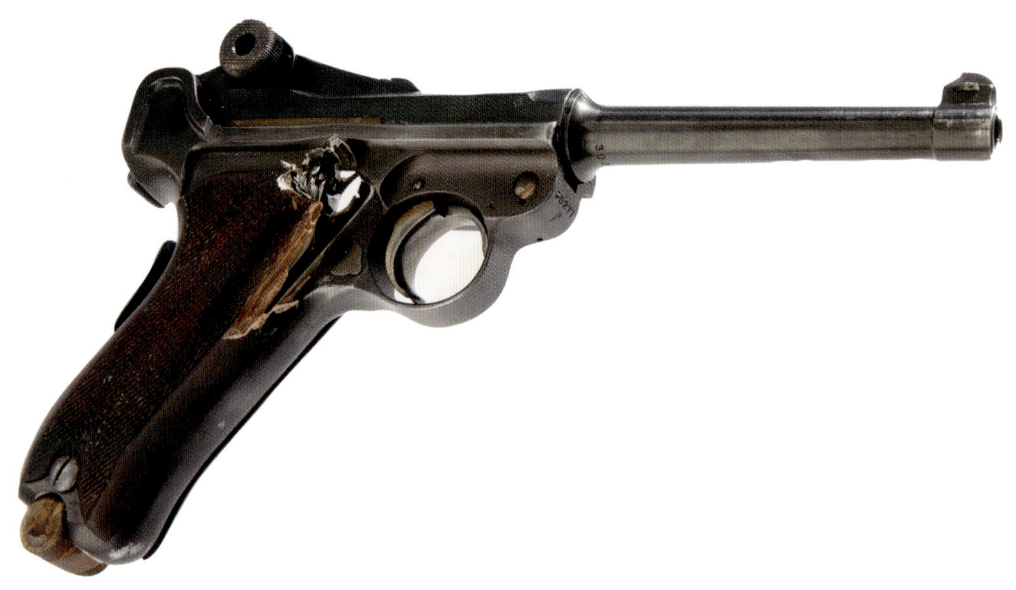

Johanna Dahm
Imagine War, 2012
gun shot with a gun
9 × 6 × 2 in.
Photo: Reinhard Zimmermann

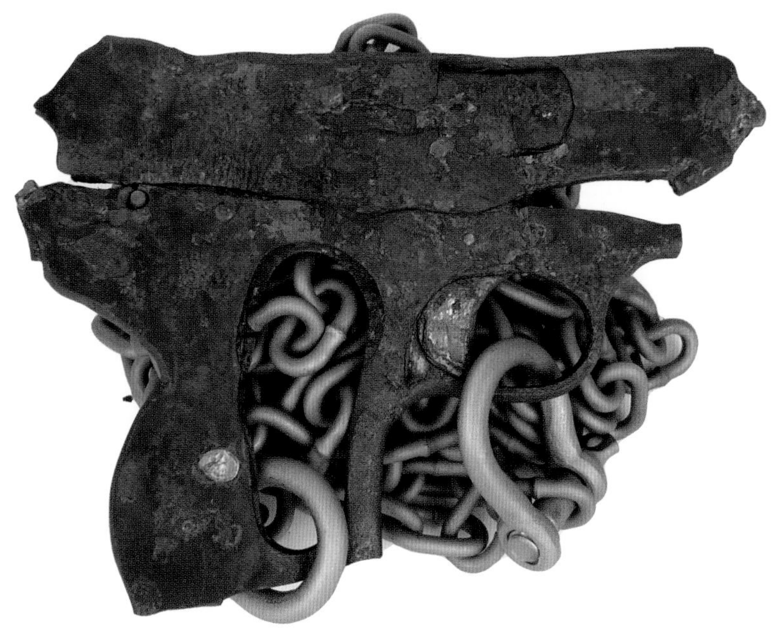

Melissa Cameron
Resilience, 2016
drop-hammer-struck gun, steel
7 × 7 × 2 in.
Photo: Melissa Cameron

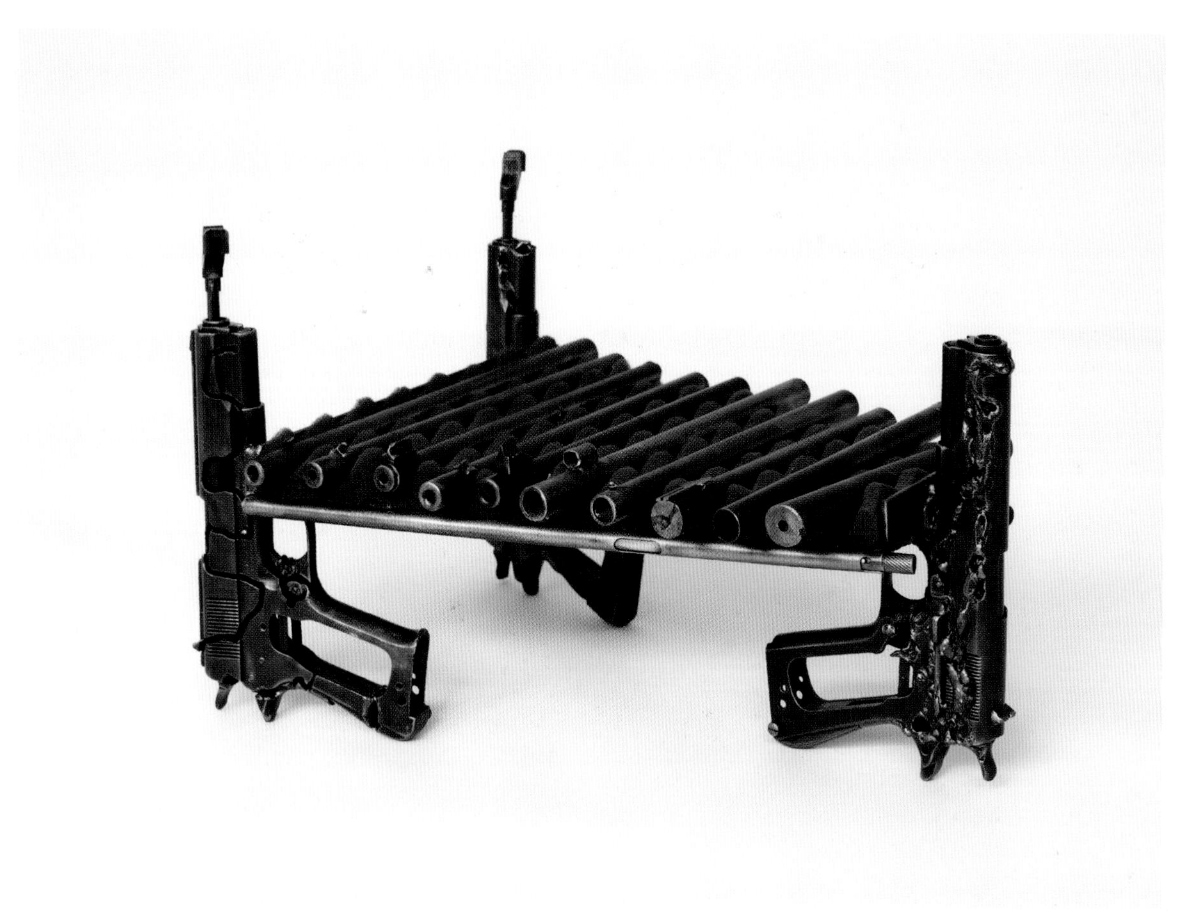

Pedro Reyes
Disarm (Xylophone XII), 2016
recycled metal
approx. 10¼ × 17¼ × 11¾ in.
Photo: Ramiro Chaves

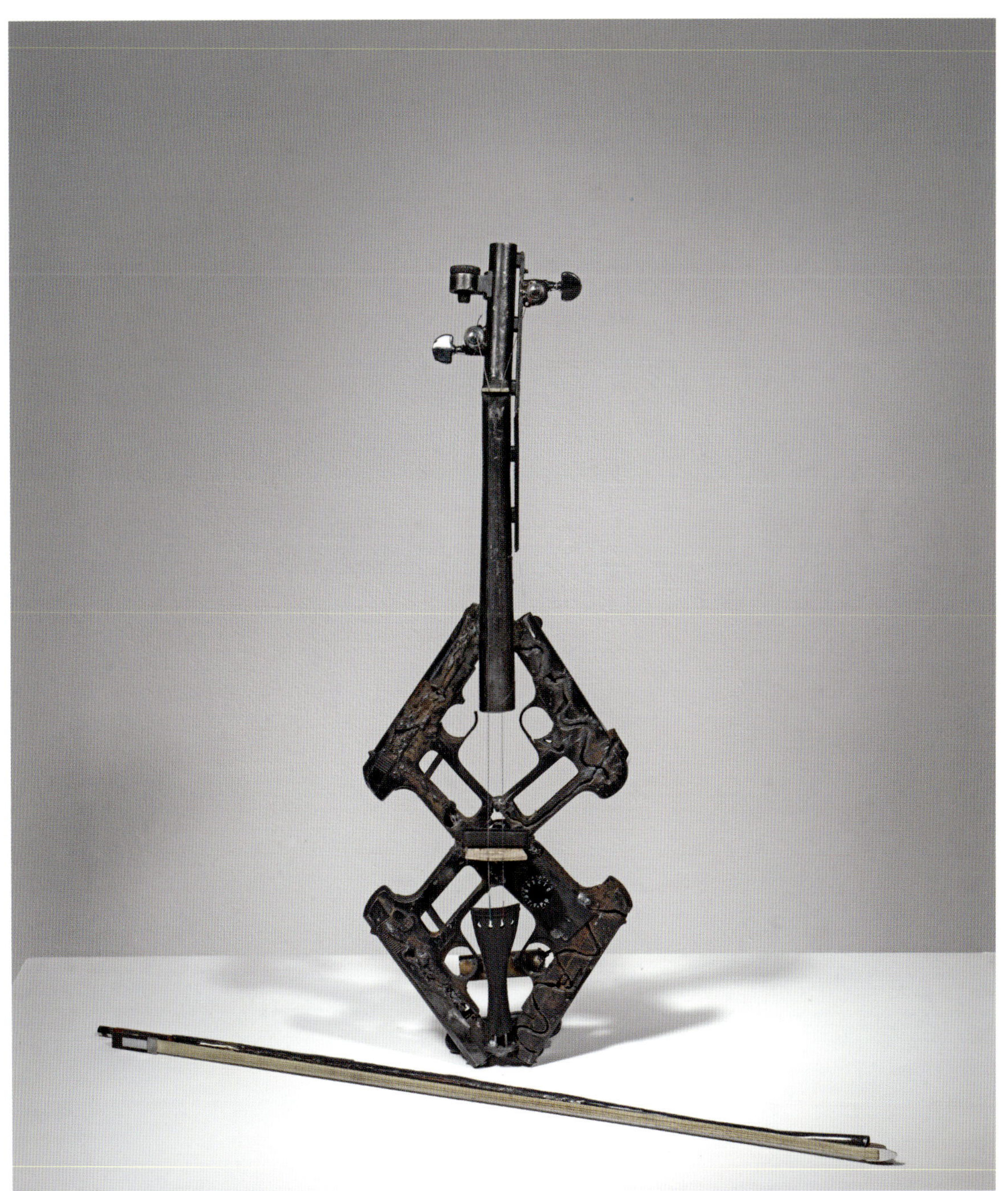

Pedro Reyes
Disarm (Violin III), 2013
recycled metal
approx. 26½ × 9 × 5 in.
Photo: Ken Adlard and Dave Morgan

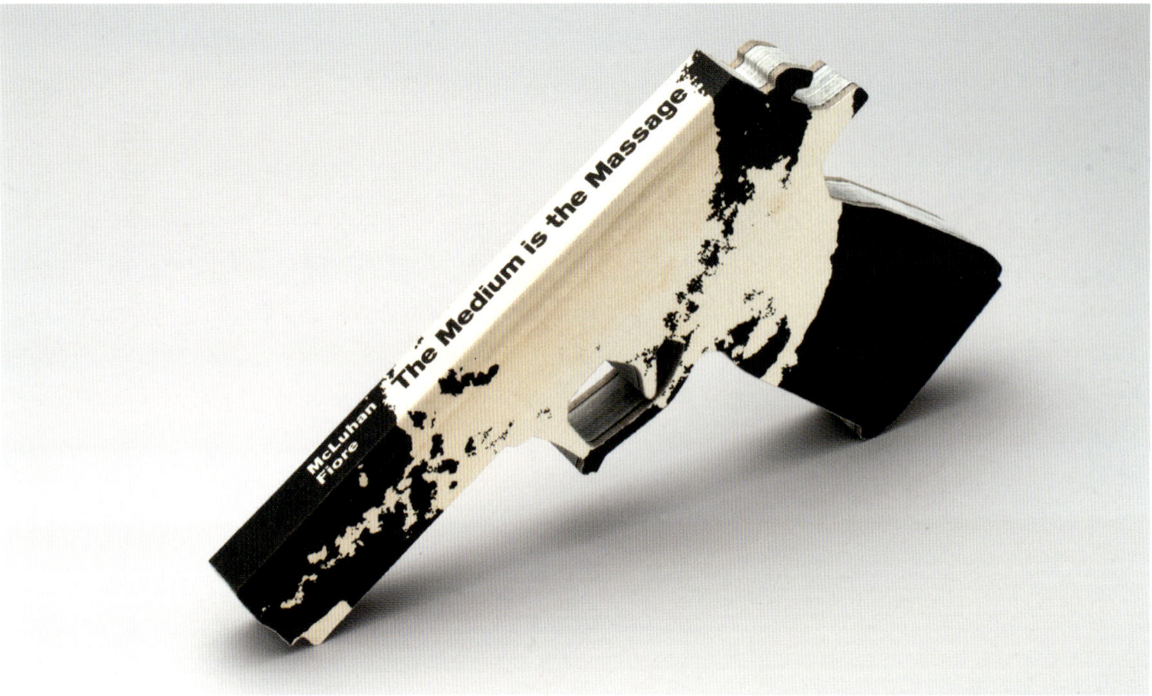

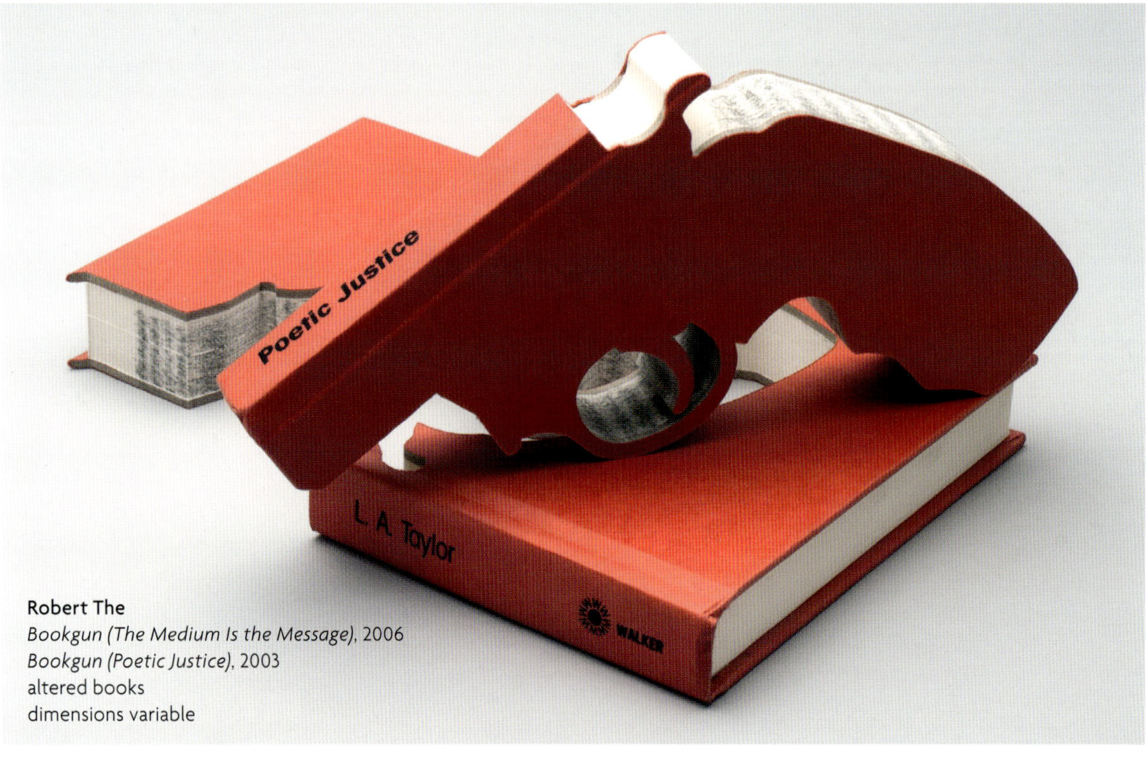

Robert The
Bookgun (The Medium Is the Message), 2006
Bookgun (Poetic Justice), 2003
altered books
dimensions variable

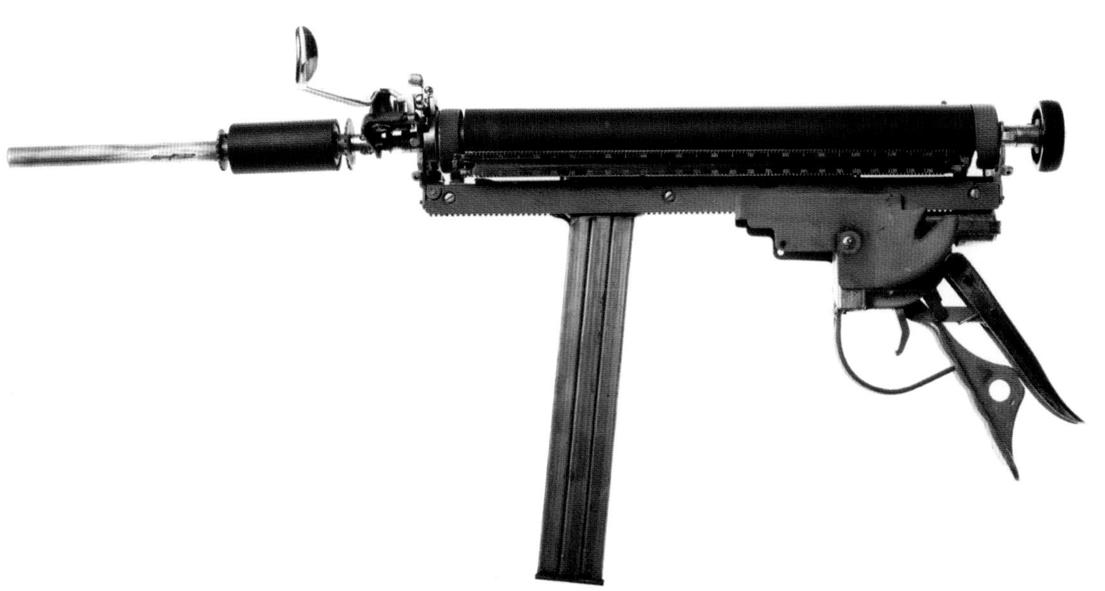

Ravi Zupa
MTSMG-RYL, 2016
antique typewriter components, stapler components, scrap steel
27 × 11 × 2 in.

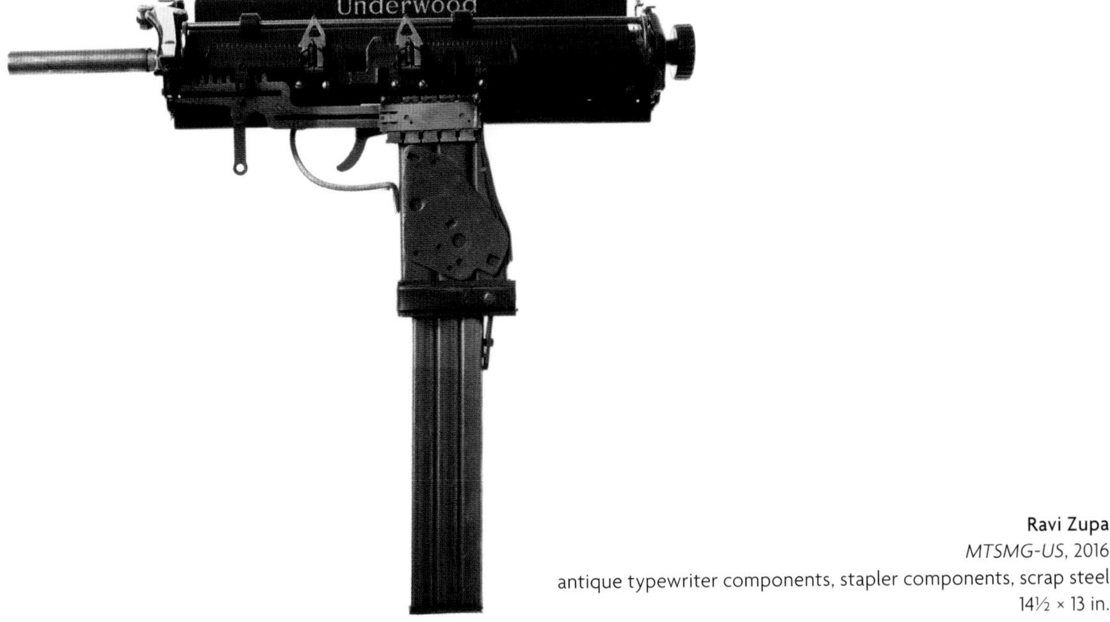

Ravi Zupa
MTSMG-US, 2016
antique typewriter components, stapler components, scrap steel
14½ × 13 in.

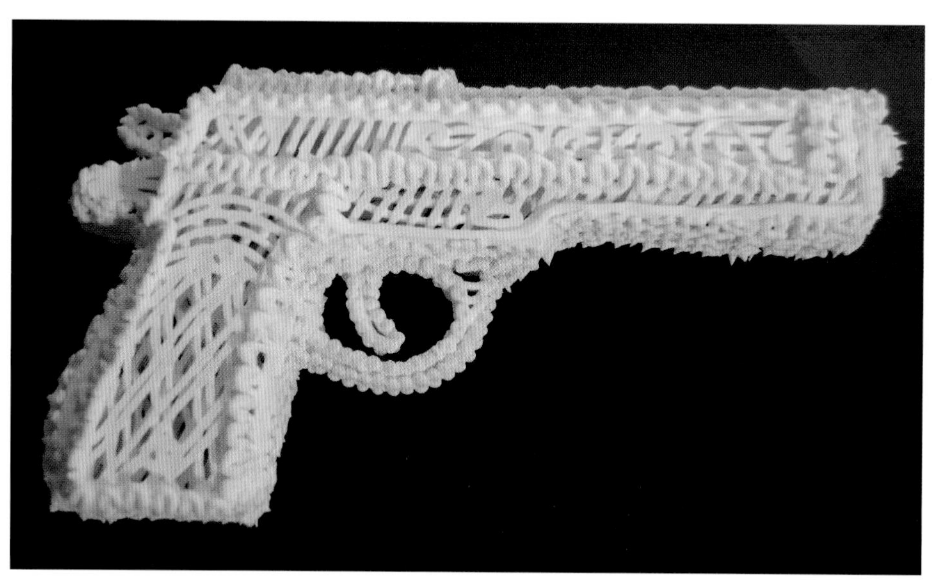

Sarah Graham
Sugar Approximation-Beretta, 2002
sugar, egg whites, wire
6 × 8 × 2 in.

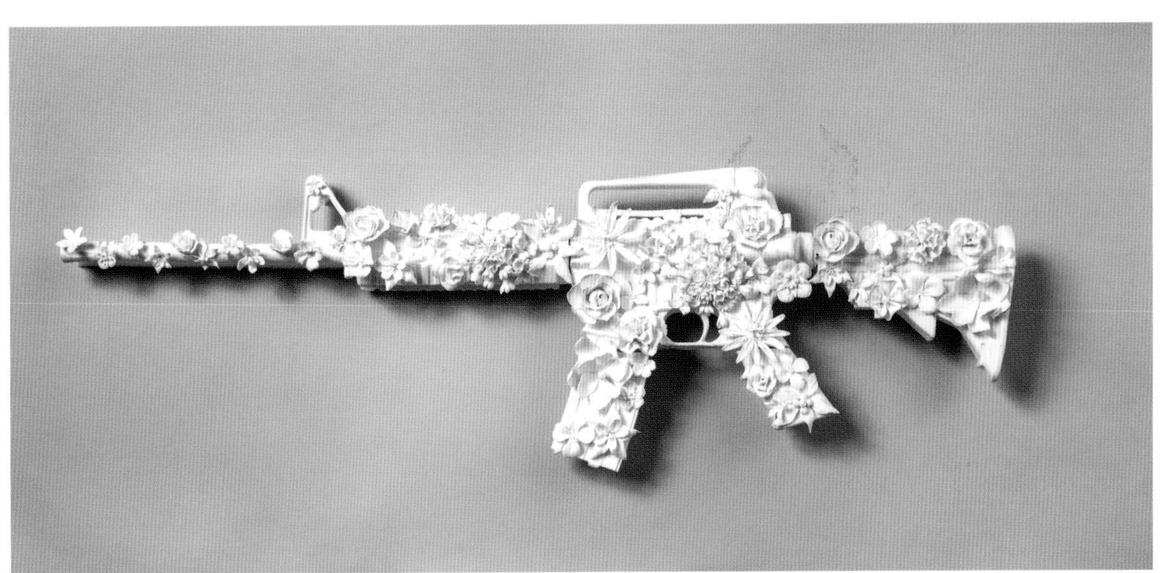

Keiko Fukazawa
AKA AR-15 2017826, 2017
porcelain
11 × 34 × 3½ in.

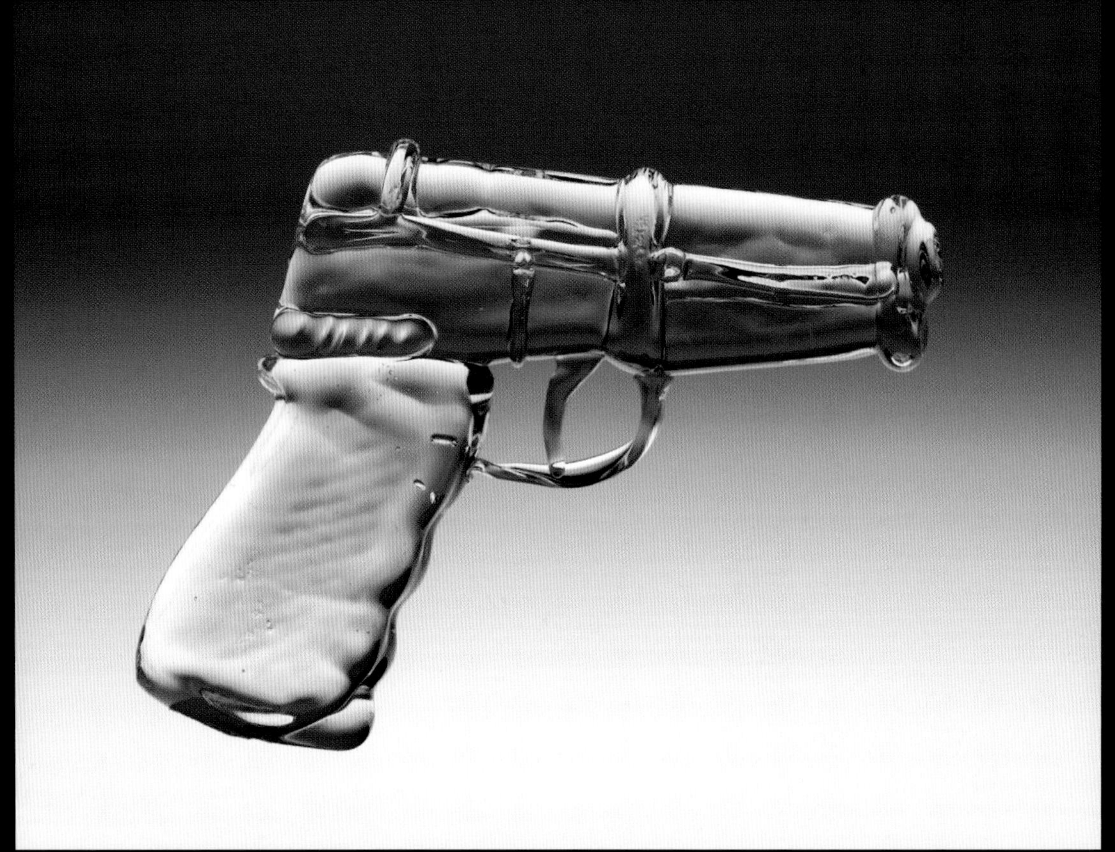

Claire Lieberman
Sharpshooter, 2010
glass
4½ × 8 × 2 in.

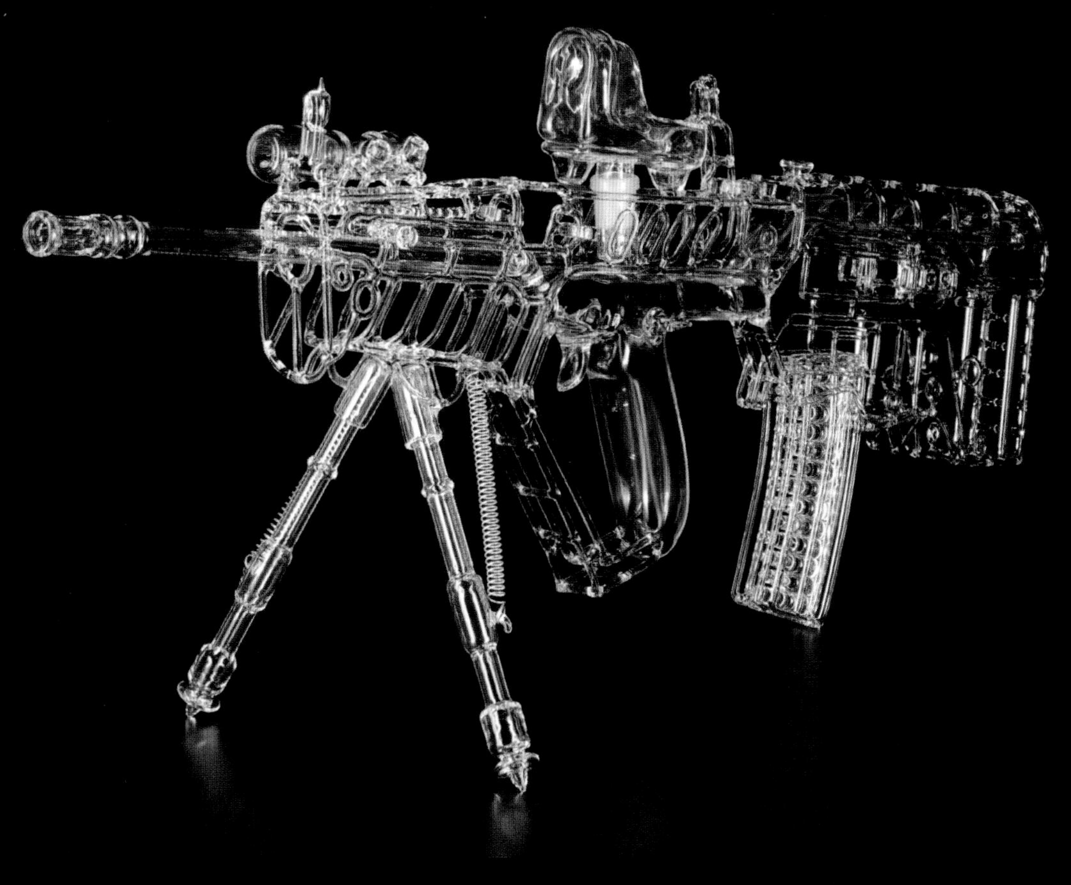

Robert Mickelsen
Star 21, from Weapons of Peace series, 2013
flame-worked glass
length 25 in.

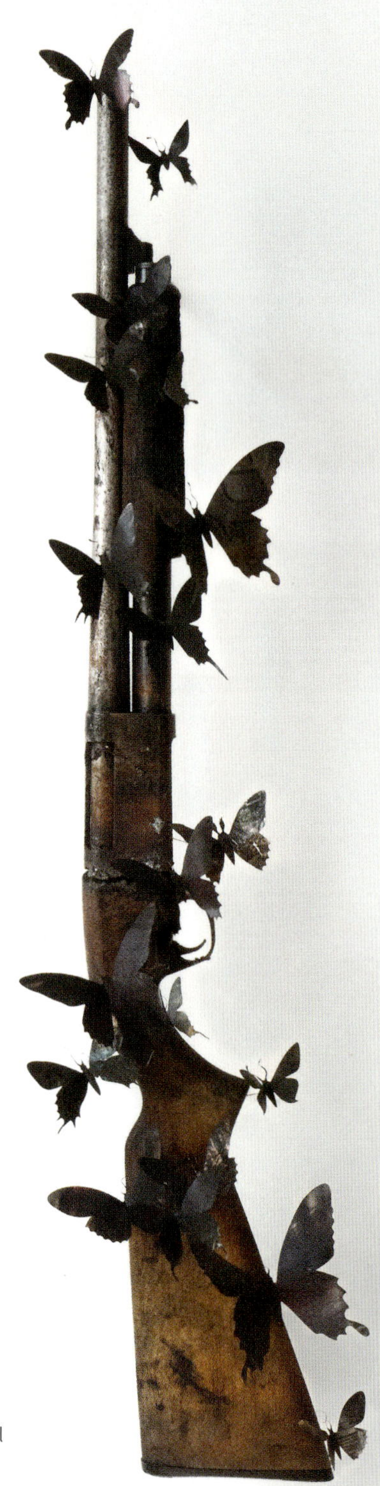

Paul Villinski
Epitaph, 2014
shotgun, aluminum (found cans), soot, steel
37 × 5¼ × 5¼ in.

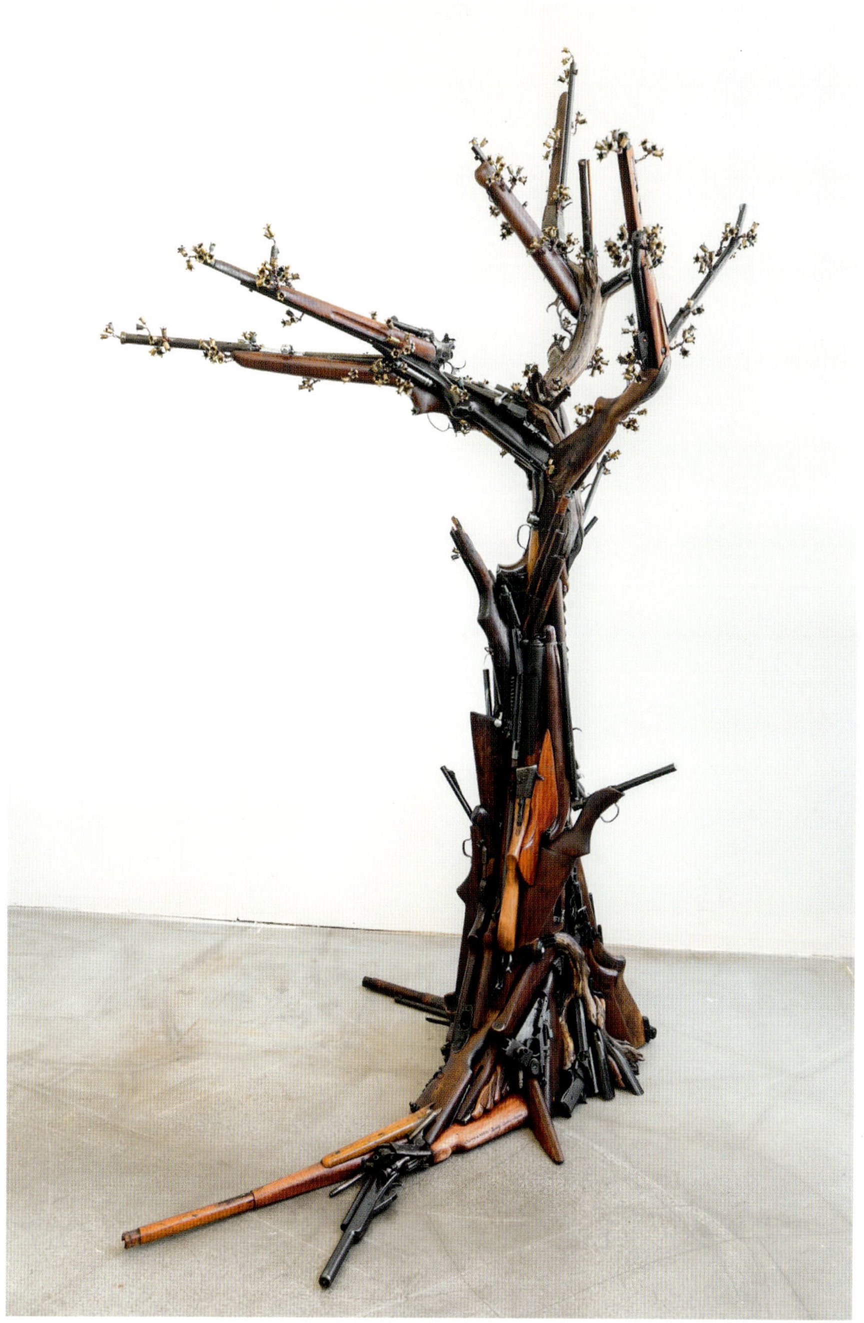

Clody Cates & Gaige Qualmann
Return to Nature, 2018
wooden rifle stocks, bullets, shell casings
9 x 3 x 5 ft.
Photo: Kane C. Andrade

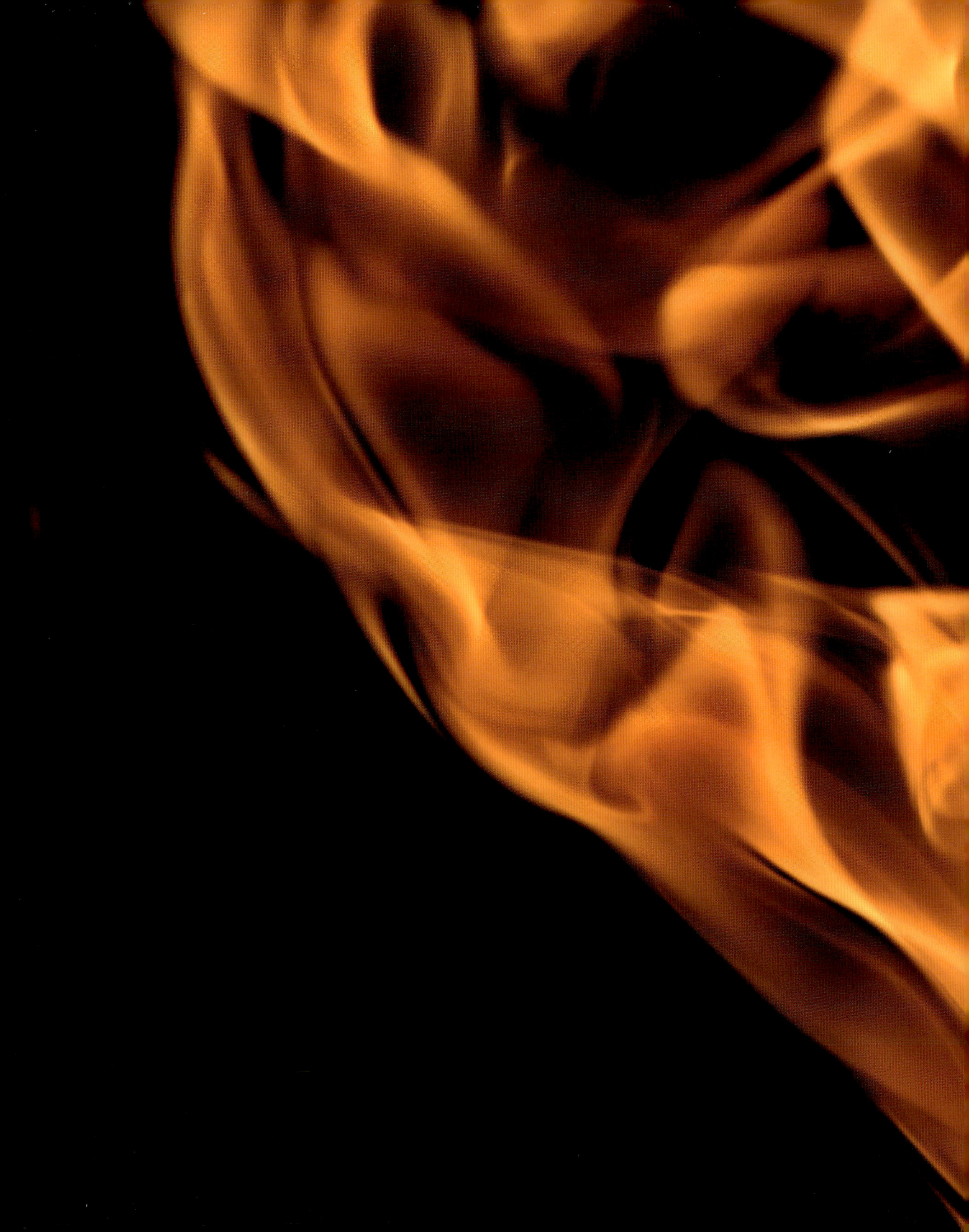

GUNNED DOWN

It is impossible to calculate the millions of humans who have died by gunshot since the invention of firearms. It is even harder to fathom the countless lives that have been maimed by this weapon over the last 1,000 years. At present, worldwide, it is known that some 250,000 die annually by guns, excluding those shot in warfare. These quarter-million deaths include suicides, accidents, and homicides, which account for the majority of deceased, particularly of young men. However, gunfire does not spare women, children, and the elderly, who too often perish in its wake. Civilian shootings, criminals, regional conflict, and terrorism all take their toll on innocent lives, and across the globe hundreds of people are fatally shot each day.

The art in this section pays homage to those killed or wounded by gun violence, and whose bodies betray the grim consequence of firearms. Here we confront images of victims, both dead and alive, who have been shot down or targeted, along with animals felled by a bullet. Together these works graphically testify that guns are indeed a matter of life and death. As declared by justice watchdog group Amnesty International, "Gun-related violence threatens our most fundamental human right, the right to life." Whereas guns have the capacity to protect lives and limbs, they also have the power to destroy both.

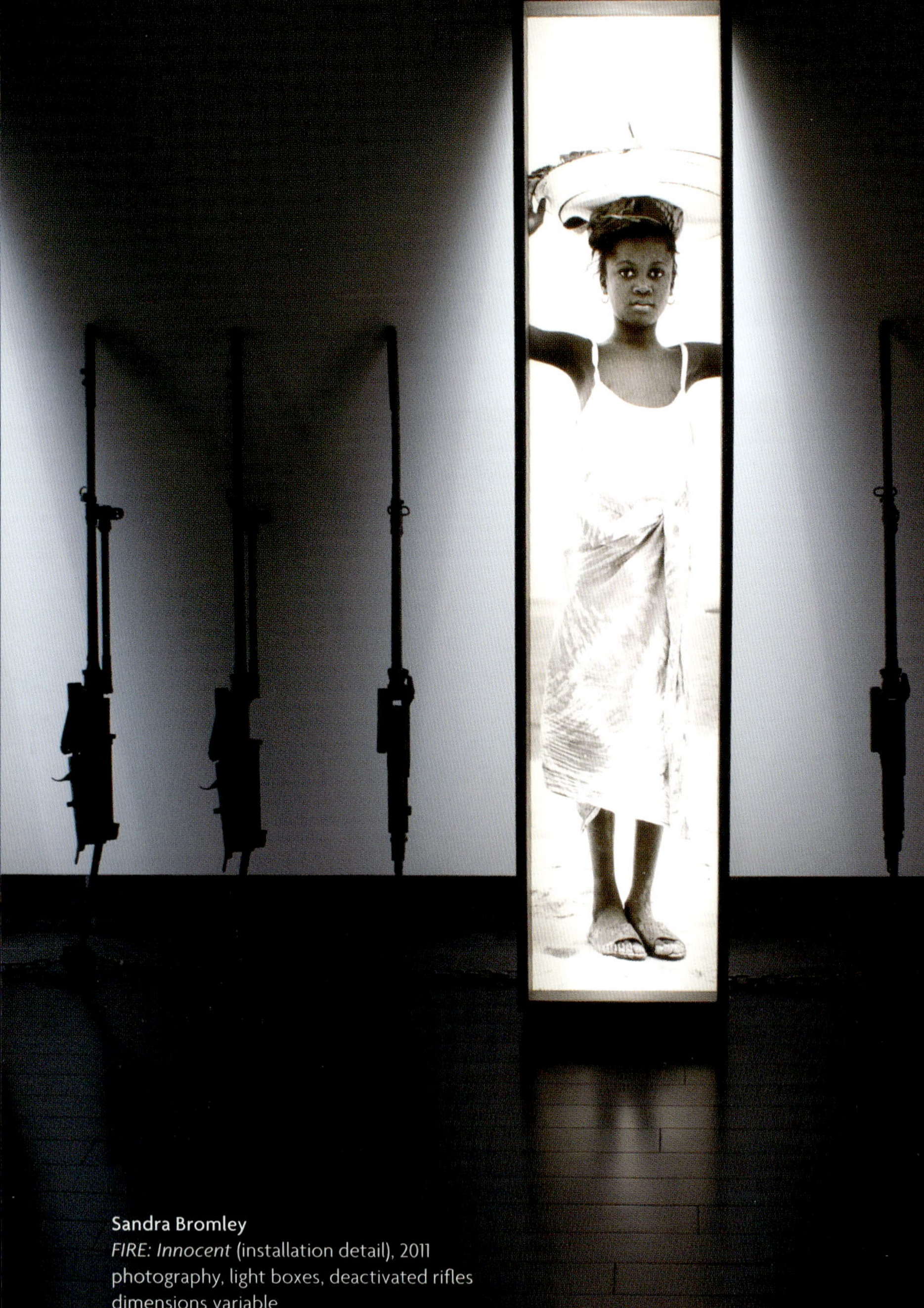

Sandra Bromley
FIRE: Innocent (installation detail), 2011
photography, light boxes, deactivated rifles
dimensions variable

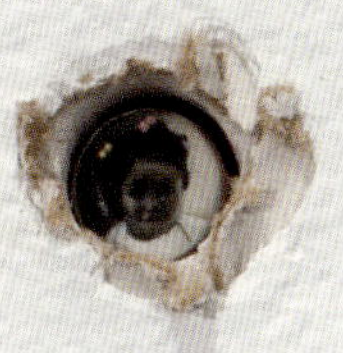

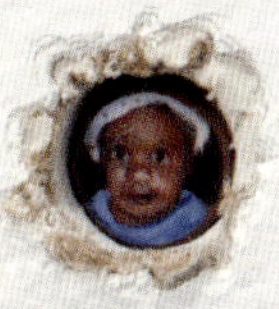

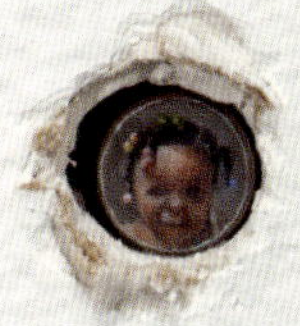

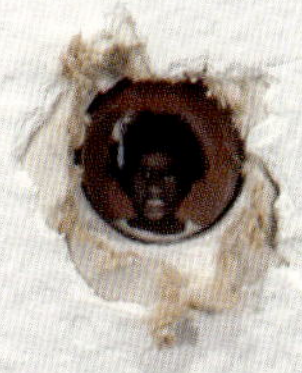

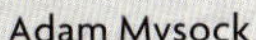

Adam Mysock
The Last Six, Under Six, Murdered by a Gun in the Sixth
(installation detail), 2014
acrylic on copper, mounted in wall
each portrait 7/16 in. (diameter of .44-caliber bullet)
Courtesy of Jonathan Ferrara Gallery, New Orleans

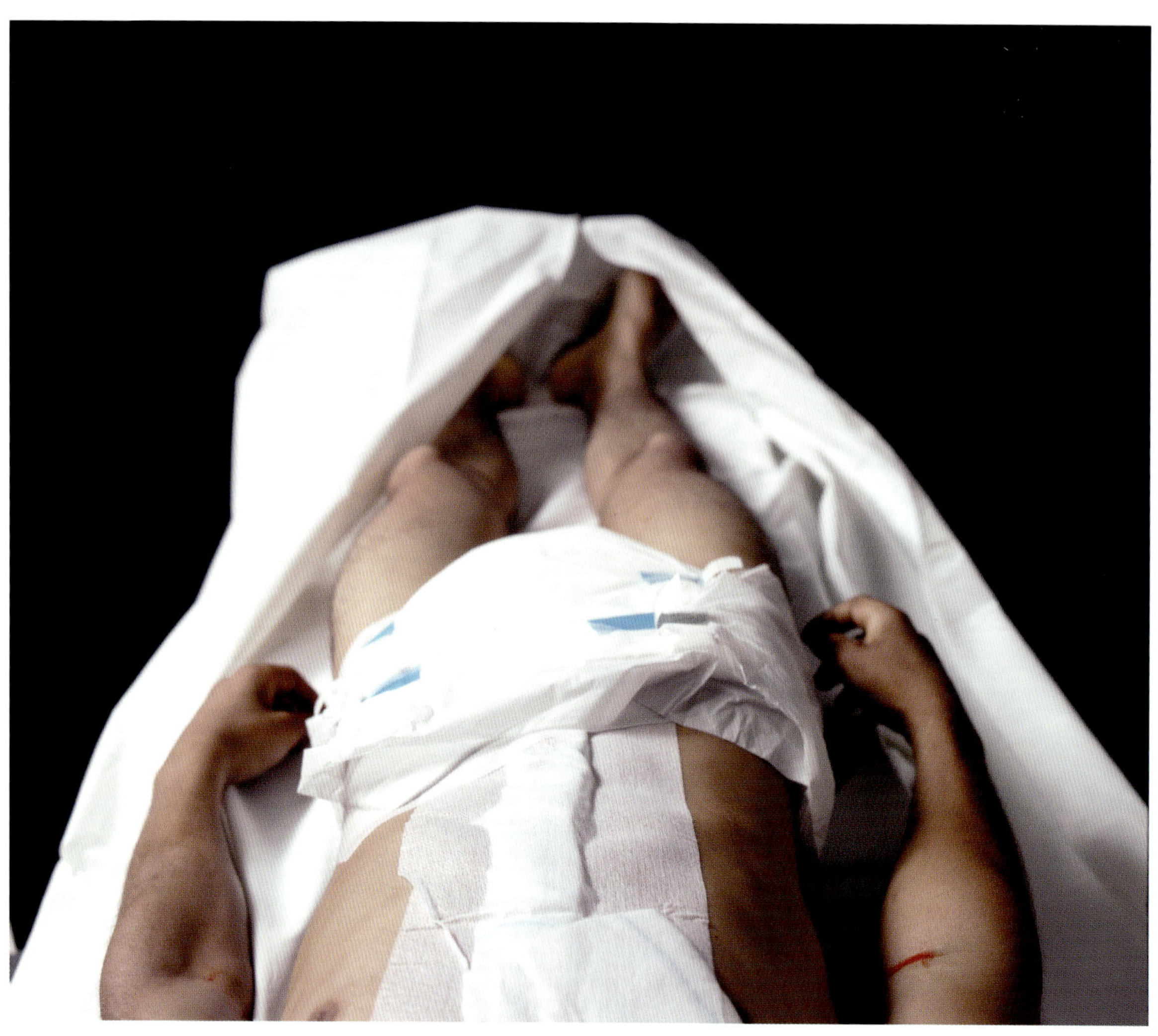

Andres Serrano
Gun Murder (The Morgue), 1992
cibachrome, Plexiglas, wooden frame
50 × 60 in.
Courtesy of the artist and Nathalie Obadia gallery

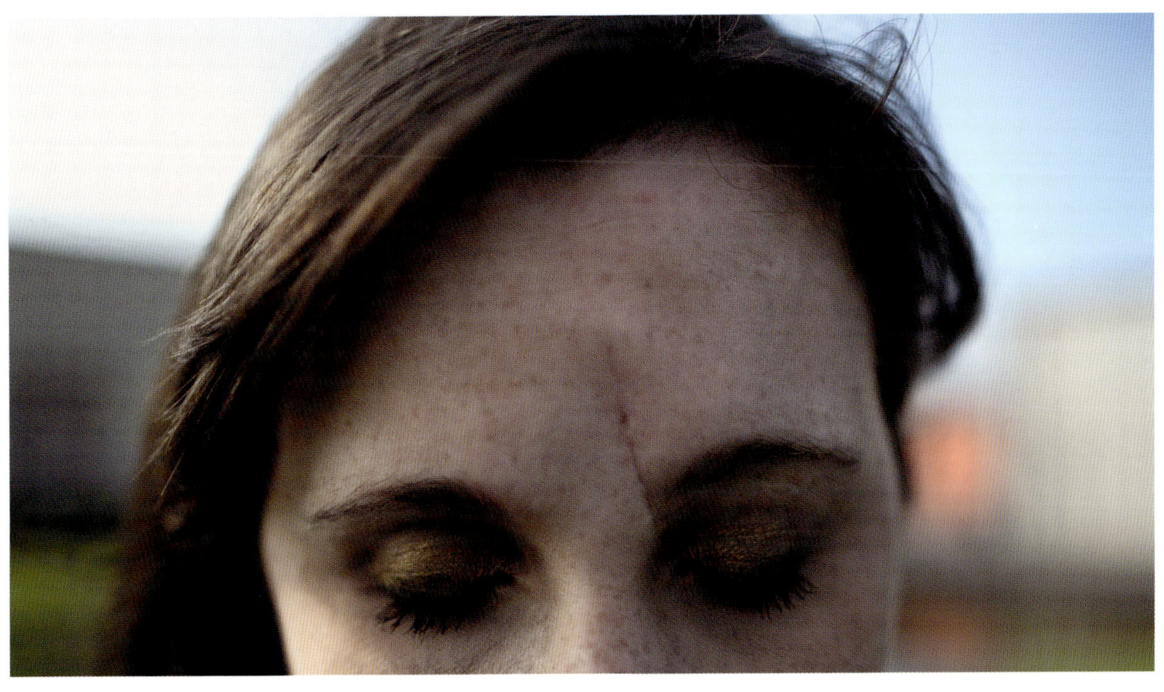

Kathy Shorr
Sara, 2015
from *SHOT: 101 Survivors of Gun Violence in America* (Brooklyn, NY: PowerHouse Books, 2017)

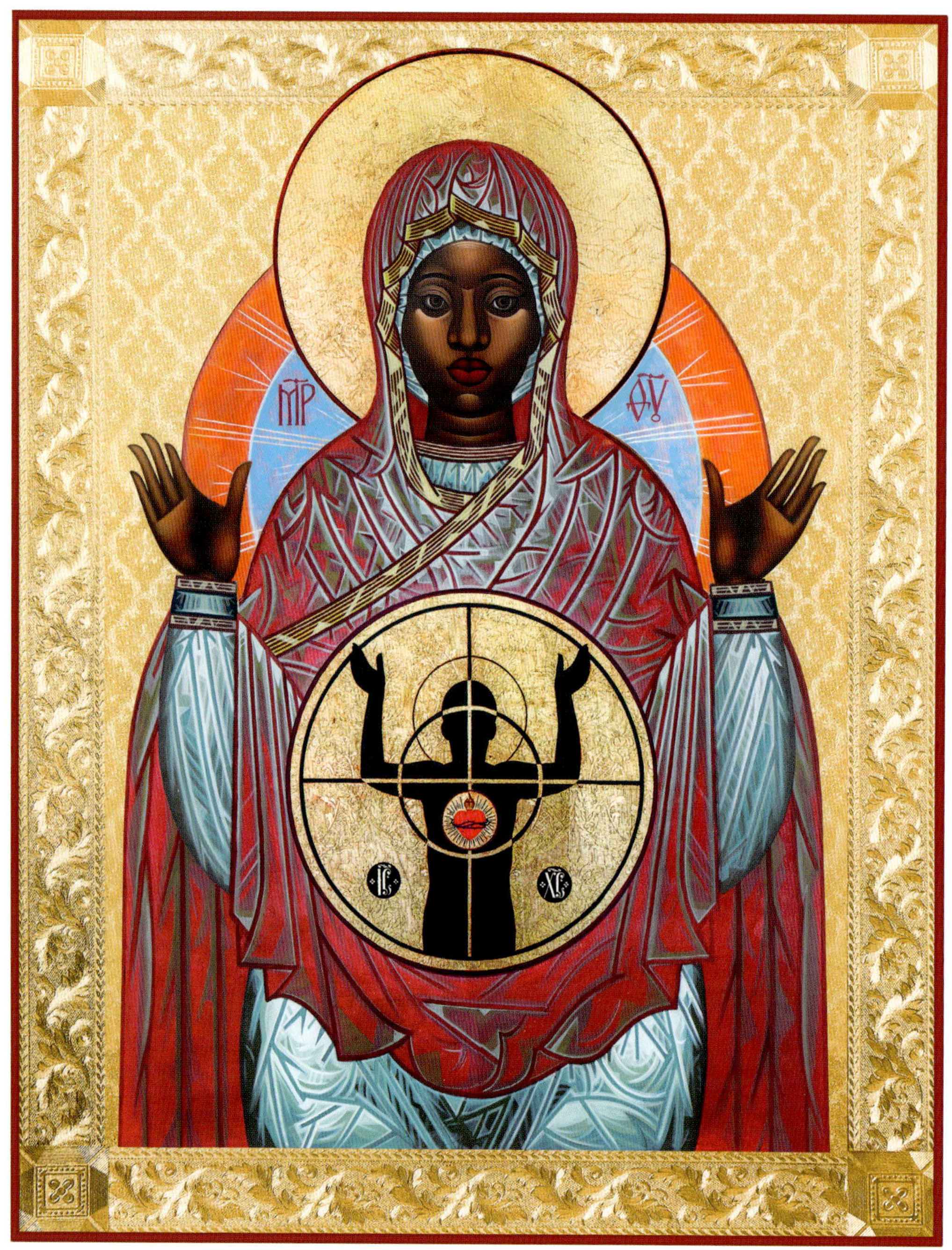

Mark Doox

Our Lady of Ferguson (All Killed by Gun Violence), 2020

acrylic, pigmented ink, gold metal leaf on red-painted and cradled wood panel

36 × 48 × 2 in.

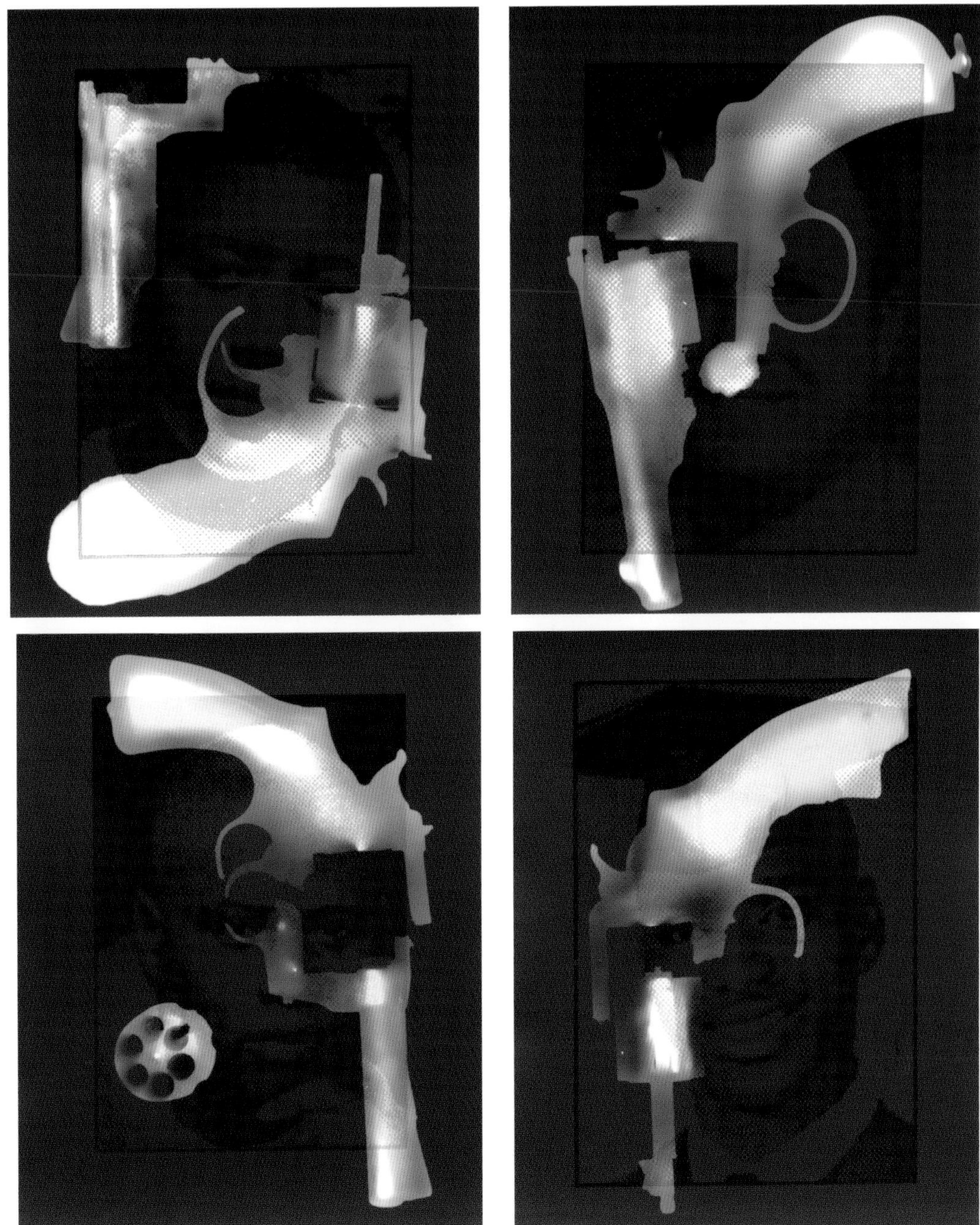

Generic Art Solutions / GAS
Antonine M. Frell Cooper. He was 22; Christopher Wayne Russell. He was 35; Zachary Gooley Marcel. He was 27; Jerome Rome Mellie Isaac. He was 28, 2002–14
screen ink on silver gelatin fiber-based paper, each 8 × 10 in.
One Hot Month series, based on *Times Picayune* obituary images from August 2002
Courtesy of Mindy Solomon Gallery, Miami

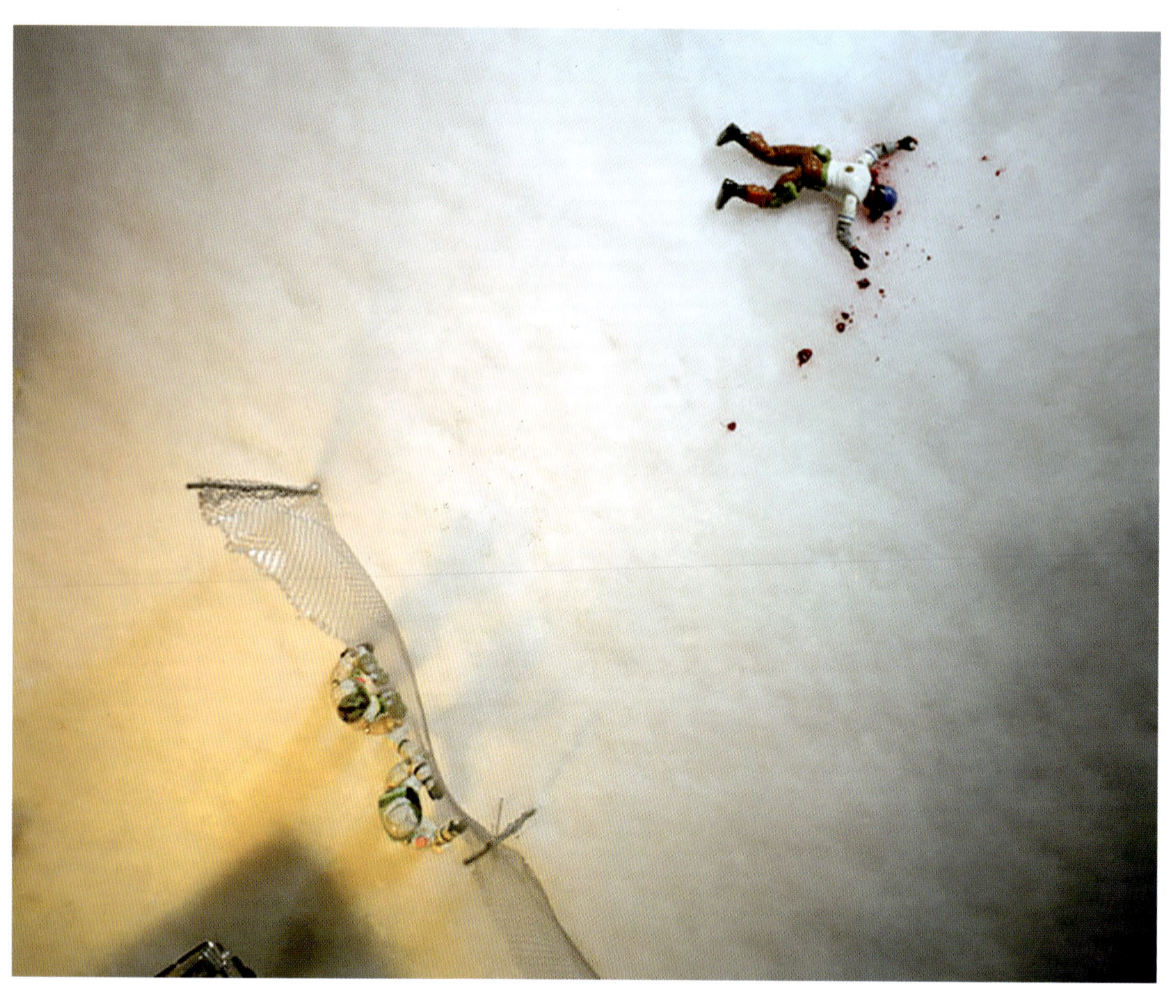

Hank Willis Thomas and Kambui Olujimi
Winter in America, 2006
film still from 4:59 video

Courtesy of the artists and Jack Shainman Gallery, New York

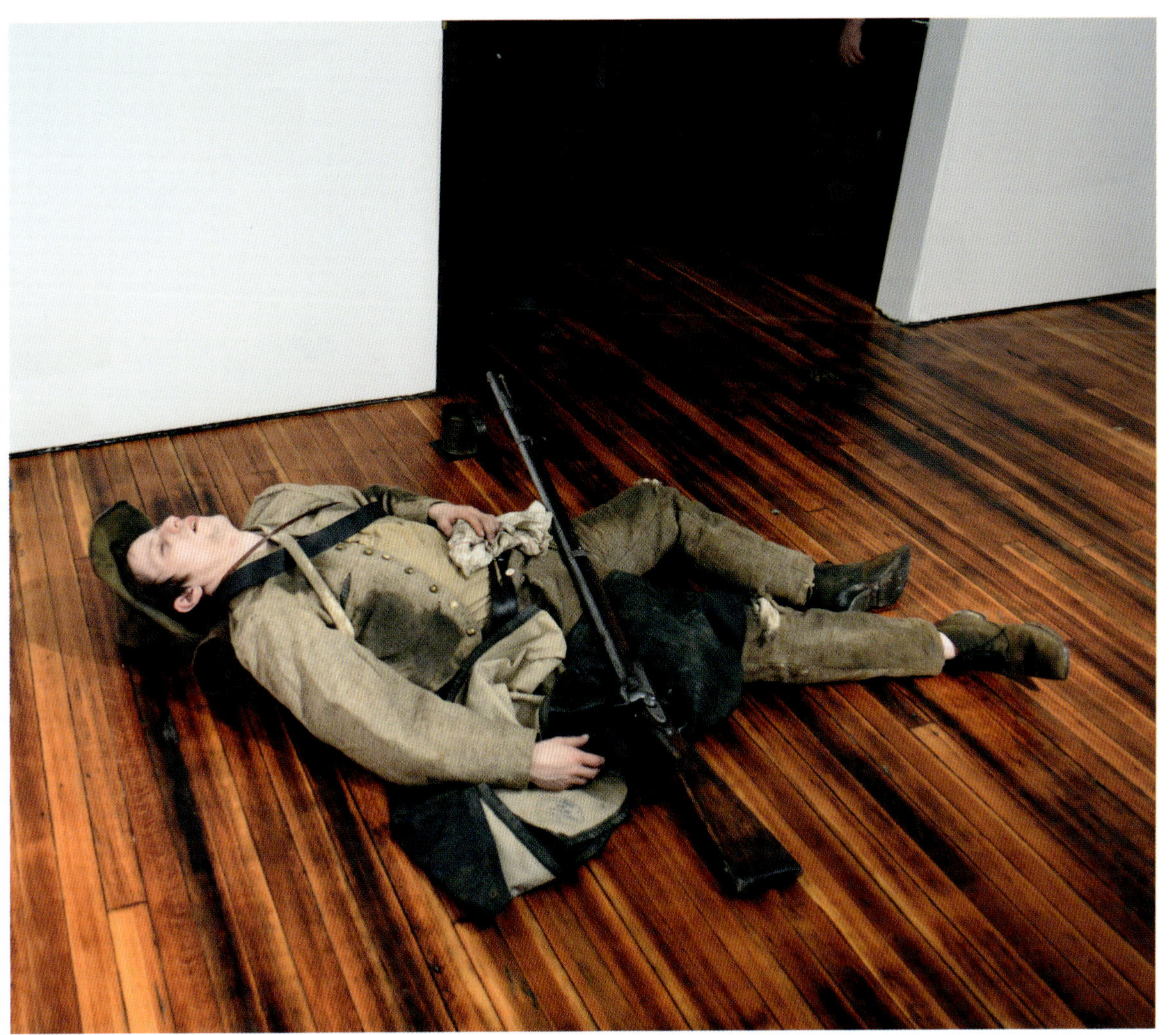

Whitney Lynn
Living History / Performing Death, 2014–15
performance series of Civil War reenactments of dead soldiers
Installation view at Sediment, Richmond, Virginia

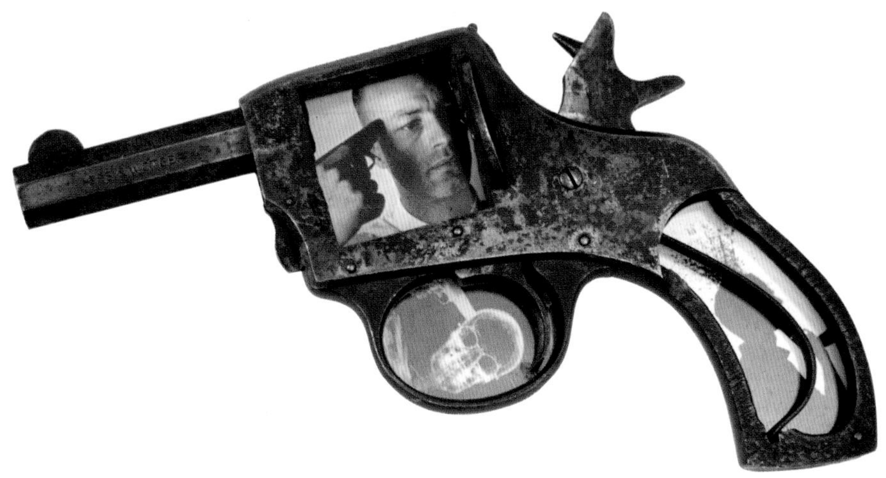

Thomas Mann
The American (Double Action) Dream, 2015
Plexiglas, digital prints, brass, copper
4 × 7 × ¾ in.

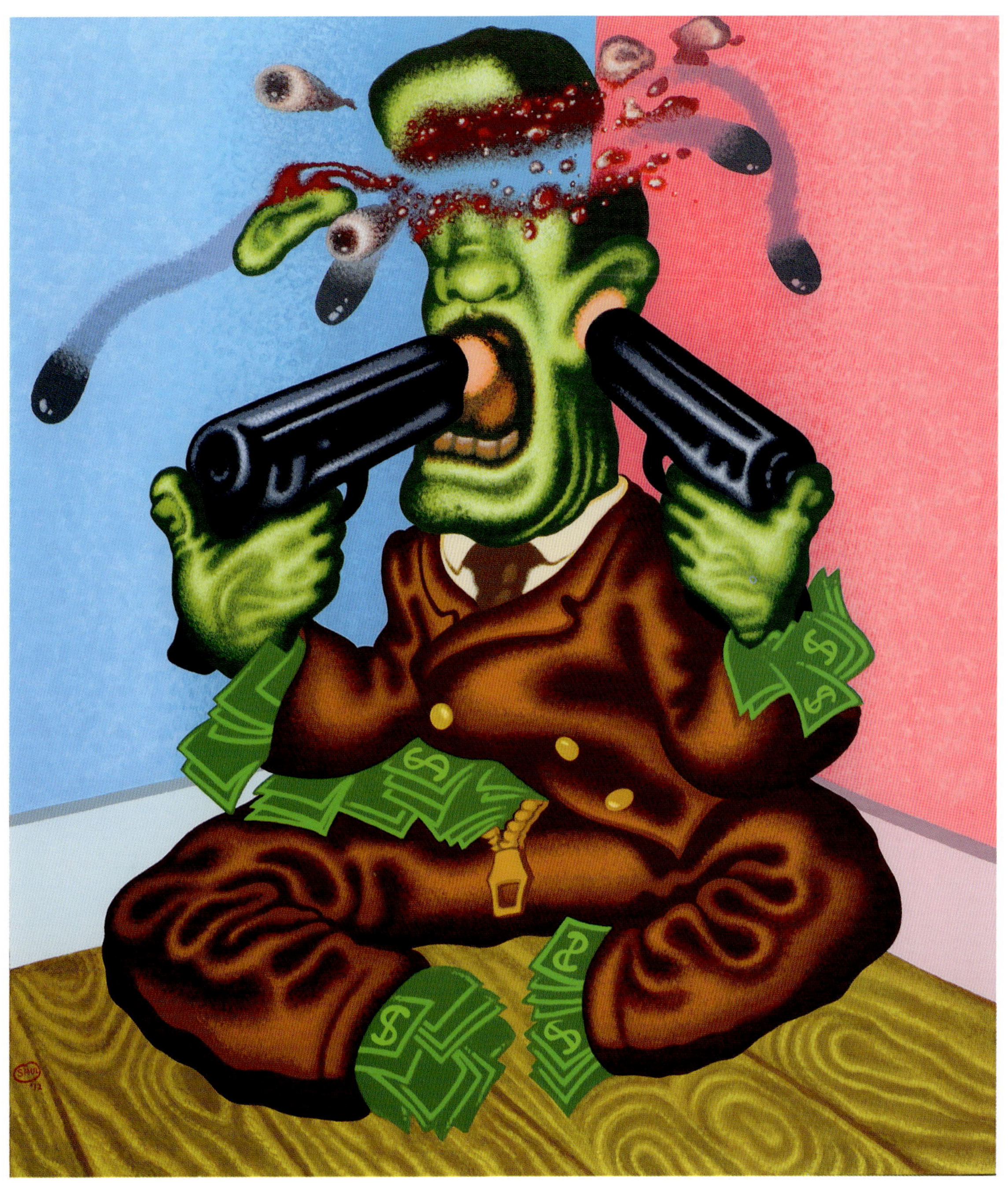

Peter Saul
Wall Street Suicide, 2012
acrylic on canvas
178 × 65 × 7 in.
Courtesy of the artist and Gary Tatintsian Gallery, Moscow

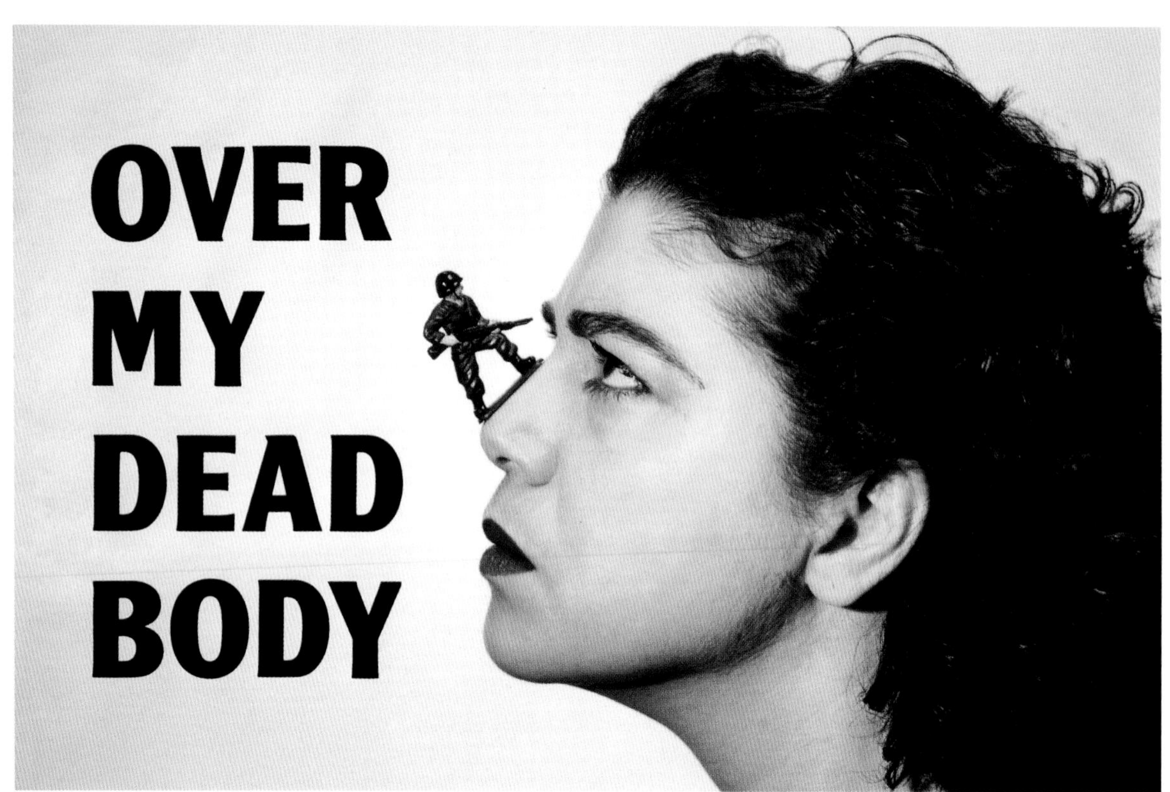

Mona Hatoum
Over My Dead Body, 1988
billboard (inkjet on paper)
80¼ × 119¾ in.

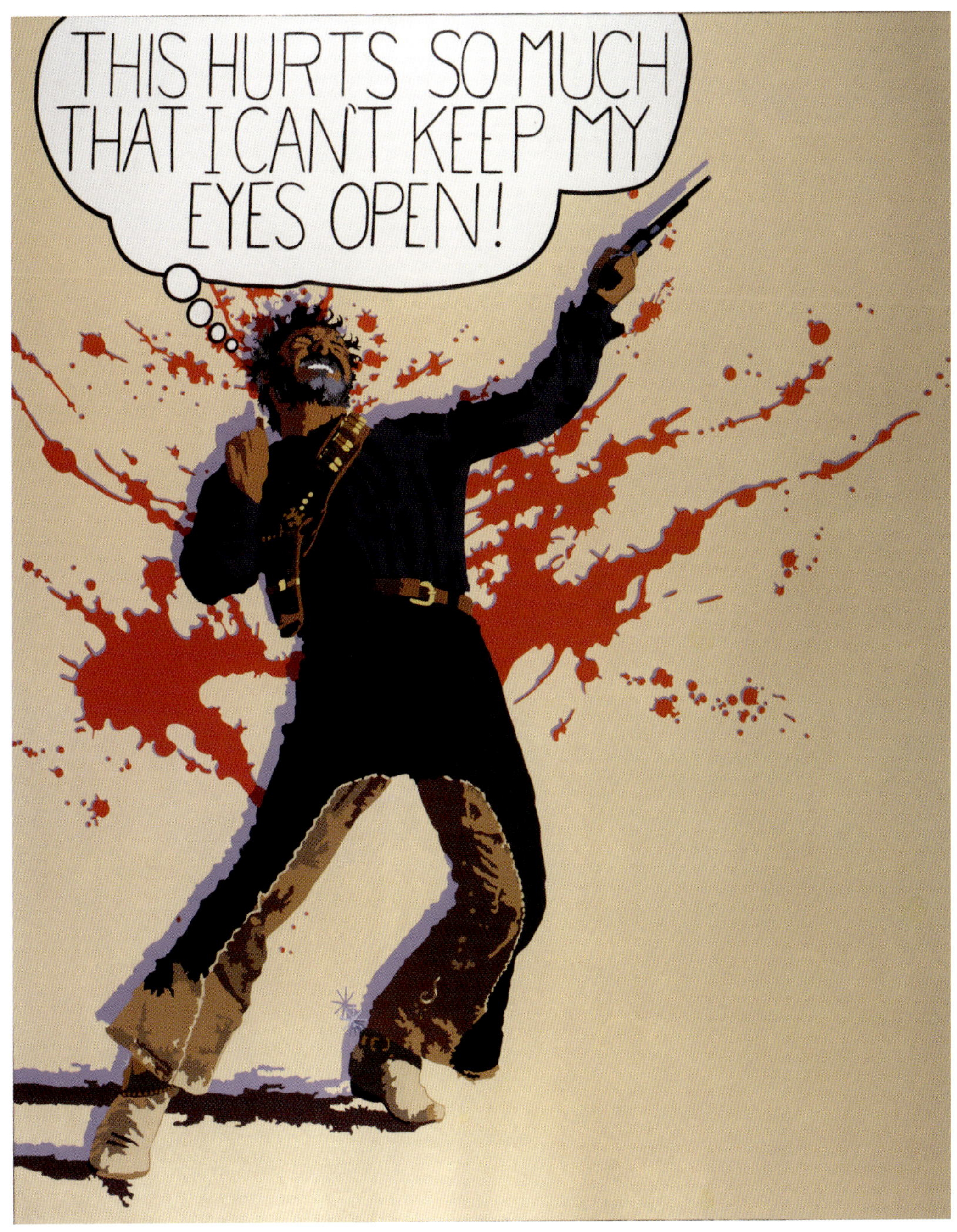

Billy Schenck
This Hurts So Much, 2005
oil on canvas
65 × 52 in.

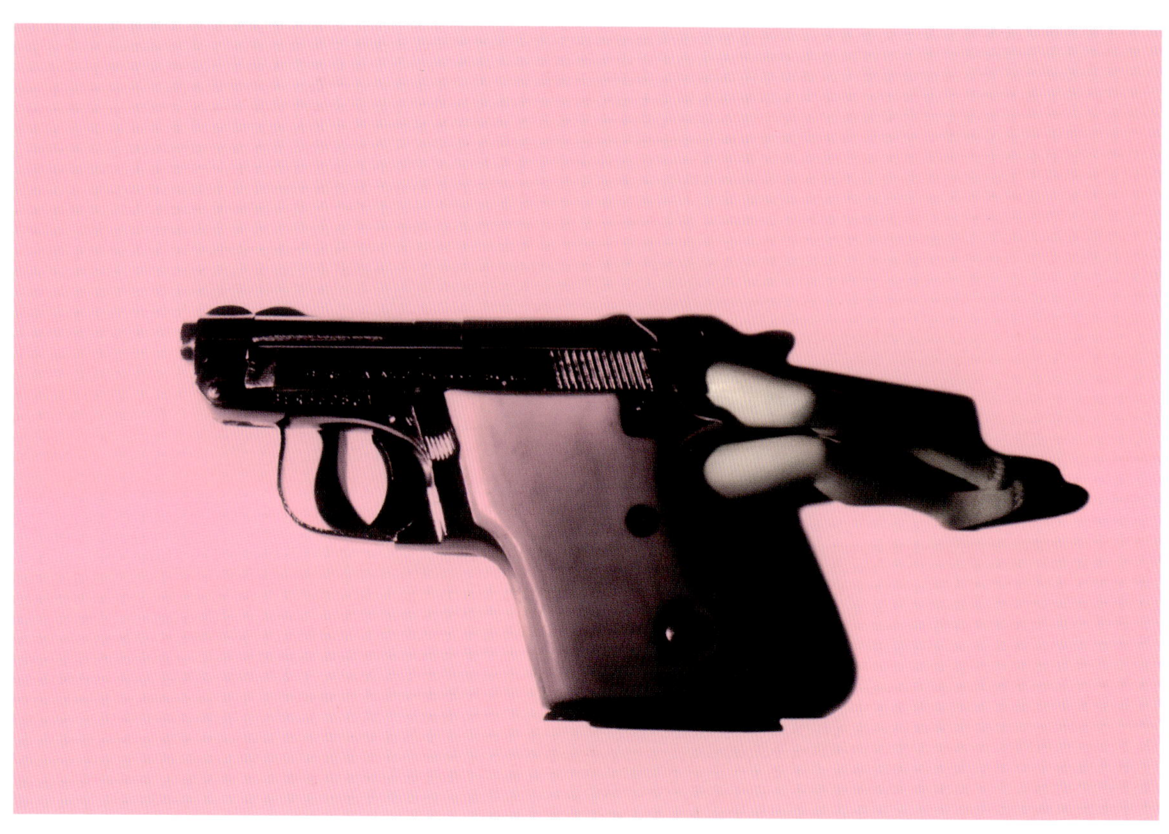

Laurie Simmons
Lying Gun / Pink, 2014
pigment print
20 × 30 in.
Edition of 1, 3 APs

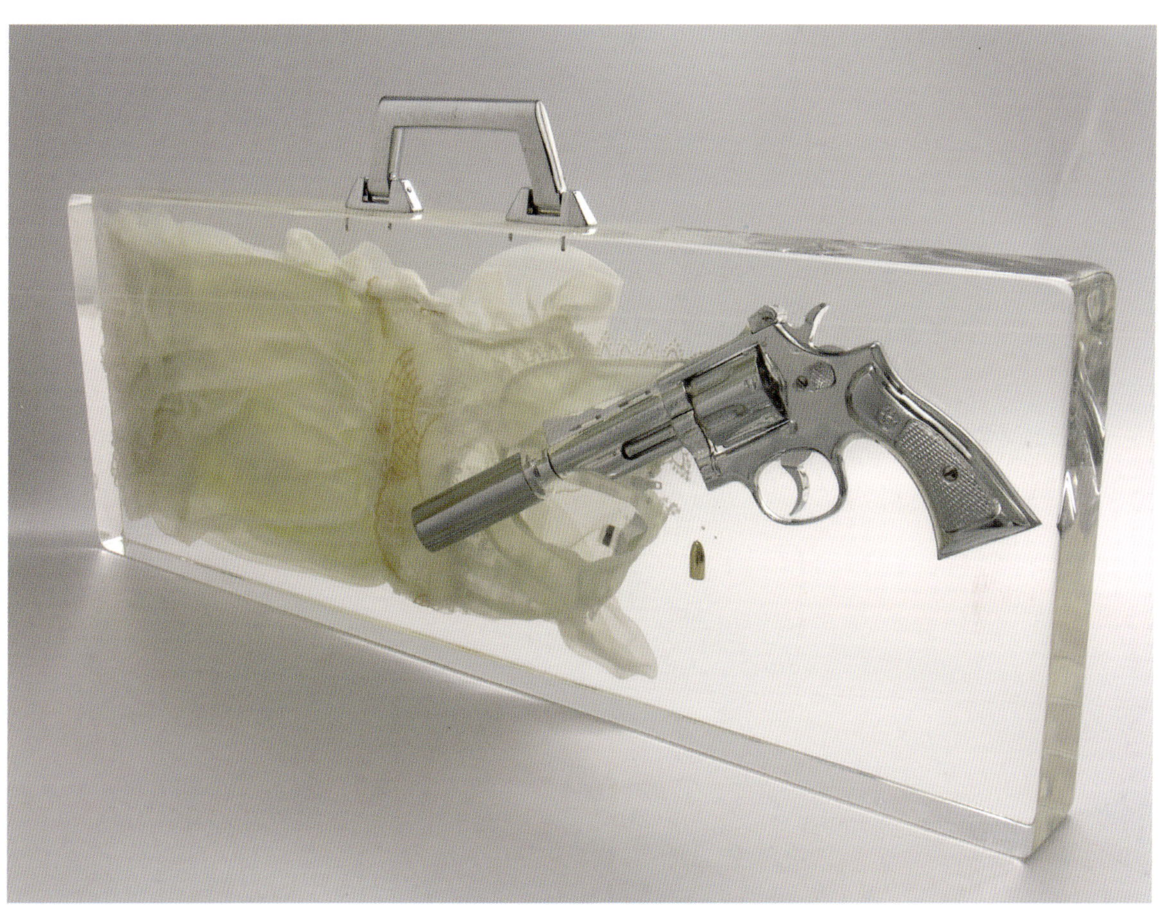

Ted Noten
Murdered Innocence, 2005
acrylic, child's christening dress, silver-plated handgun with silencer, pearl, diamond, golden bullet
9½ × 26¾ × 2 in.
Photo: Ted Noten

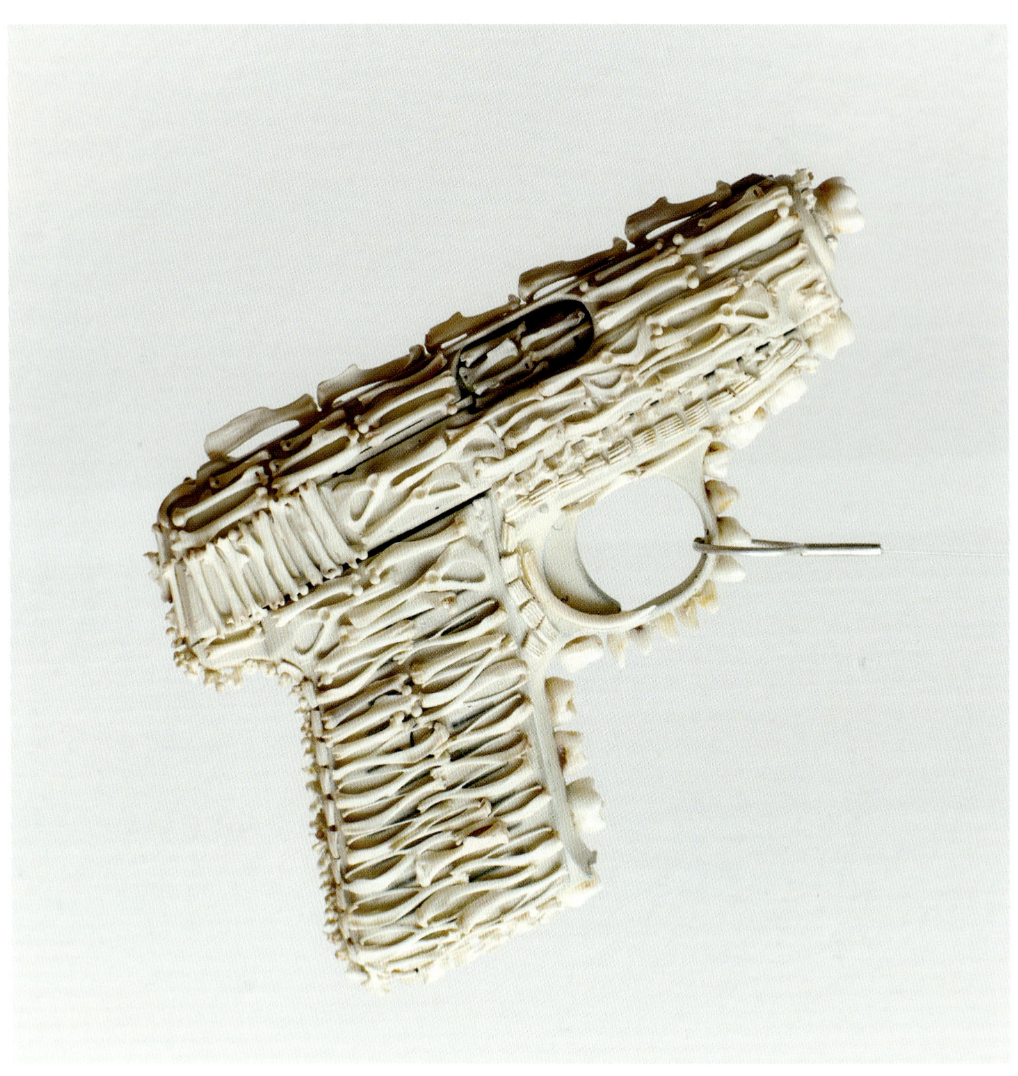

Sandra Enterline
Baby Bones (In Memory of Sandy Hook), 2015
handgun, baby teeth, rodent bones, paint
4 × 6 × 1¼ in.
Photo: David Martinez

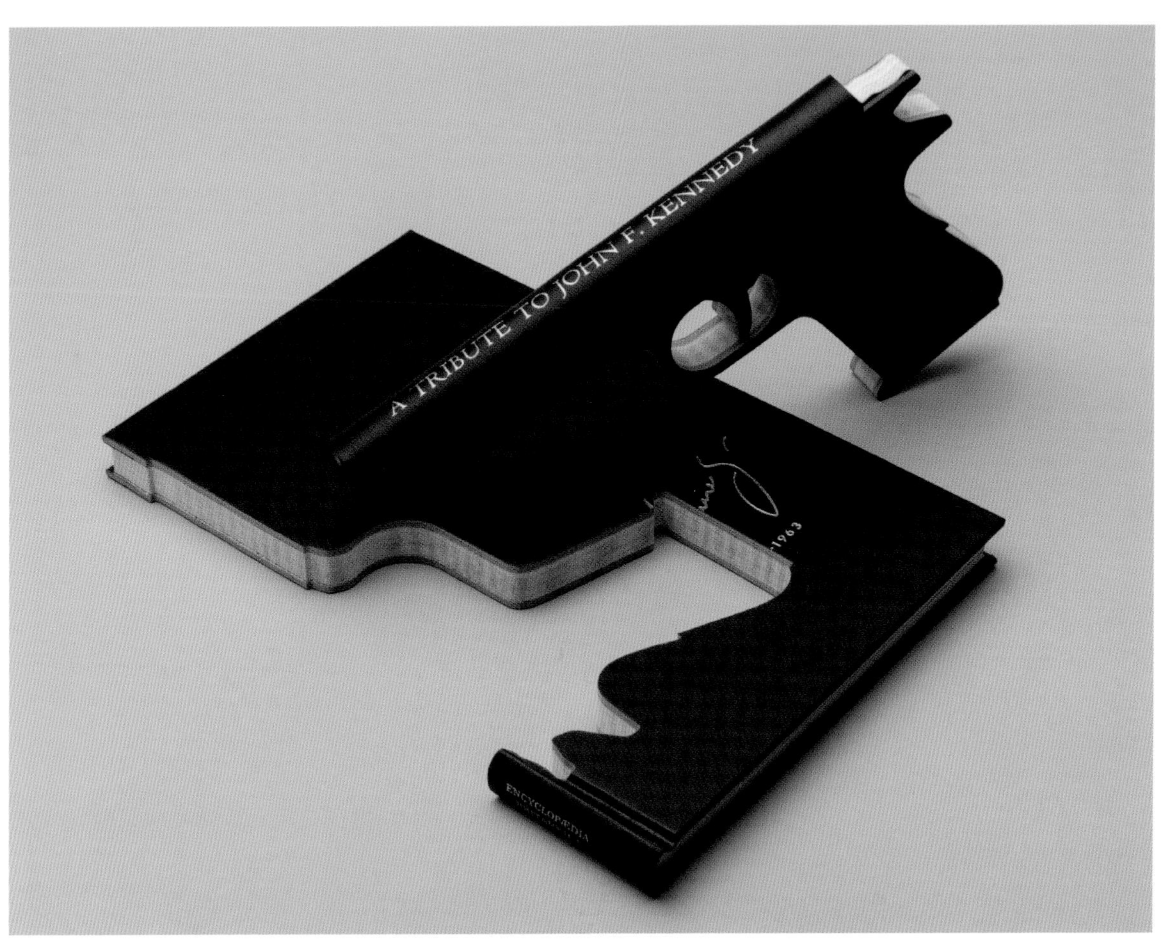

Robert The
Bookgun (A Tribute to John F. Kennedy), 1995
altered book
9¼ × 6½ × in.

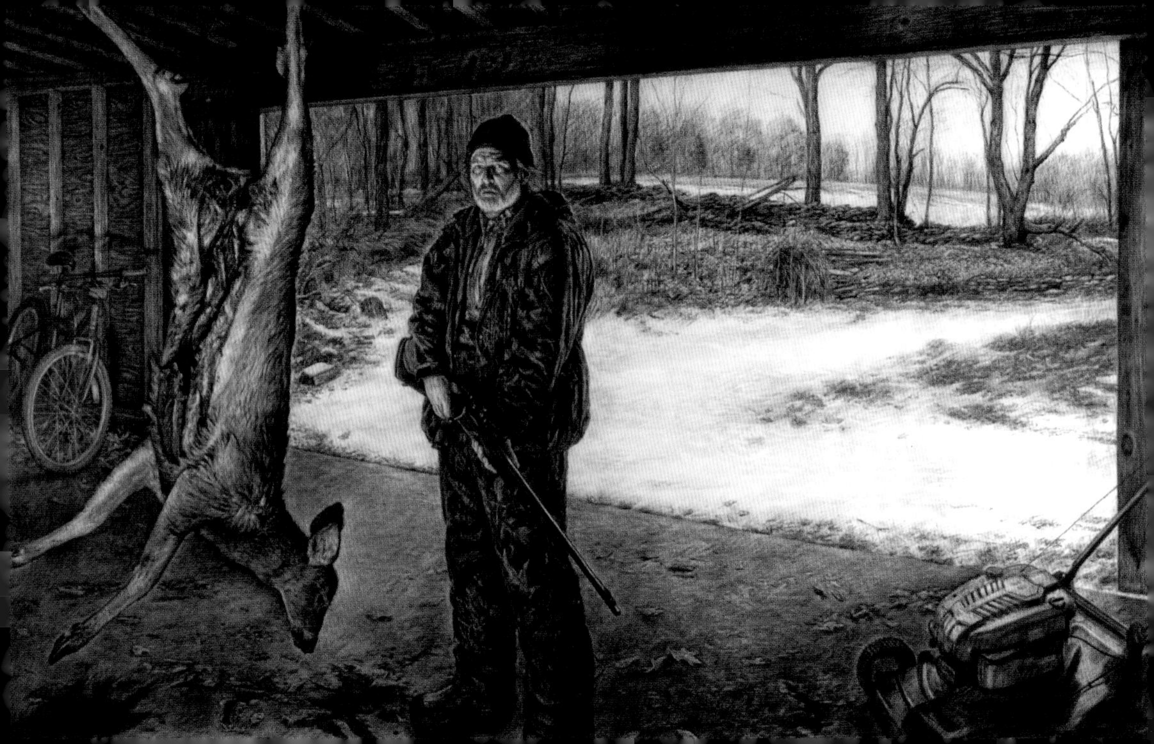

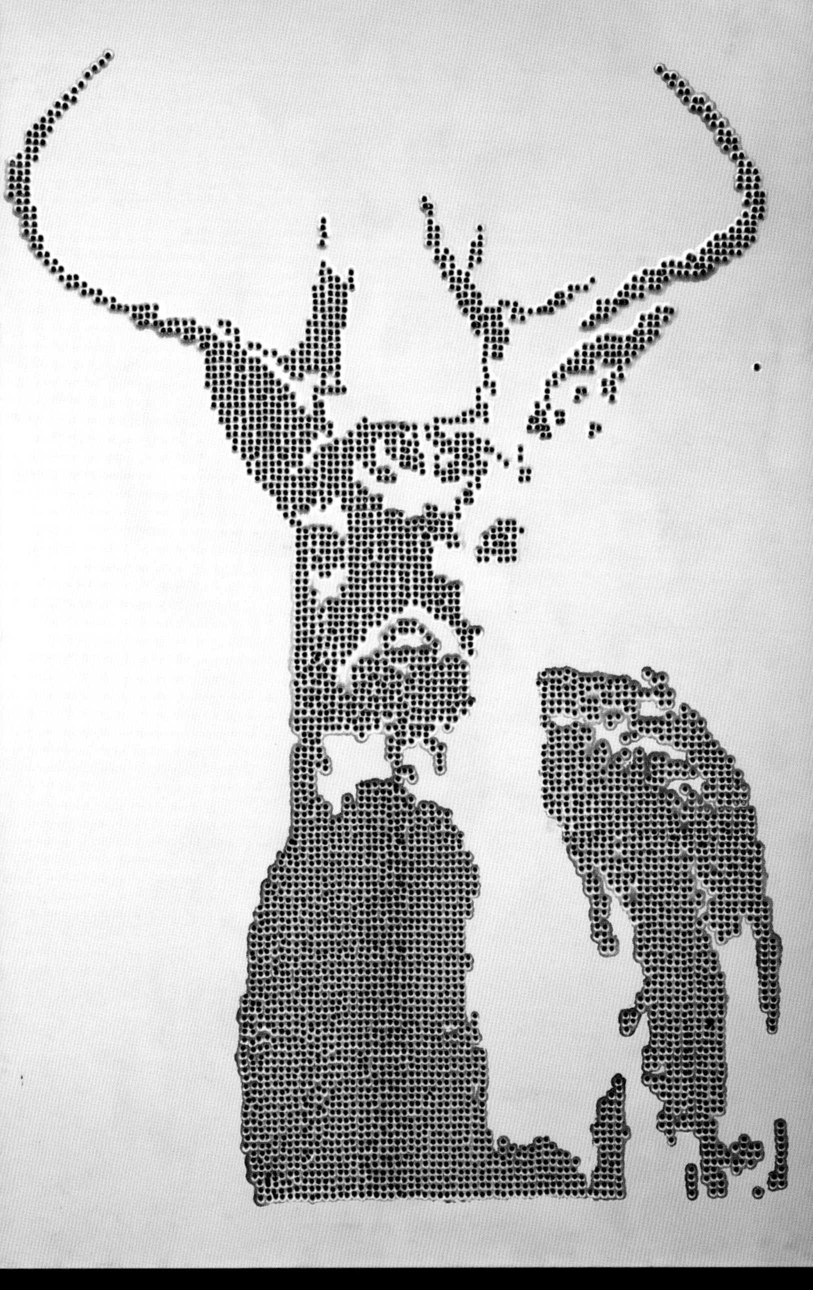

Walton Creel
Deer, from Deweaponizing the Gun series, 2003
.22-caliber bullets shot into painted aluminum panel
72 × 48 in.

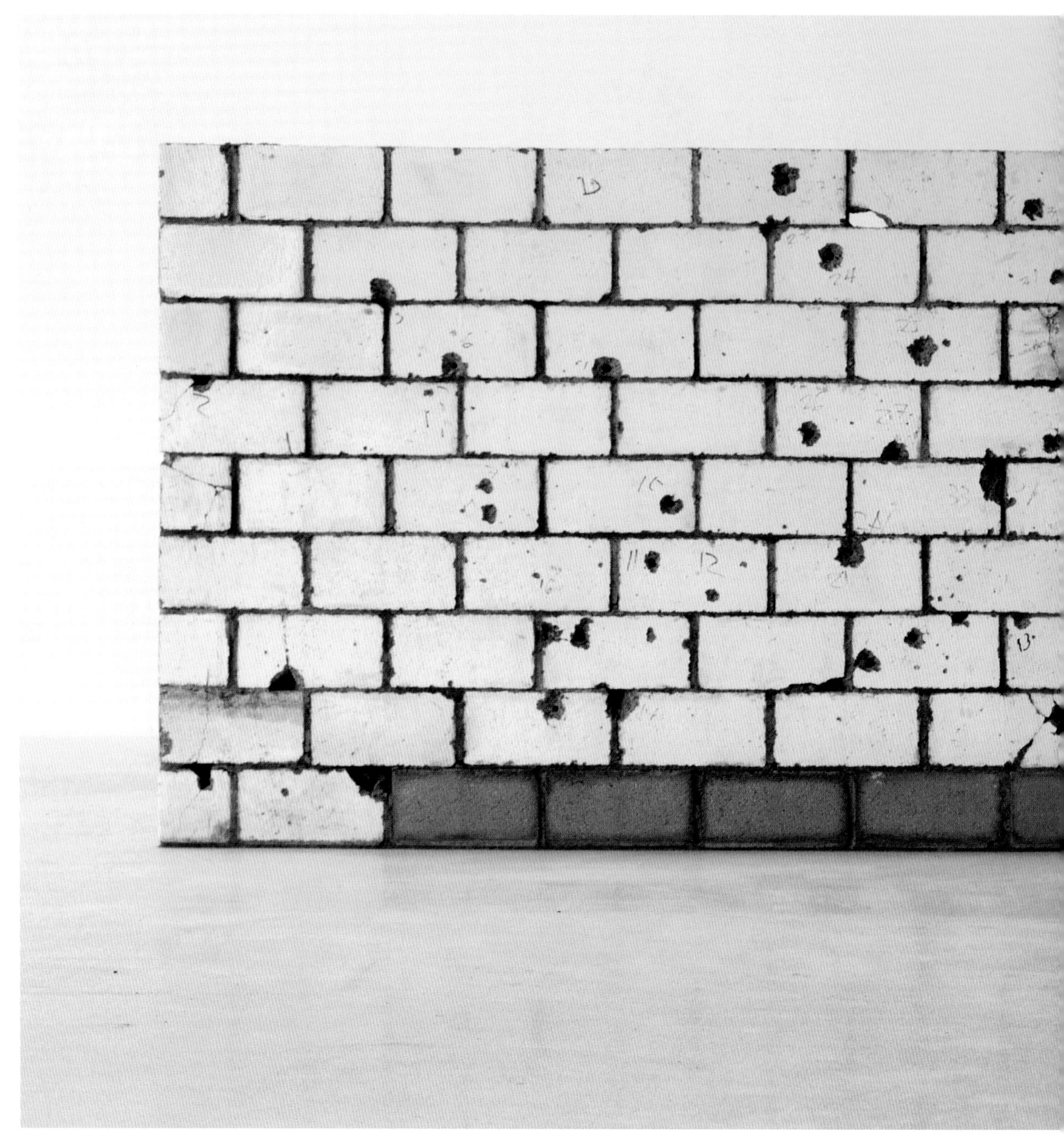

Teresa Margolles
Muro baleado (Culiacán), 2009
wall from Culiacán in front of which two police officers were shot
Installation view from "Frontera," MUSEION Bolzano, Italy, 2011
Courtesy of Gabinete TM / James Cohan, New York
Photo: Rafael Burillo

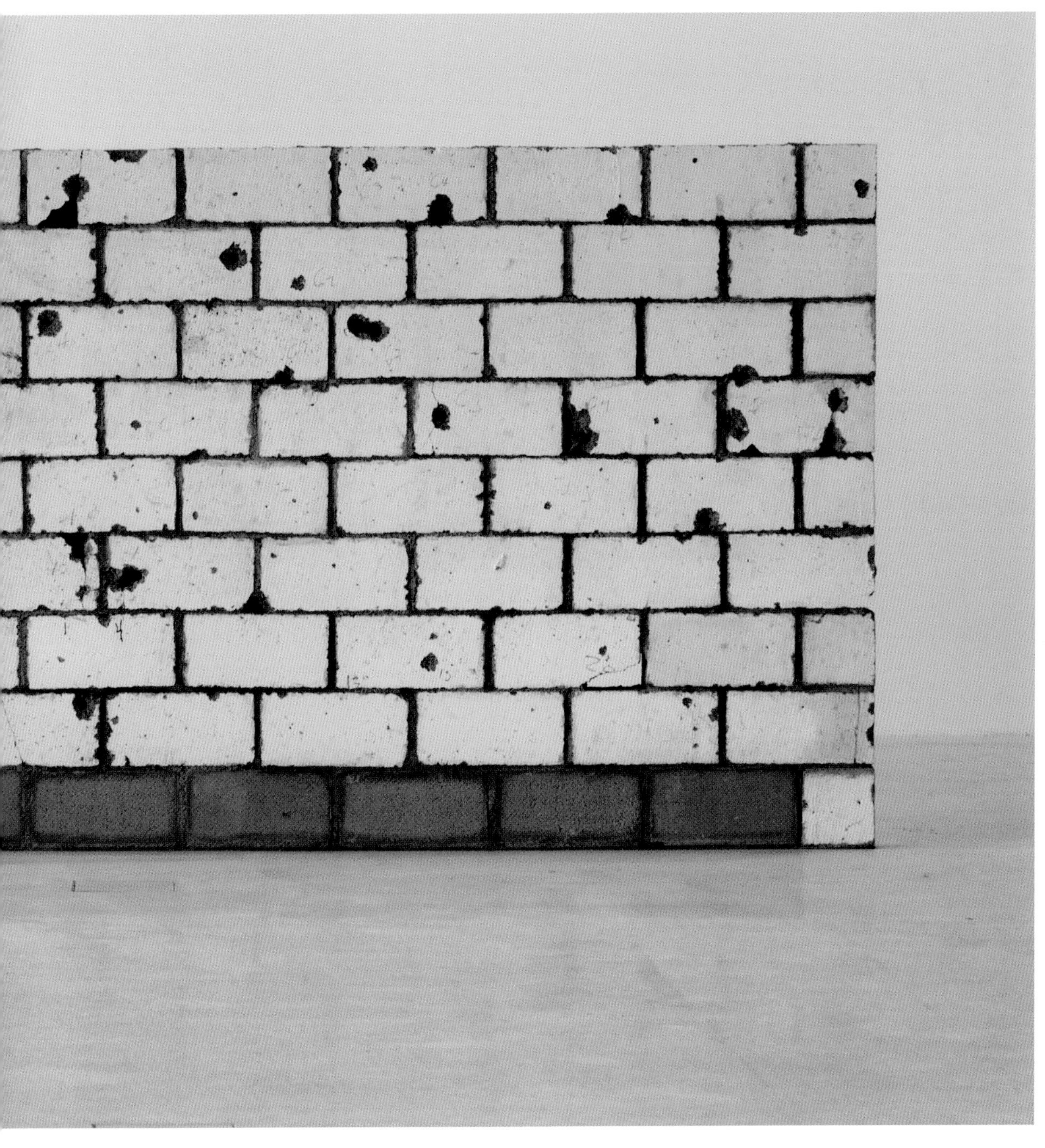

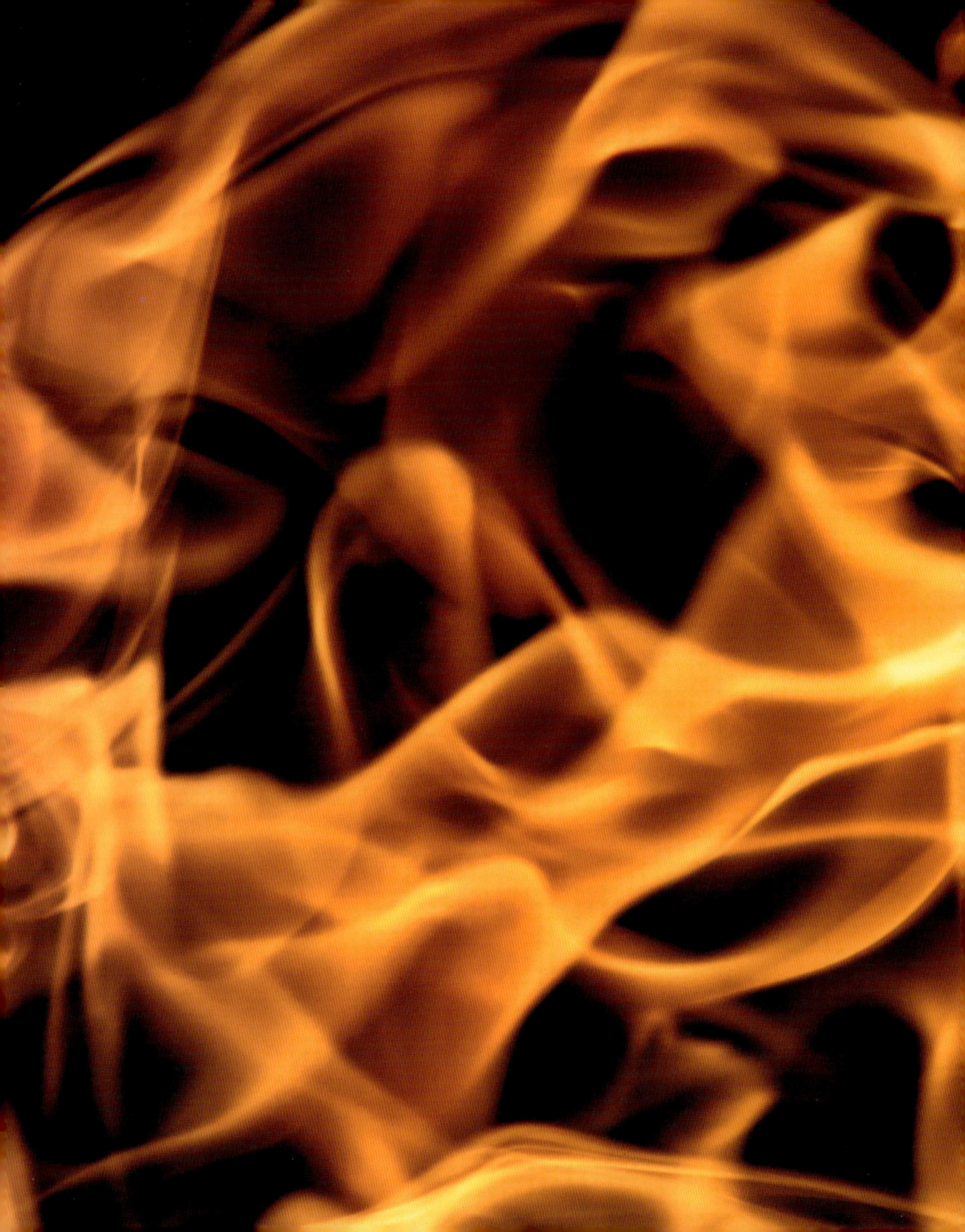

GUN LICENSE

According to popular wisdom, there are three subjects to avoid in polite company and at the workplace: religion, politics, and sex. This etiquette rule can be traced to *Hill's Manual of Social and Business Forms,* first published in 1873. As the guide instructs, "Do not discuss politics or religion in general company. . . . To discuss those topics is to arouse feeling without any good result." Admittedly, the works shown here provoke more emotions than good results but likewise expose the heated import of such issues in our lives. When these hot-button items are combined with guns, they yield a heady brew. All three taboo topics—along with money, drugs, and race—are tackled by this section's artists, who grant themselves creative license to enter the fray.

The union of guns and religion would seem unlikely, if not ungodly. Yet, violence and religion have intermingled for centuries, with holy wars waged for religious ends. The link between sex and guns is more readily apparent. Marketers know that sexiness sells, especially when promoting the projectile potency of guns. Firearms are also requisite gear for sex traffickers and other illegal cartels. And politics have become nearly synonymous with guns, which are one of the most partisan issues today. As these fearless artists reveal, avoiding the subjects of religion, sex, politics, and firearms may be polite, but it is not prudent.

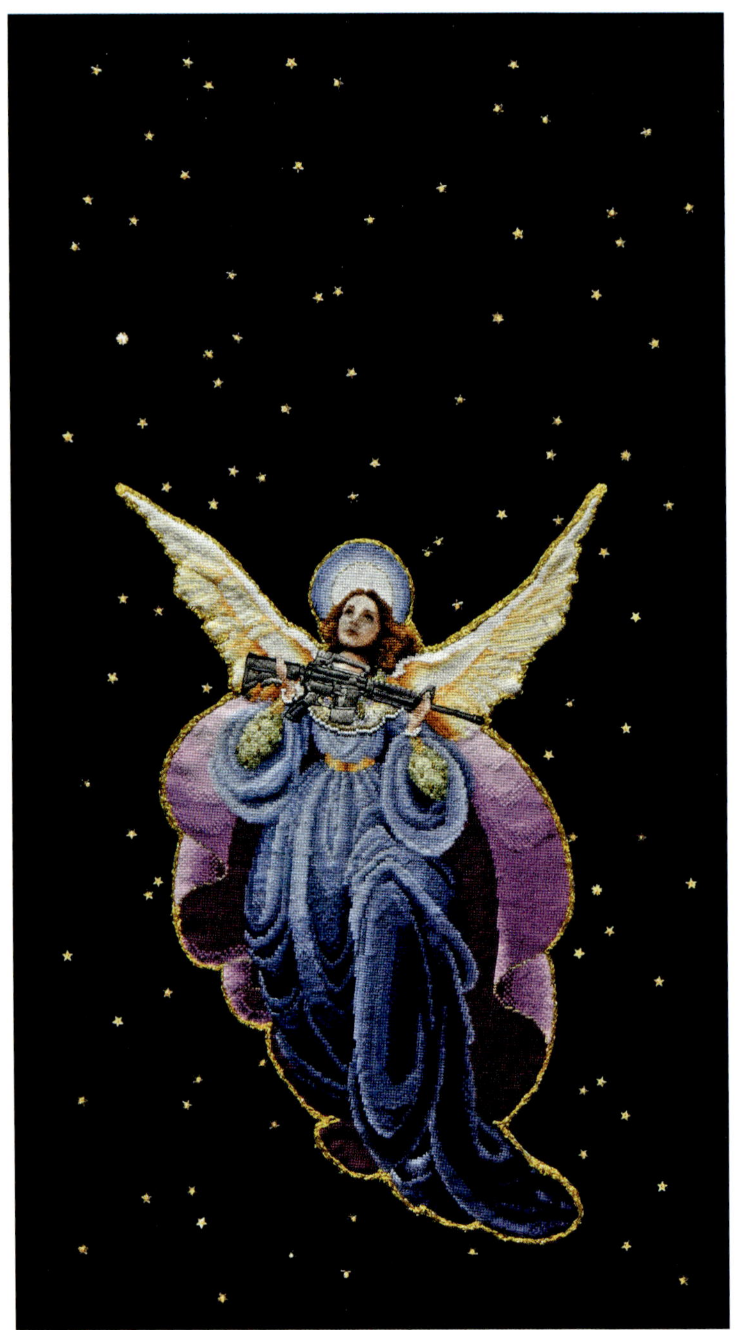

Kate Kretz
One Day in America, 2018
embroidery on found cross-stitch, 96 beads & sequins (one for every gun death per day in the US)
28 × 16 in.
Photo: Greg Staley

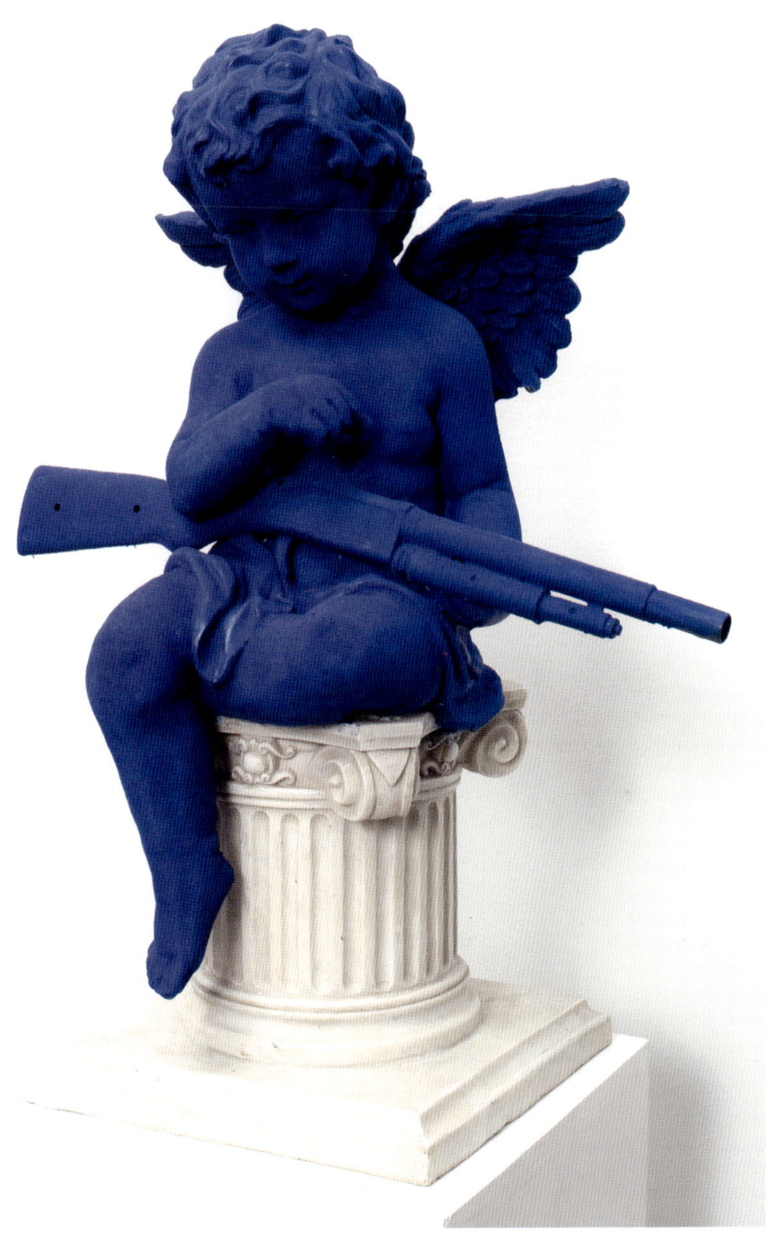

Willie Cole
Medicine Man, 2010
cast resin, flocking, paint
23¼ × 17¼ × 11 in.
Photo: Jason Mandella
Image courtesy of Alexander and Bonin, New York

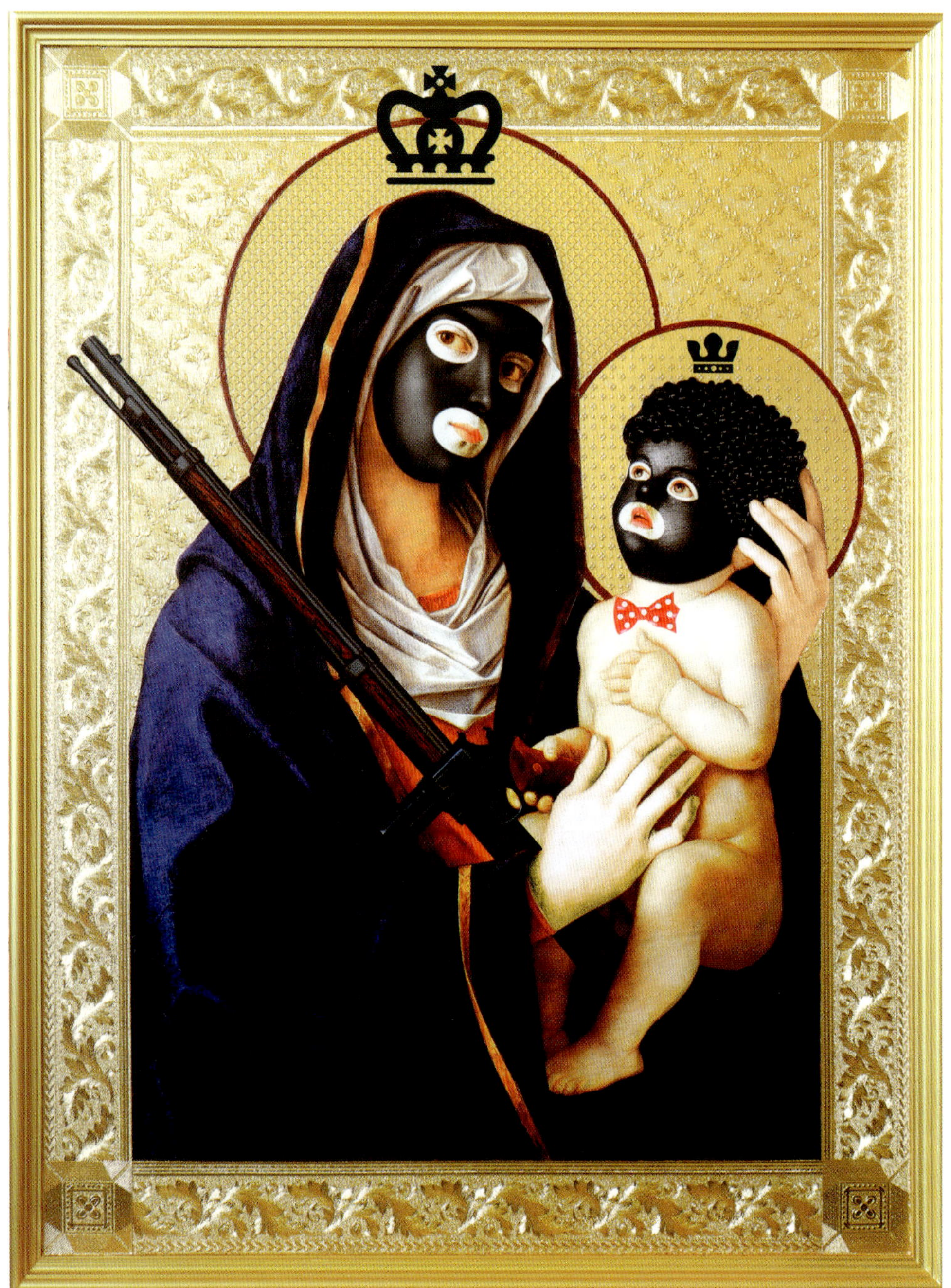

Mark Doox
Madonna and Child of Minstrelsy and 2nd Amendment Solutions, 2019
acrylic, pigmented ink, gold metal leaf on gold-framed and cradled wood panel
36 × 48 × 2 in.

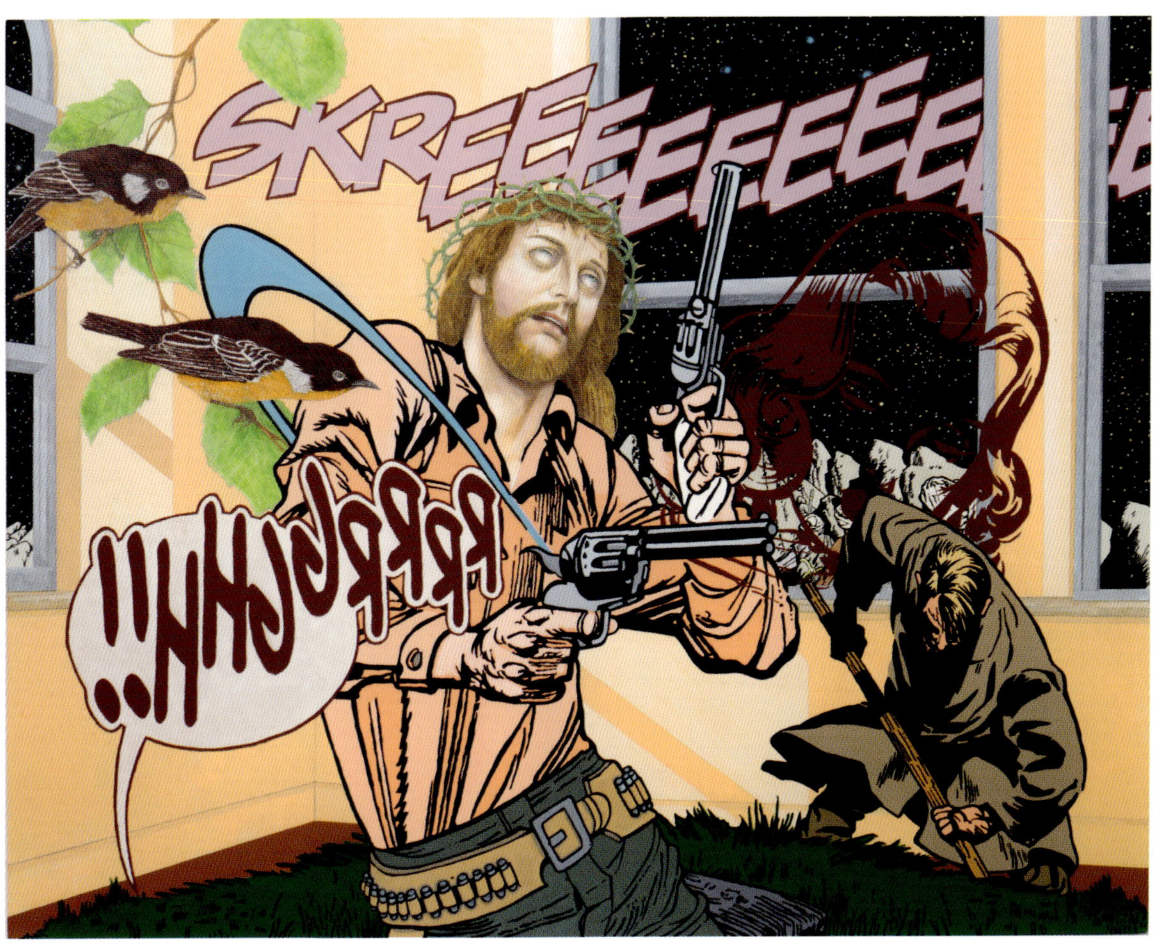

Jerry Kearns
SKREEEEE!, 2010
acrylic on canvas
72 × 92 in.

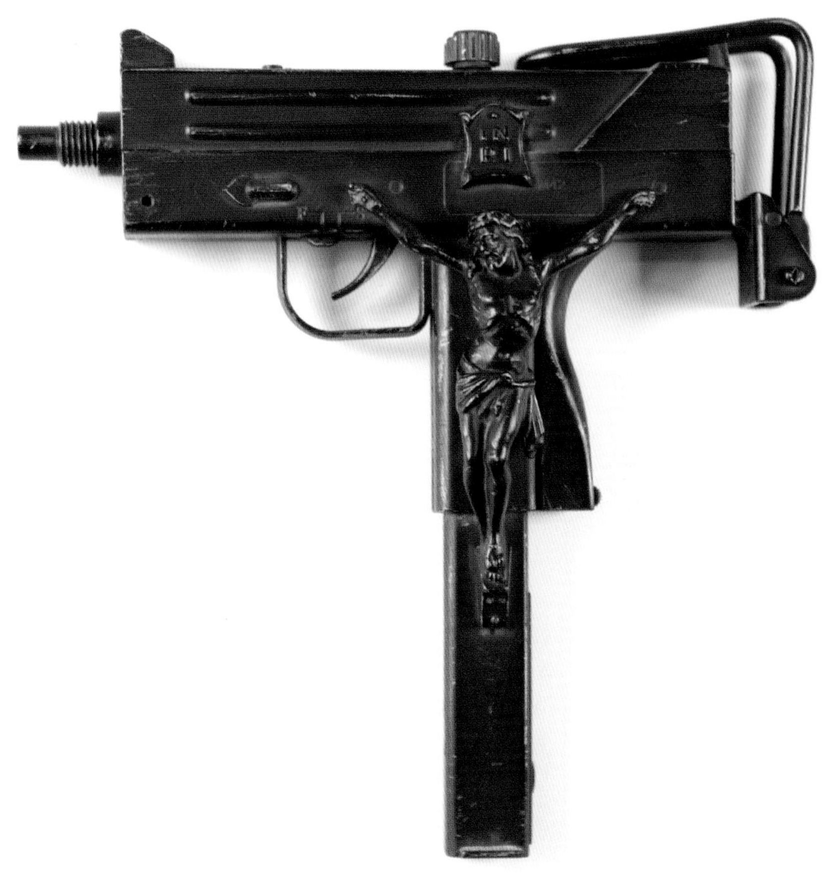

Seyo Cizmic
With God on Our Side, 2007
antiqued Uzi replica pistol with hand-carved crucifix
10½ × 10½ × 2 in.

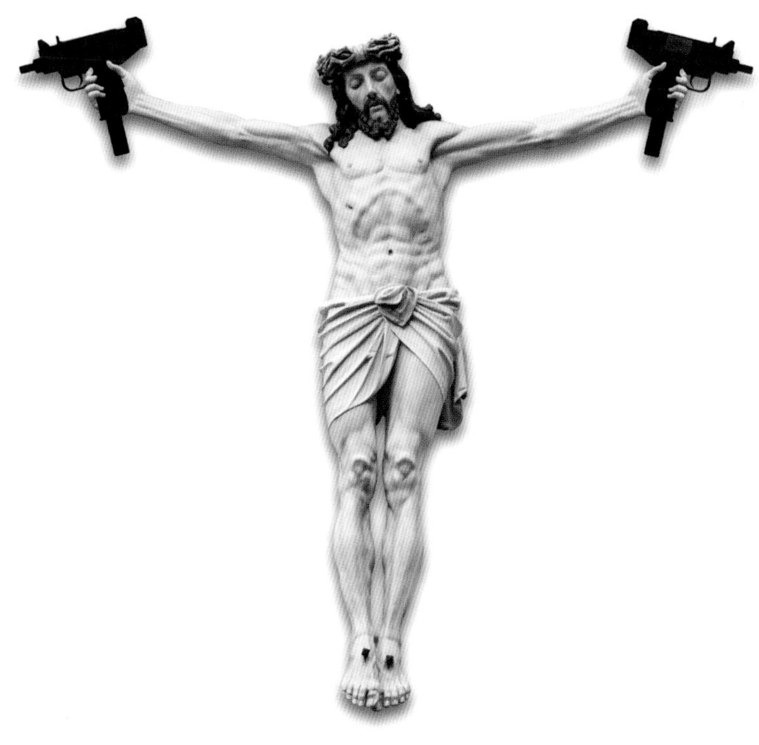

Magnus Gjoen
Mala Fide, 2012
archival pigment inks on paper
27½ × 27½ in.

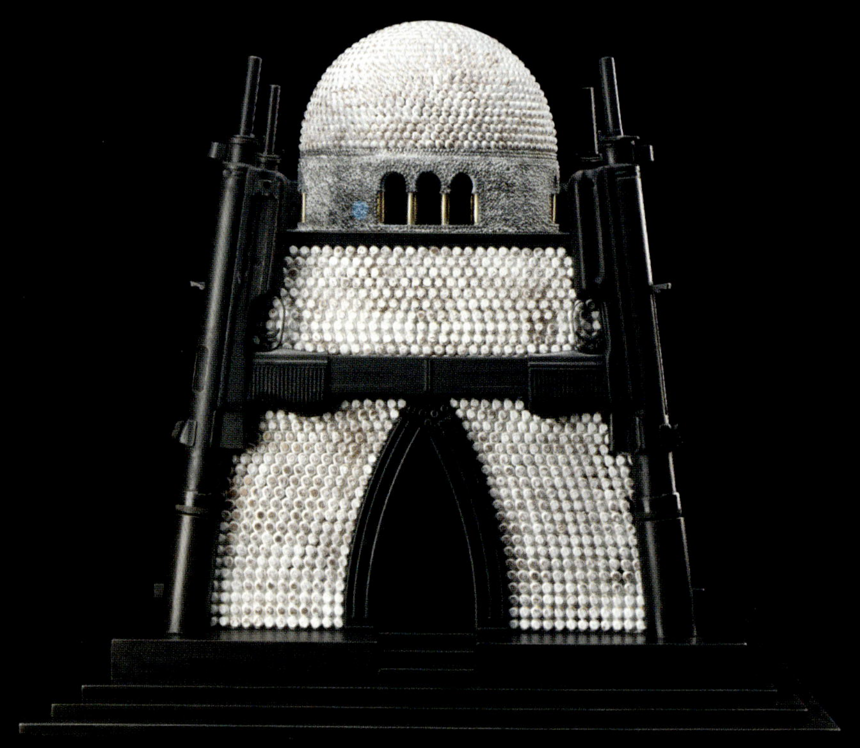

Al Farrow
Mausoleum I (After National Mausoleum of Pakistan), 2007
guns, gun magazines, bullets, shell casings, lead shot, steel
27¾ × 30 × 30 in.
Collection of Jeffrey N. Dauber & Marc A. Levin, San Francisco
Photo: Jock McDonald; courtesy of Catharine Clark, San Francisco

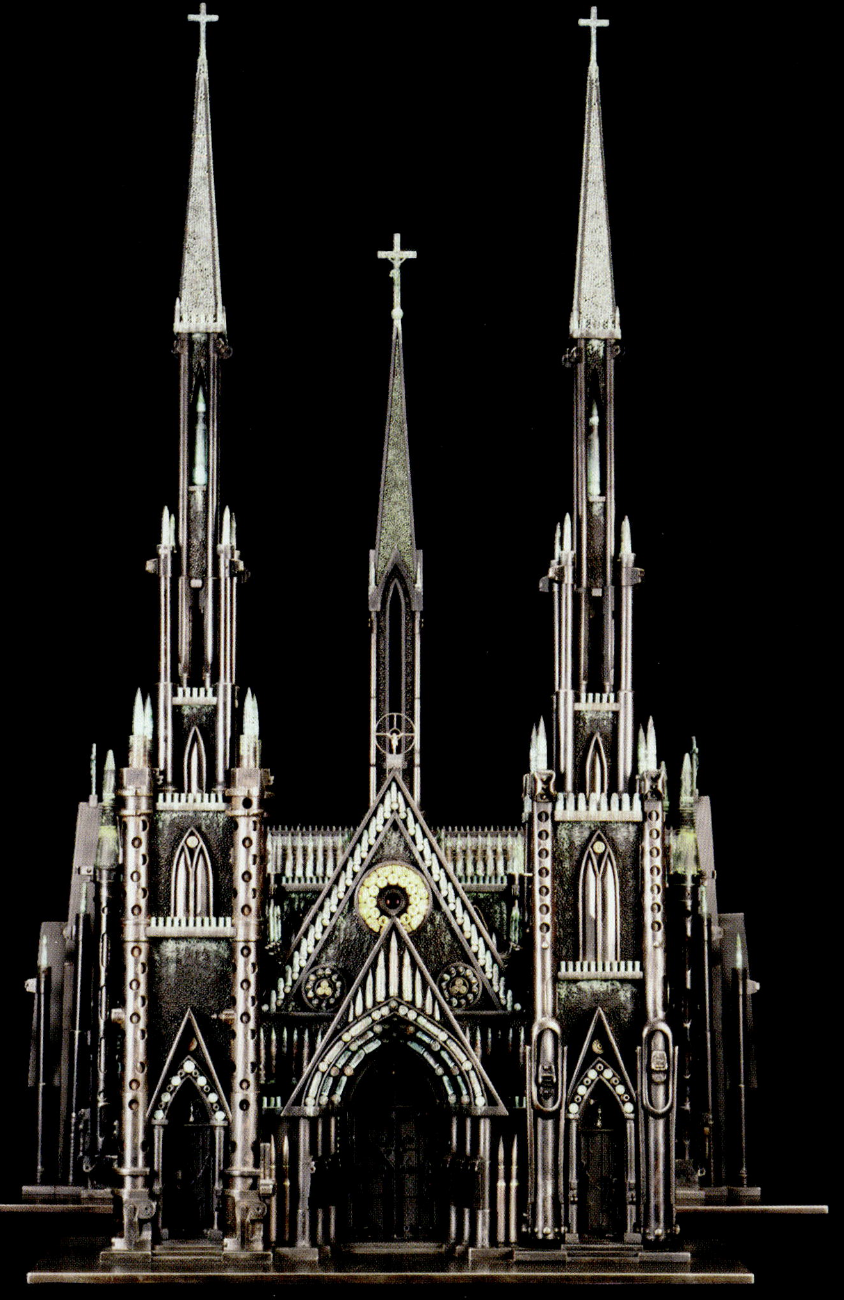

Al Farrow
The Spine and Tooth of Santo Guerro, 2007
guns, gun parts, bayonets, bullets, shell casings, lead shot,
steel, glass, bone, tooth, crucifixes, antique textile
64 × 50½ × 74 in.
Collection of the Fine Arts Museums of San Francisco
Photo: Jock McDonald; courtesy of Catharine Clark, San Francisco

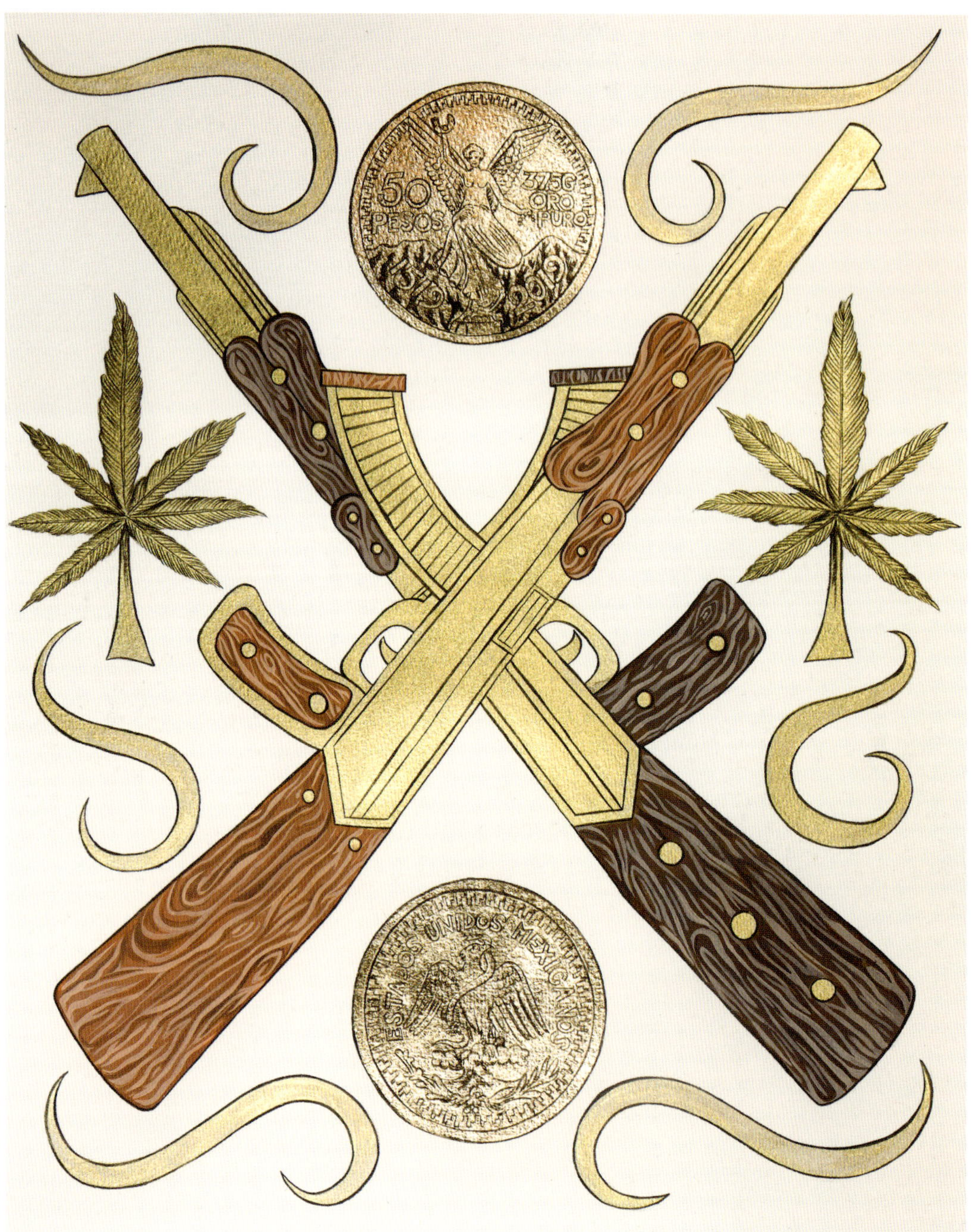

Eduardo Sarabia
Oro, 2018
acrylic, gold leaf, india ink, and gold on paper
21¼ × 17¼ in.
© Eduardo Sarabia; courtesy of Maureen Paley, London

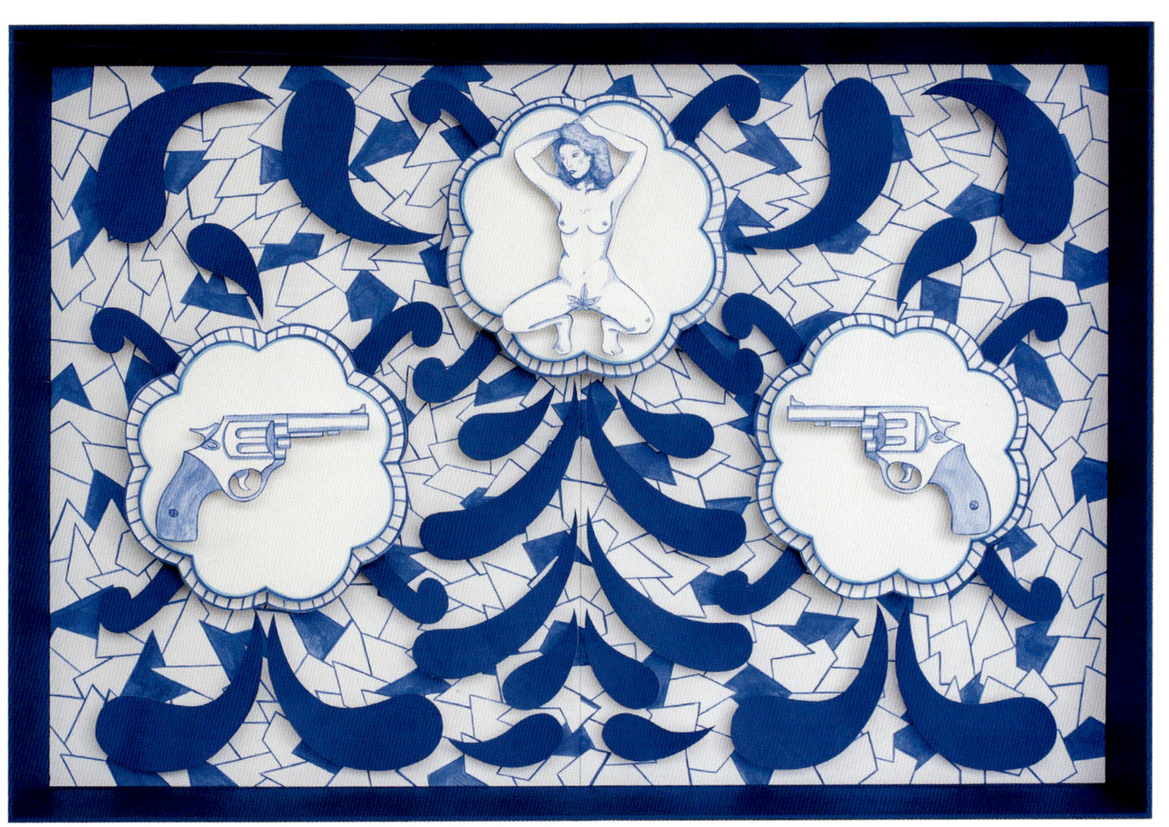

Eduardo Sarabia
La china no tiene pelos en la lengua, 2015
acrylic on paper
17¼ × 25¼ × 2¾ in.
© Eduardo Sarabia; courtesy Maureen Paley, London

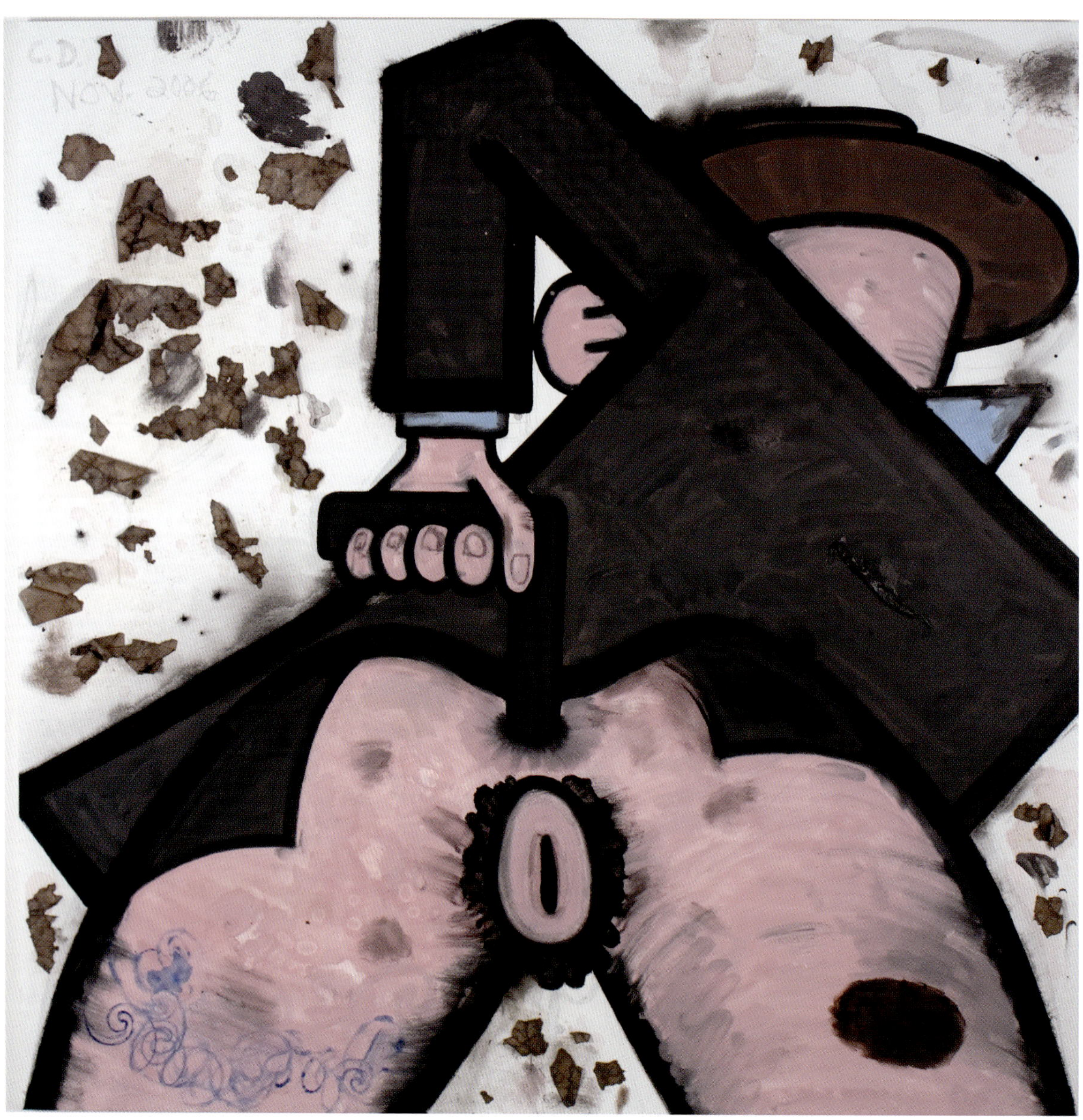

Carroll Dunham
Square Mule, 2006
mixed media on linen
74¾ × 74¾ in.

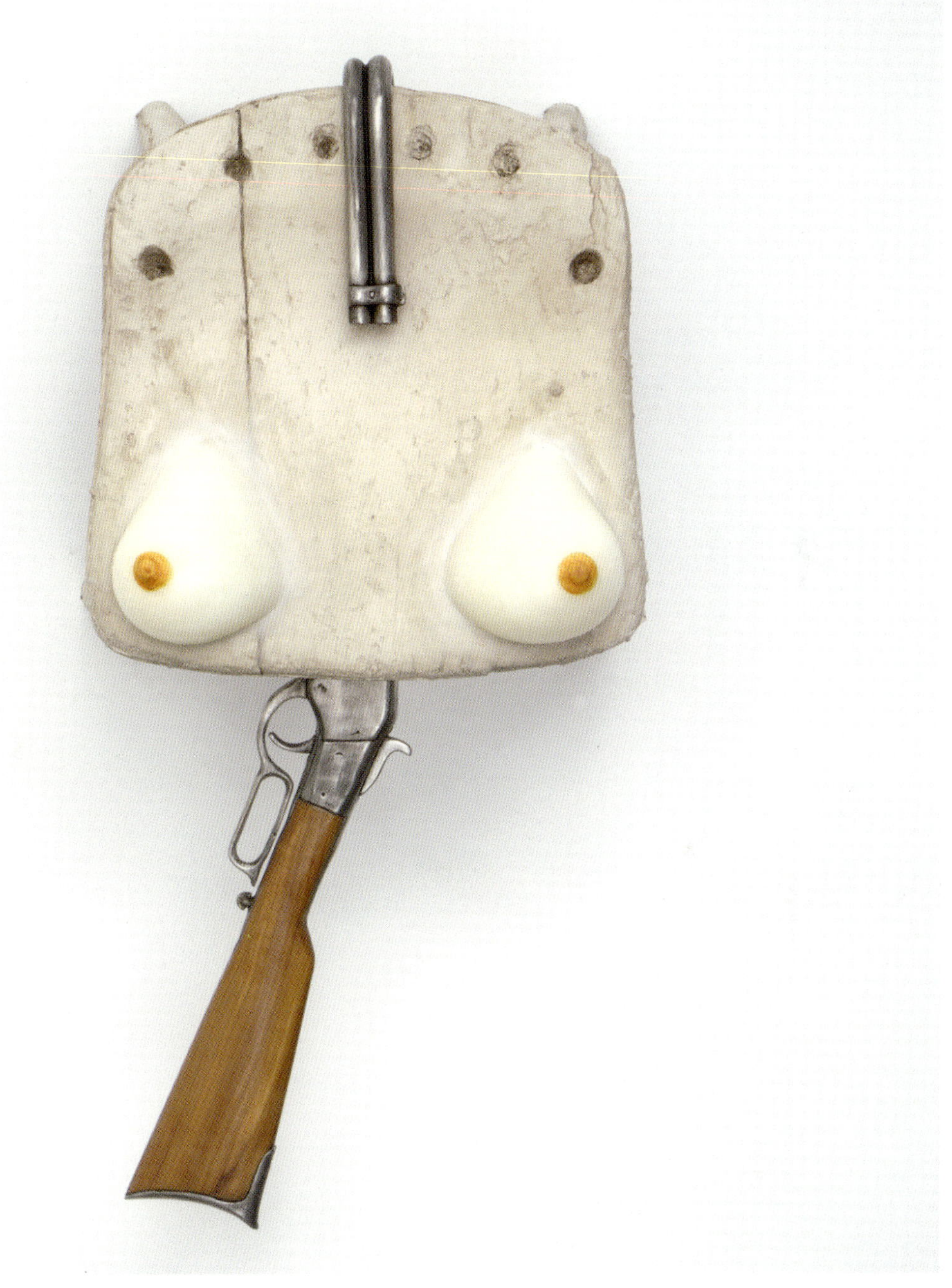

Robert Gober
Untitled, 2007–08
applewood, pewter, cast gypsum polymer, beeswax, paint, pigment
31¾ × 16½ × 18 in.
© Robert Gober, courtesy of Matthew Marks Gallery

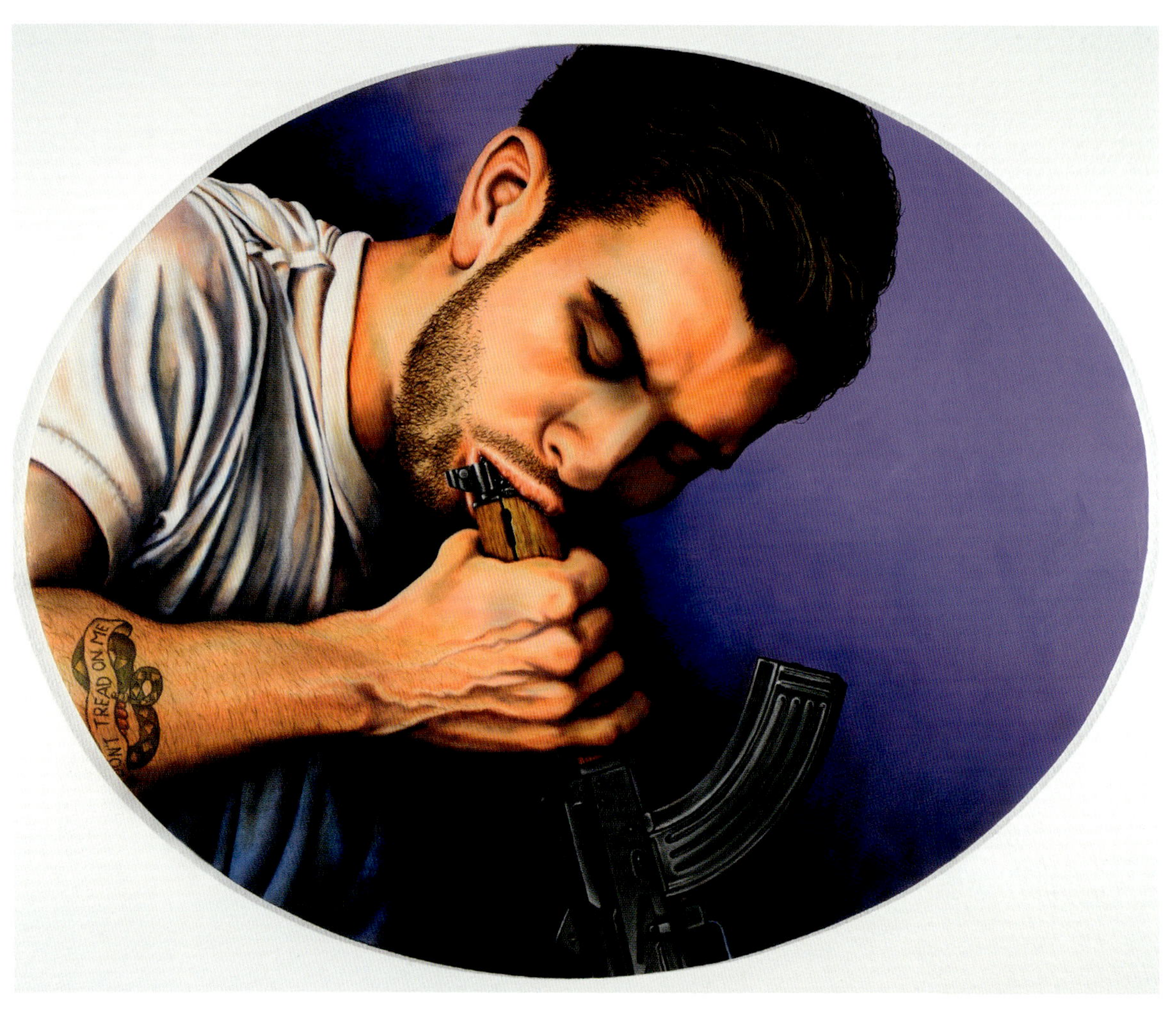

Kate Kretz
Gunlicker II, 2015
oil and acrylic on gatorboard
16 × 20 in.
Photo: Greg Staley

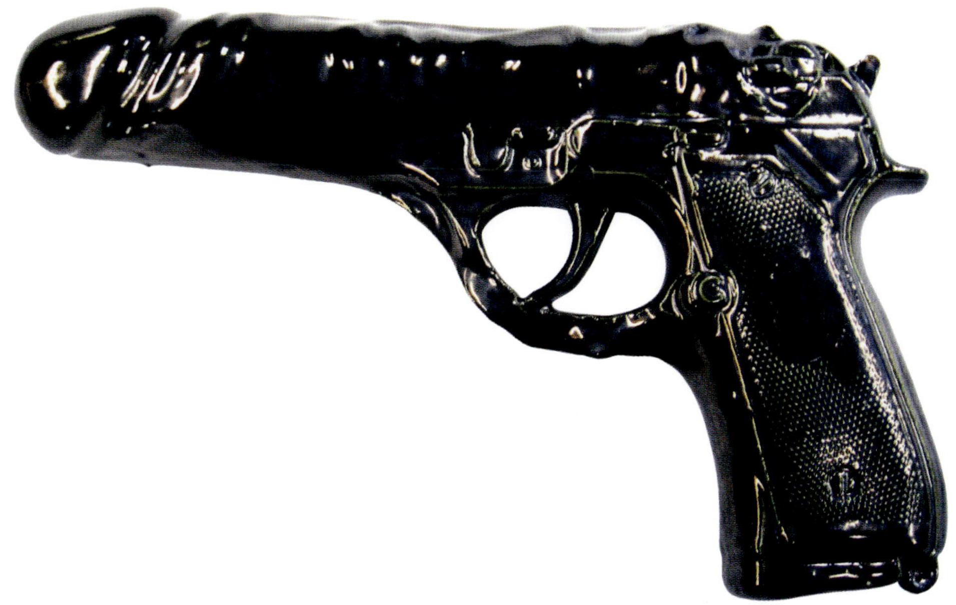

Marnika Shelton
Cocked, 2008
ceramic
8 × 4½ × 1½ in.

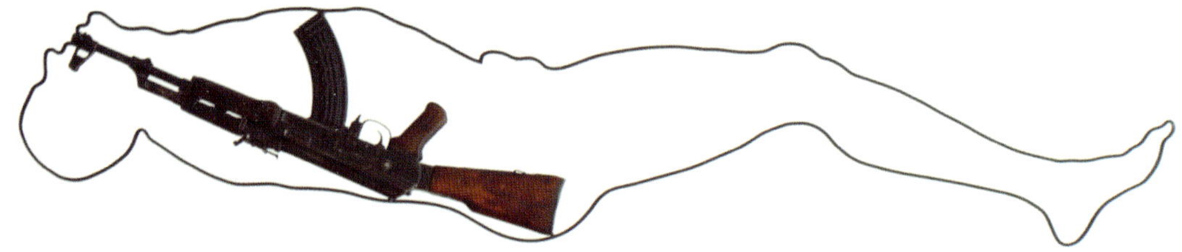

Antony Gormley
Silence, 2012
square section: mild steel bar, and AK 47
15¾ × 78¾ × 2¾ in.

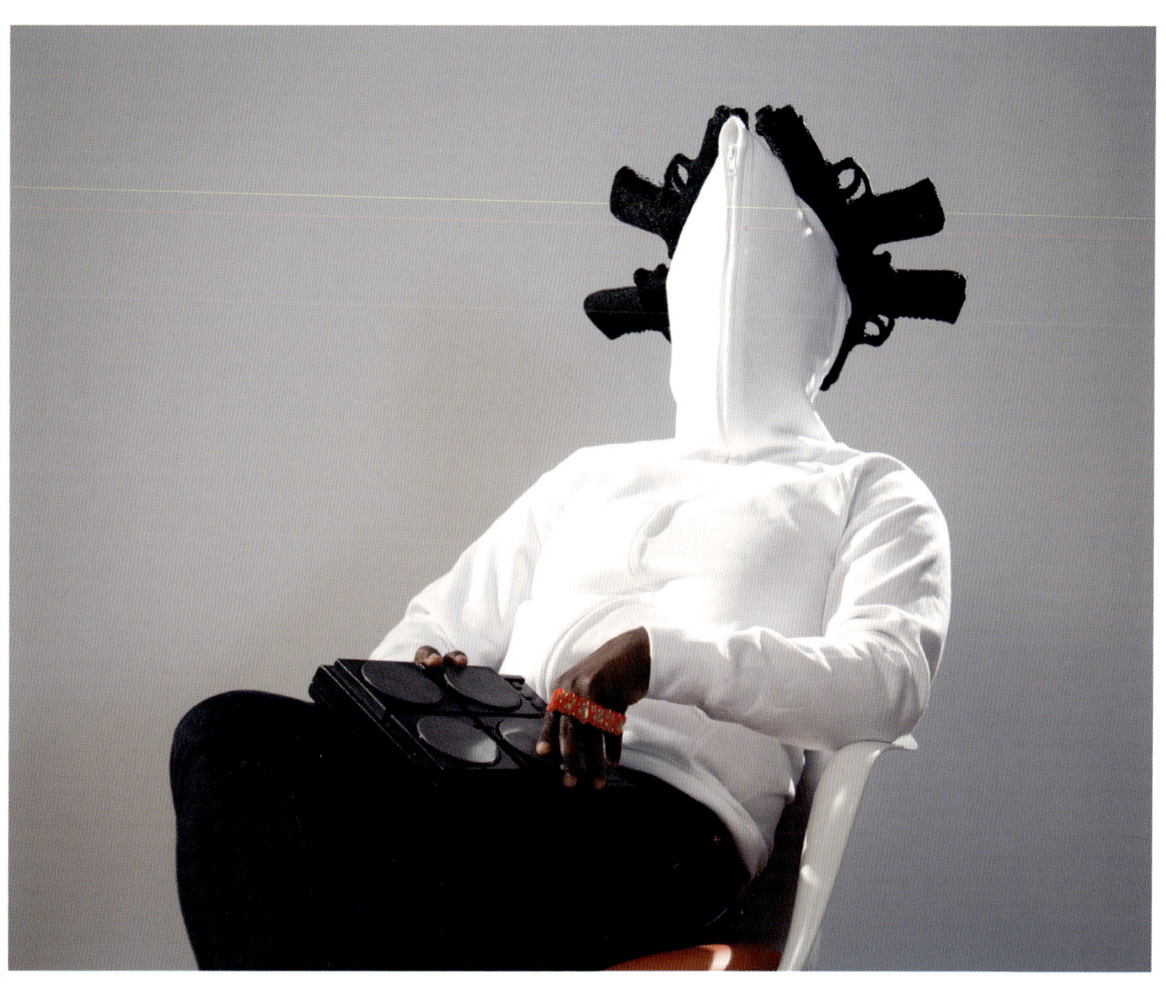

Robert Pruitt, in collaboration with The Fabric Workshop and Museum, Philadelphia
Untitled photographs (detail), 2011
archival pigment prints on rag paper
72 × 88 in. overall; detail, 25 × 31 × 1 in.
Edition of 5, 2 APs
Courtesy of the artist and Koplin Del Dio Gallery, Seattle, WA

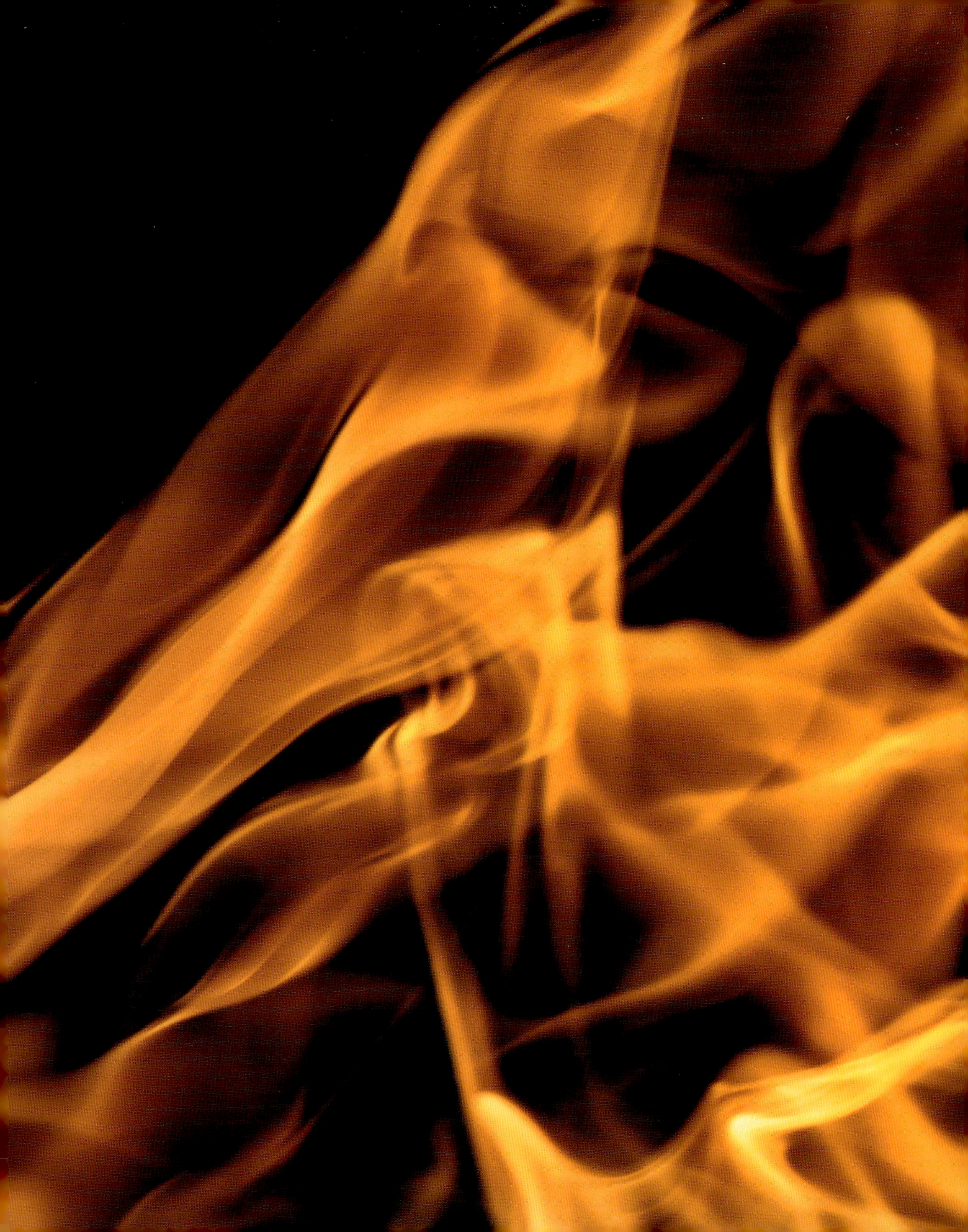

THE ARMORY

Armories and arsenals are storage locales for weapons and ammunition. Whether military or civilian, public or private, an armory safeguards arms for future attack and defense. The stockpiling of firearms across the globe has shifted from militaries to individuals during recent decades. Indeed, of the estimated one billion guns in current global circulation, 85% are in civilian hands. In the United States, about 3 percent of Americans own nearly half the country's 270 million guns. These so-called super-owners possess an average of seventeen guns each, with some owning upward of 3,000 weapons, as does Coloradoan Mel Bernstein, dubbed the "most armed man in America." The works featured in this section reflect the drive to amass arms in proportions that border on irrational.

Such hoarding of pistols, rifles, machine guns, and ammo has fueled a veritable private arms race. As with escalations between nation-states, there are implicit rivalries in this weaponry surge. The growth of citizen armories raises uneasy questions about the ultimate aims for these firearms—is it the government, criminal gangs, a marked social group, other super-owners, or some nebulous outside enemy? And what does the rampant quest for ever more firepower spell for the future? With the arms race running apace with the human race, who will win in the end?

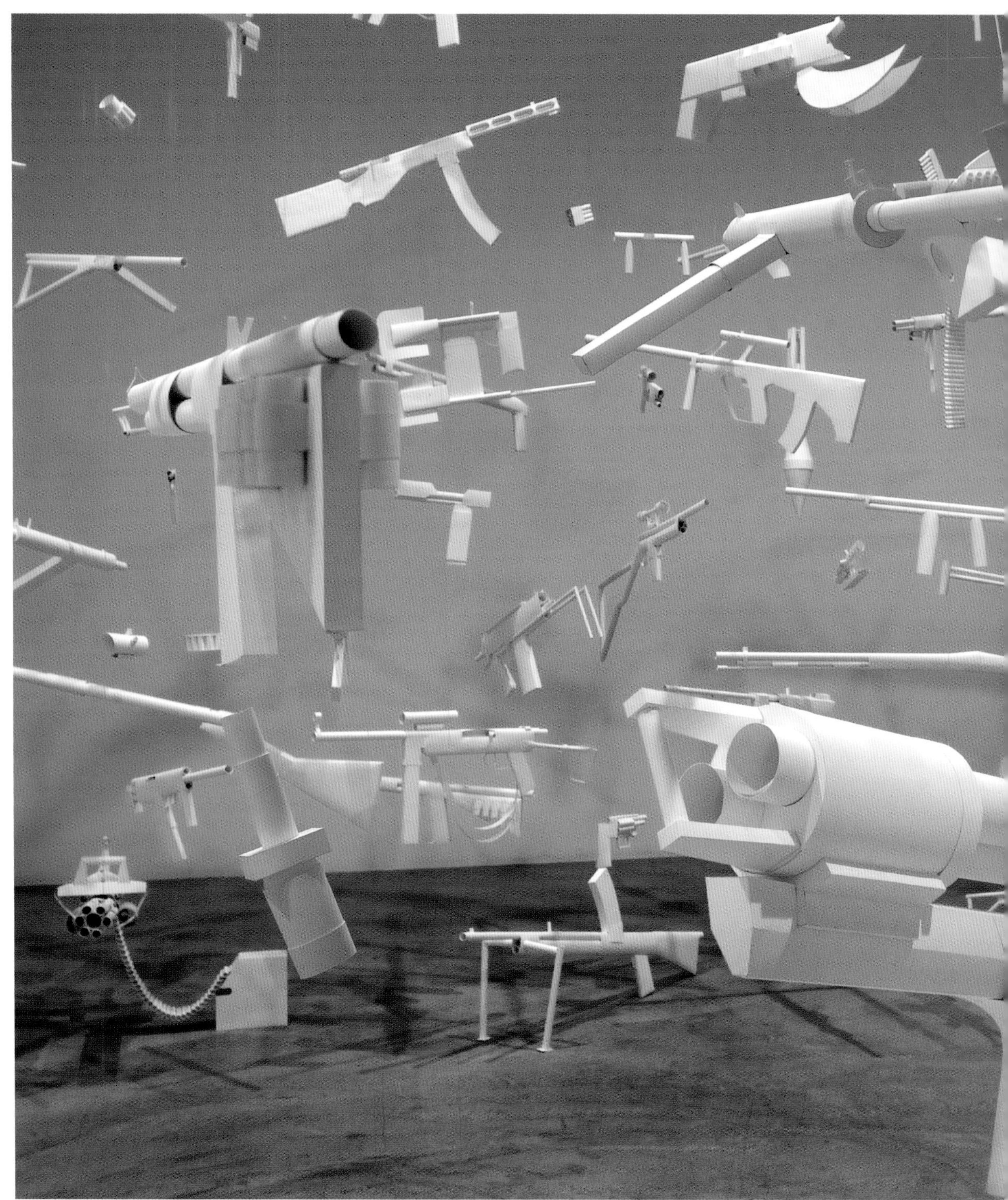

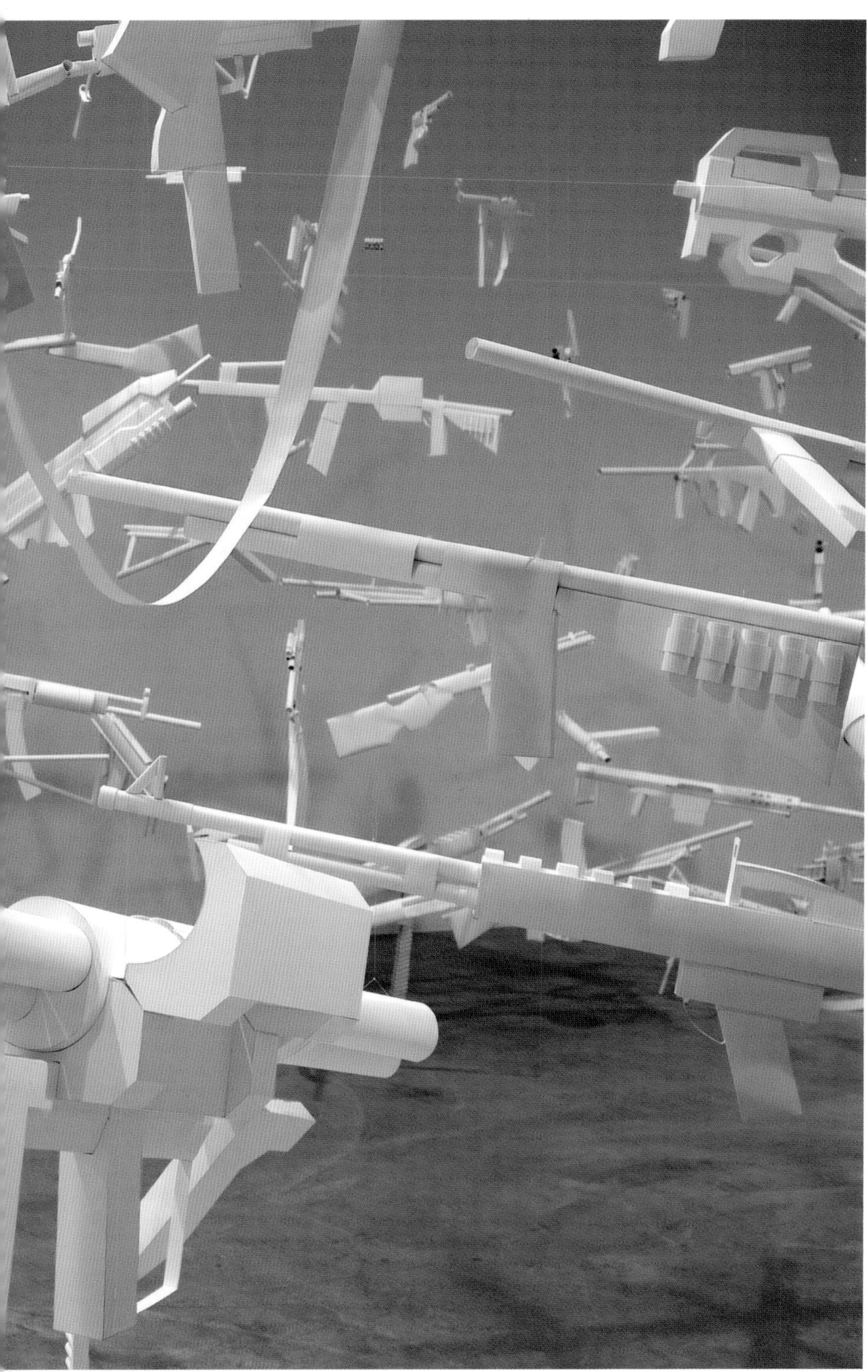

Sarah Frost
Arsenal, 2010
paper, tape, monofilament,
glue, video stills (300 units)
dimensions variable
Installation view at
Contemporary Art Museum
Saint Louis

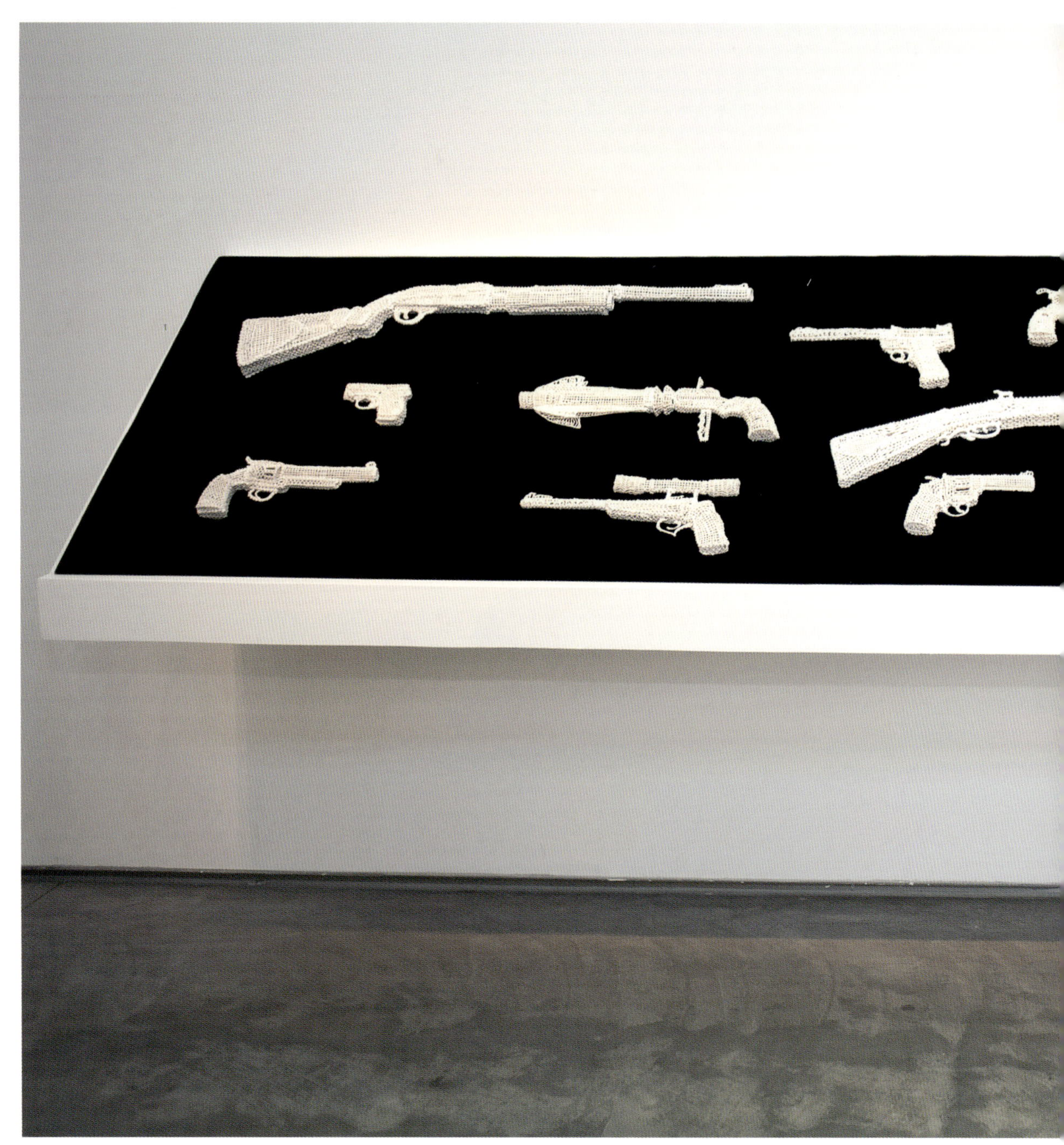

Susan Graham
My Dad's Gun Collection, 2012
porcelain
installation of 17 guns
2 × 12 × 3½ ft.

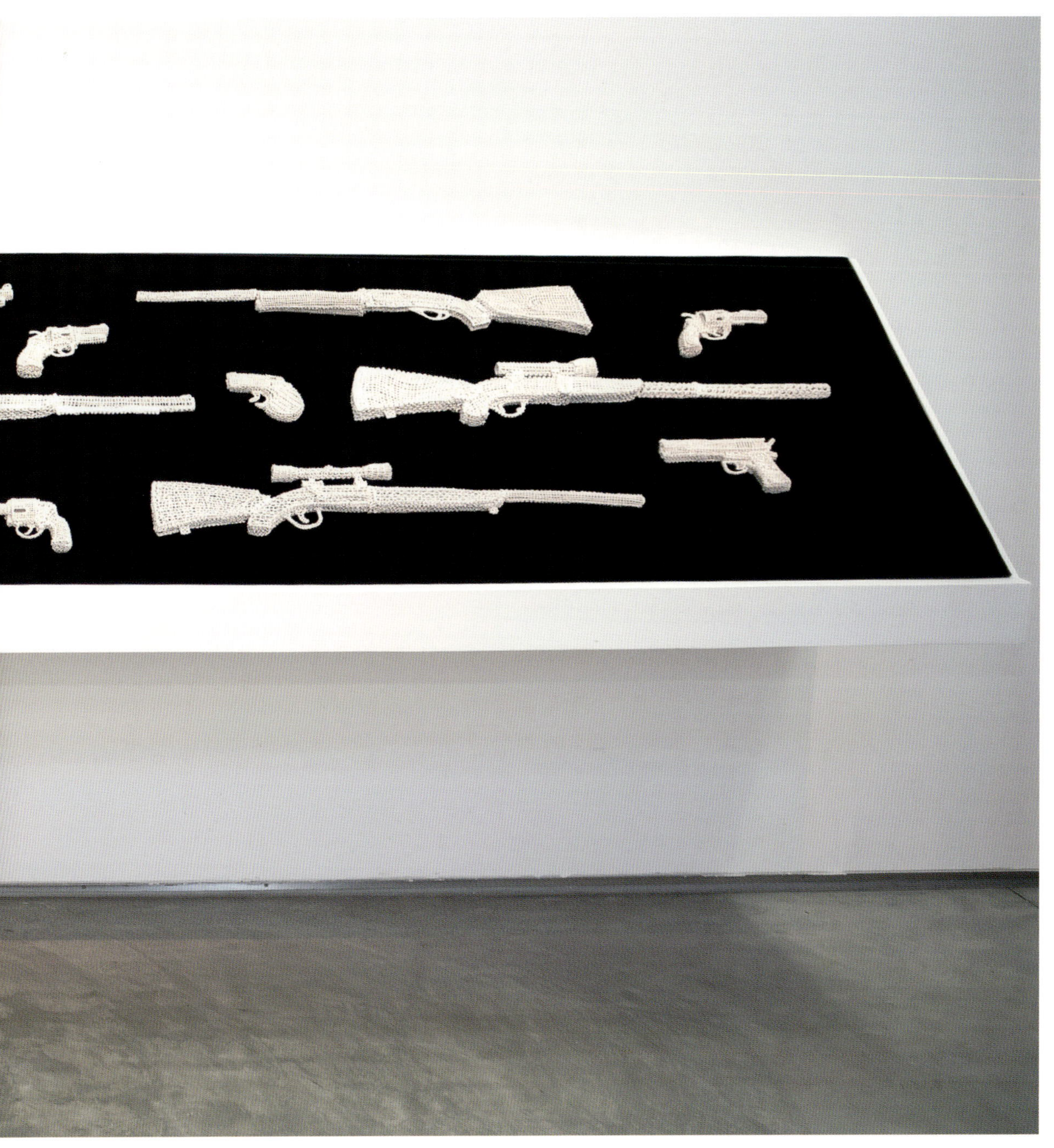

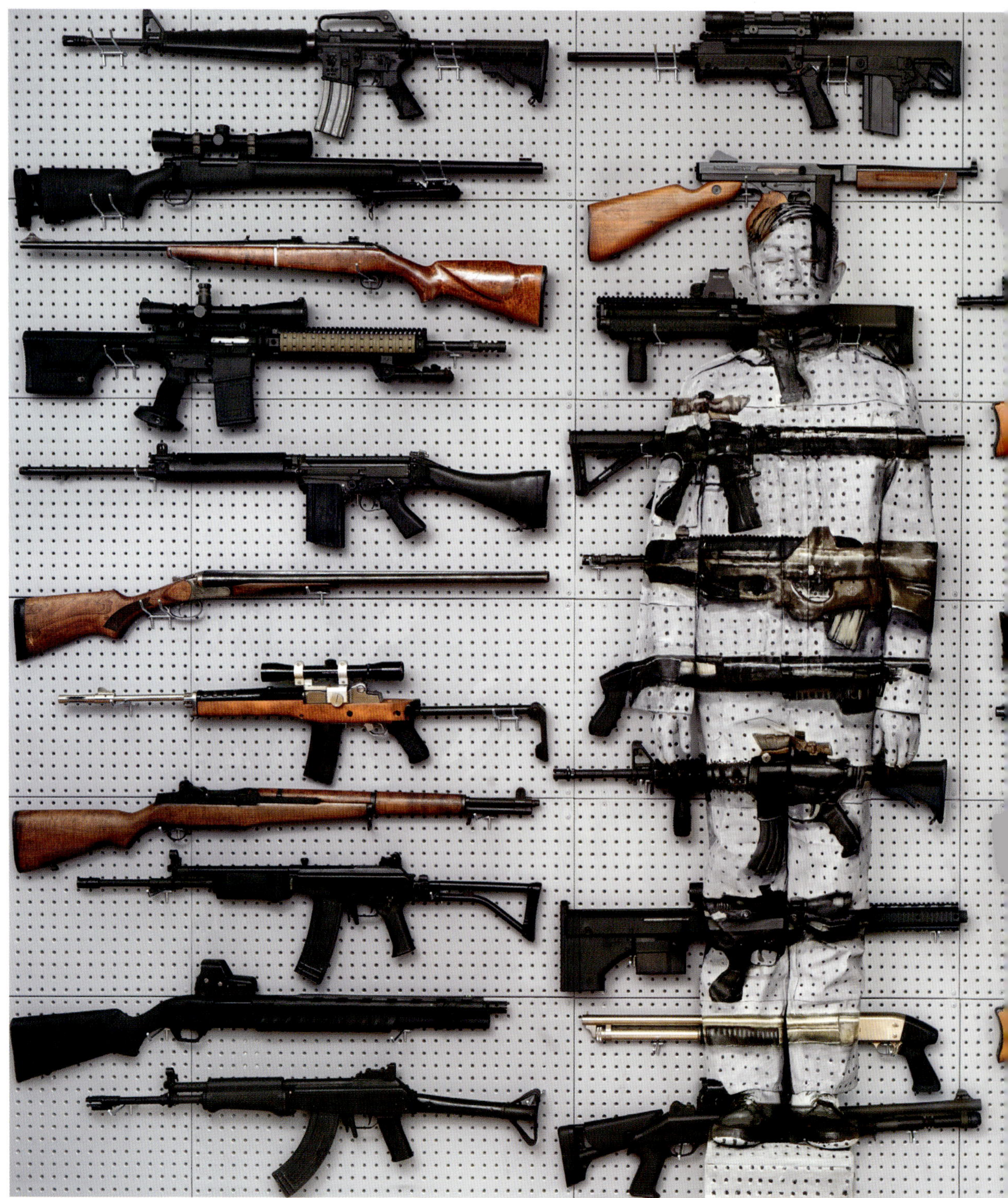

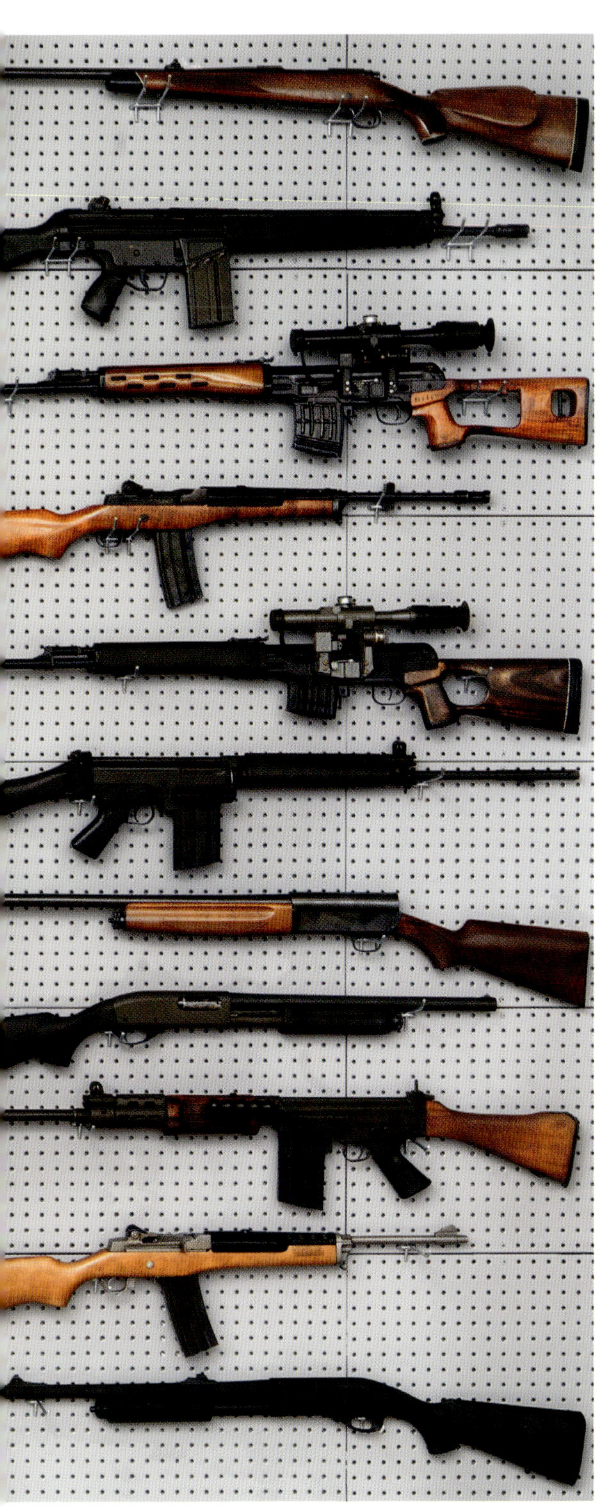

Liu Bolin
Hiding in New York No. 9—Gun Rack, 2013
archival pigment print
44¼ × 59 in.
Courtesy of Liu Bolin and Liu Bolin Art Studio

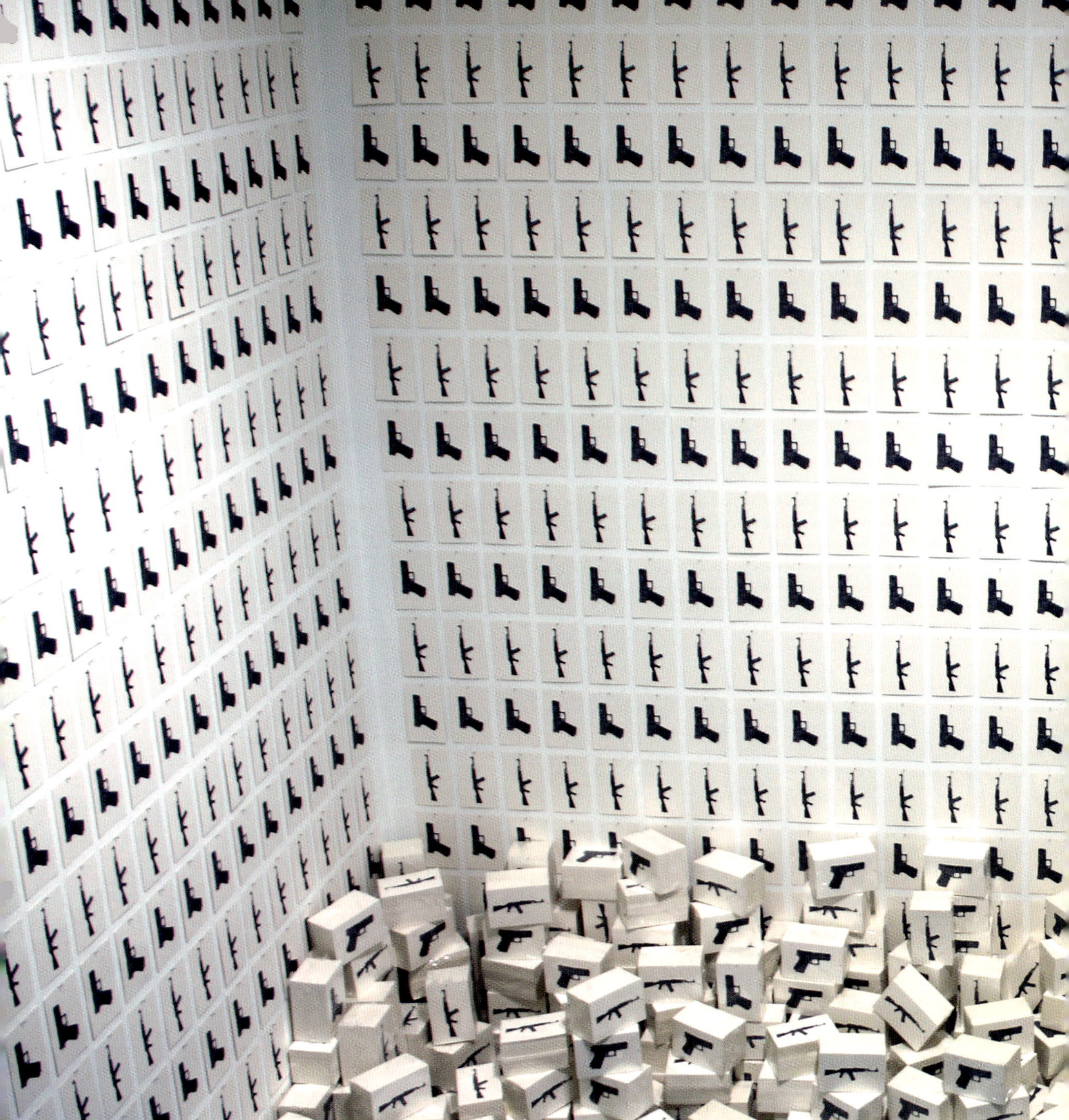

Linda Bond
Inventory, 2011–present
190,000 offset-printed 6 × 4 in. cards, each for one cache of US weapons gone missing in Iraq
Installation view at Brattleboro Museum & Art Center, Vermont
Photo courtesy of Brattleboro Museum & Art Center

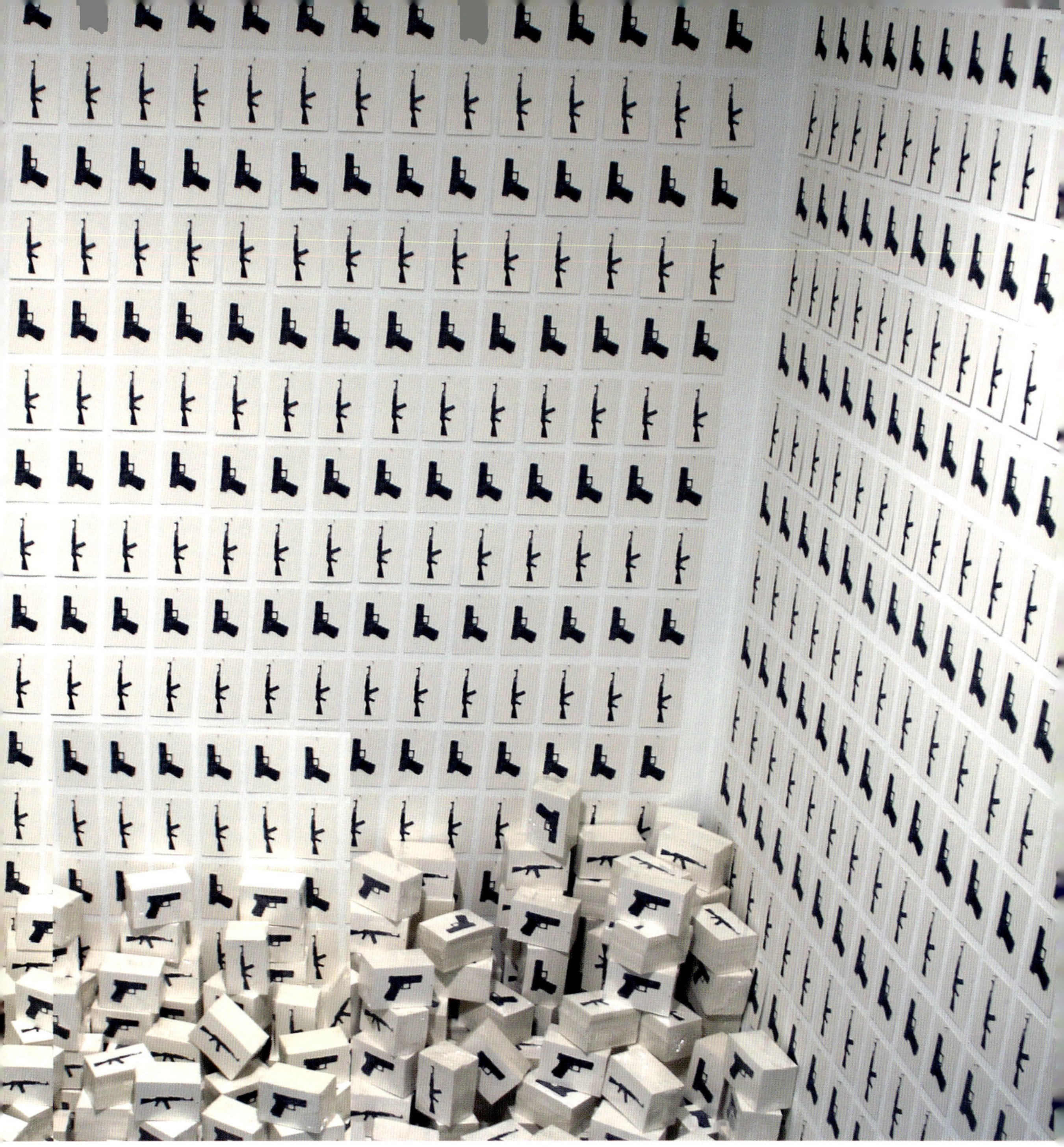

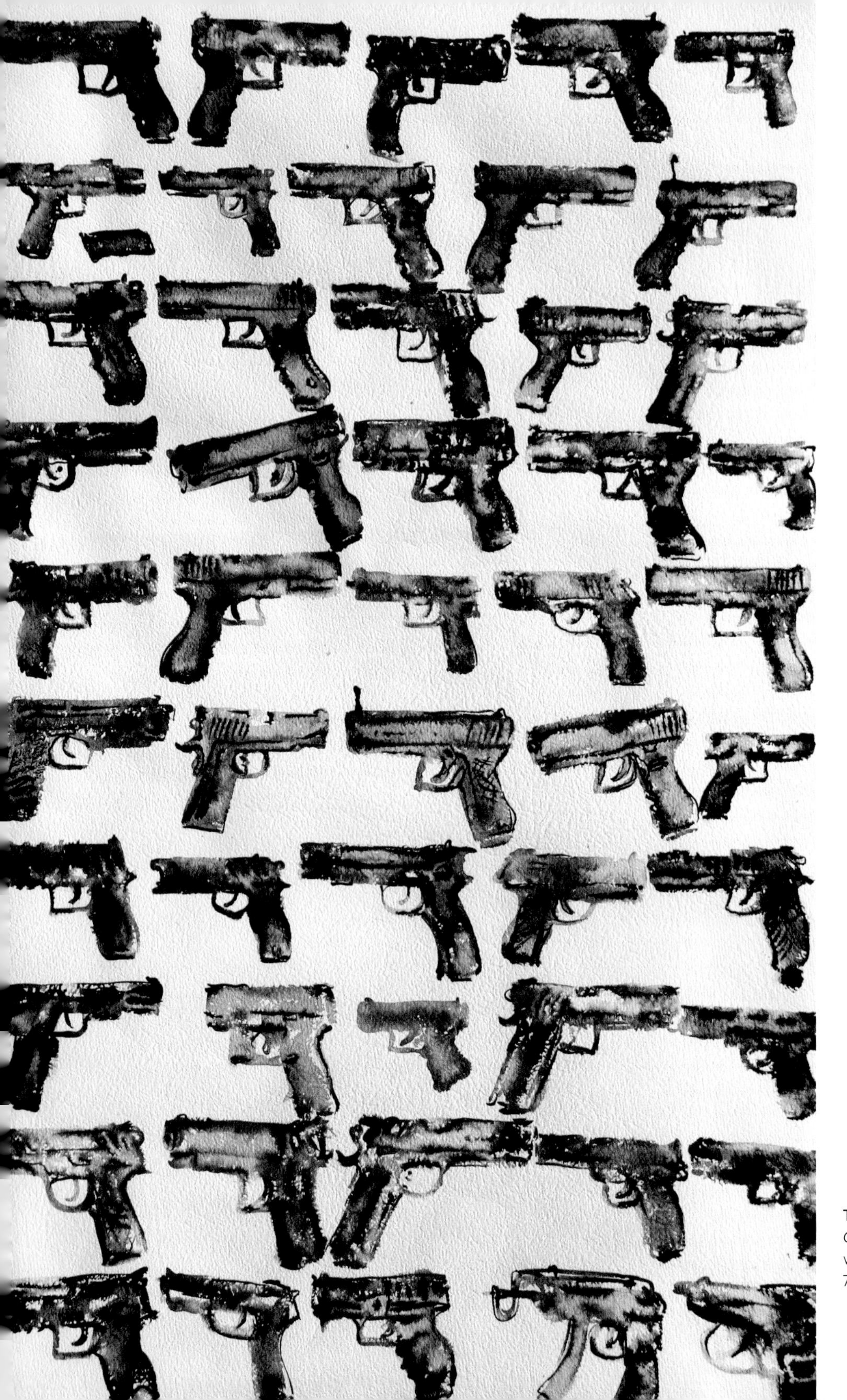

Tawan Wattuya
Guns, 2017
watercolor on paper
78¾ × 118 in.

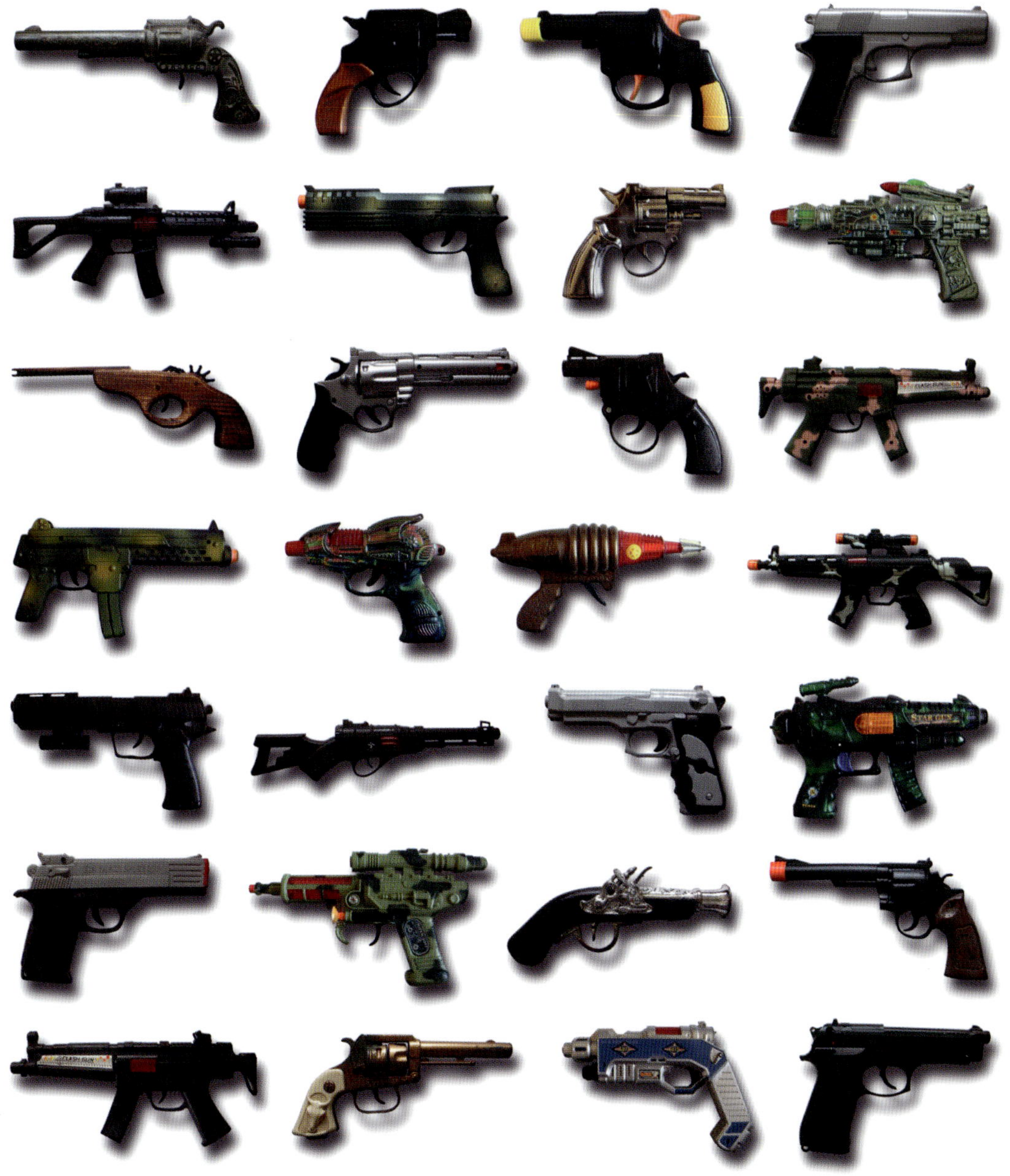

Bruce Mahalski
Military Action Set (age 3+), 2005
inkjet print of toy guns bought at discount stores in New Zealand
34¾ × 46¾ in.

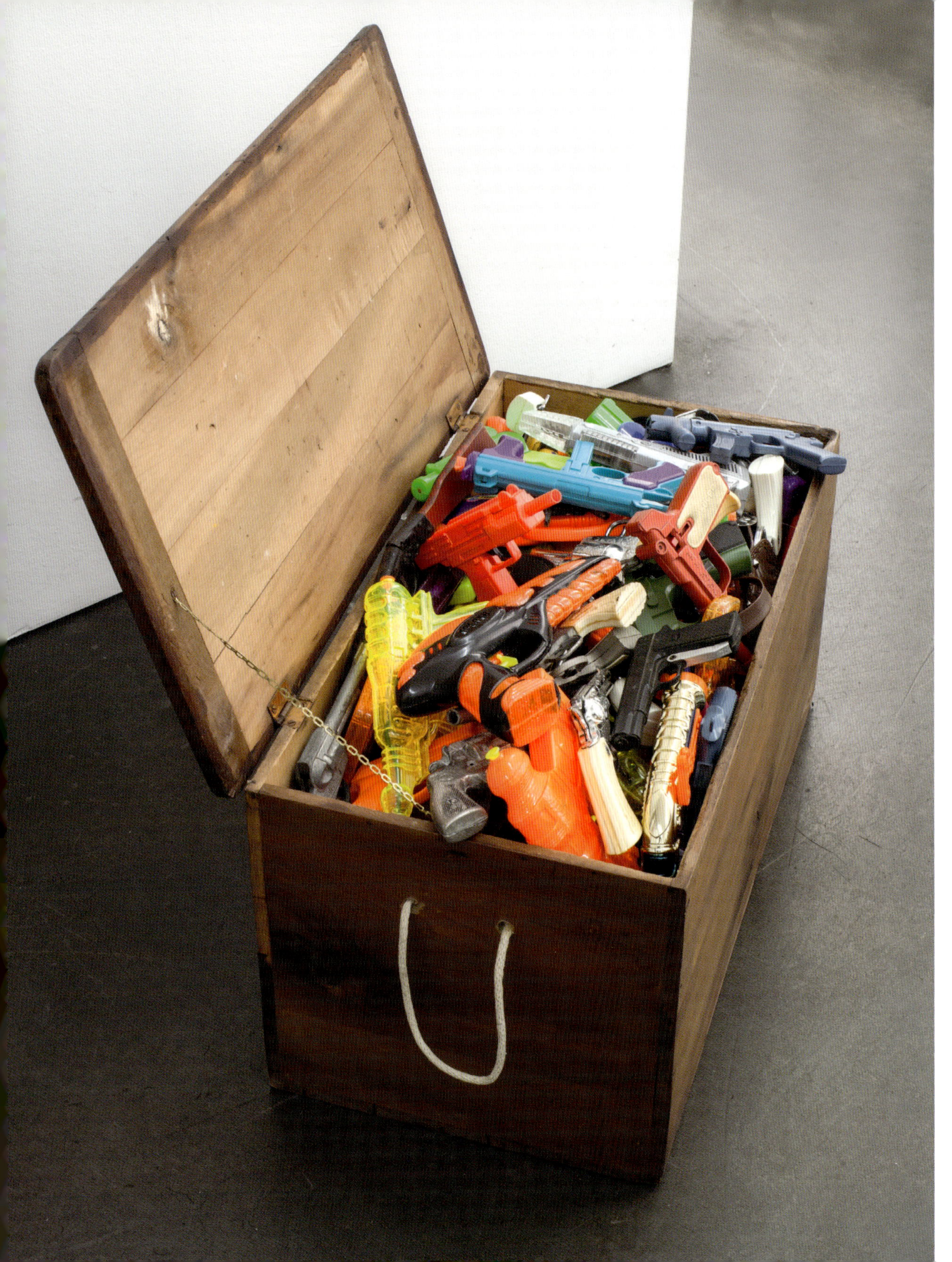

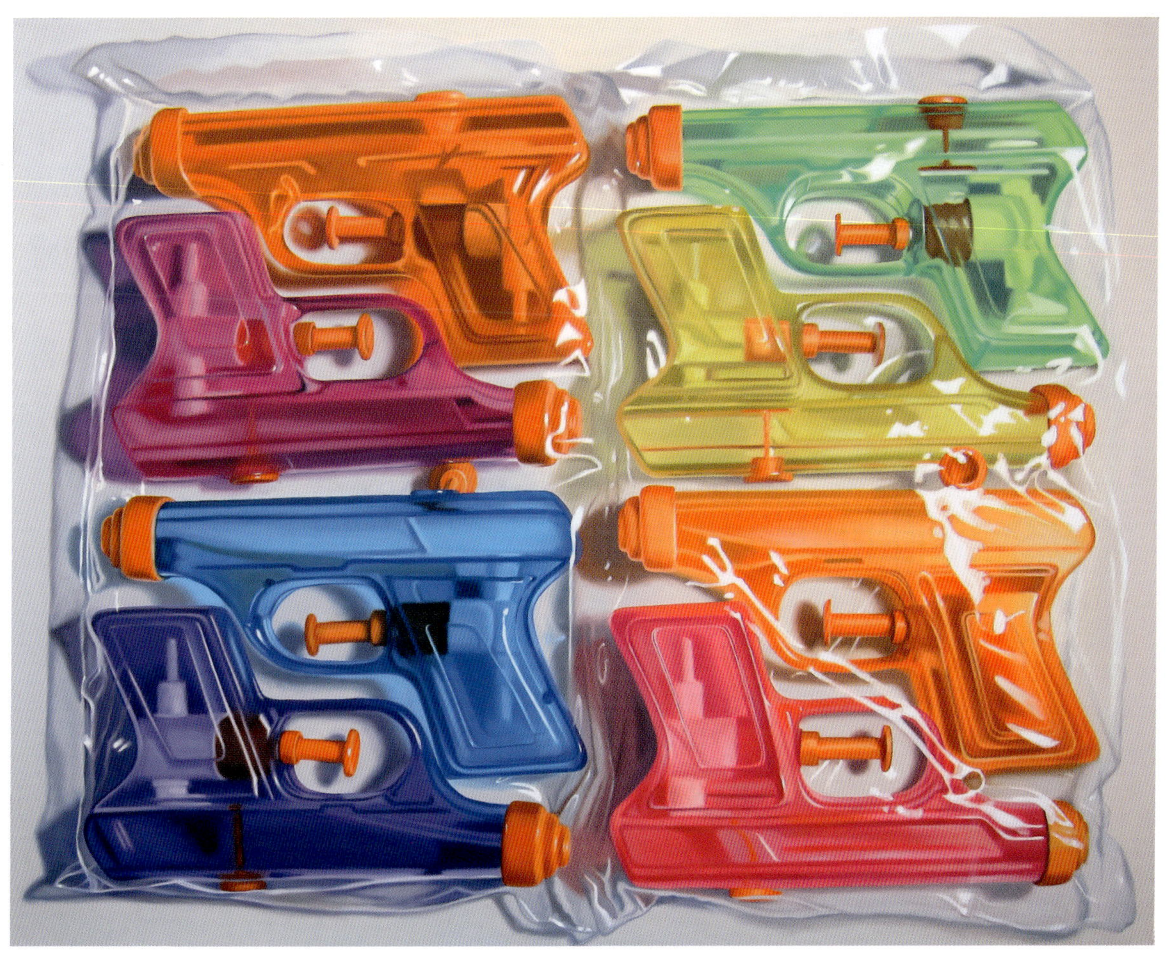

Shannon Cannings
Arsenal, 2015
oil on canvas
55 × 70 in.

Mark Dion
Toy Box, 2008
139 toy guns, wooden box
Courtesy of the artist and Galerie Nagel Draxler, Berlin/Cologne/Munich
Photo: Simon Vogel

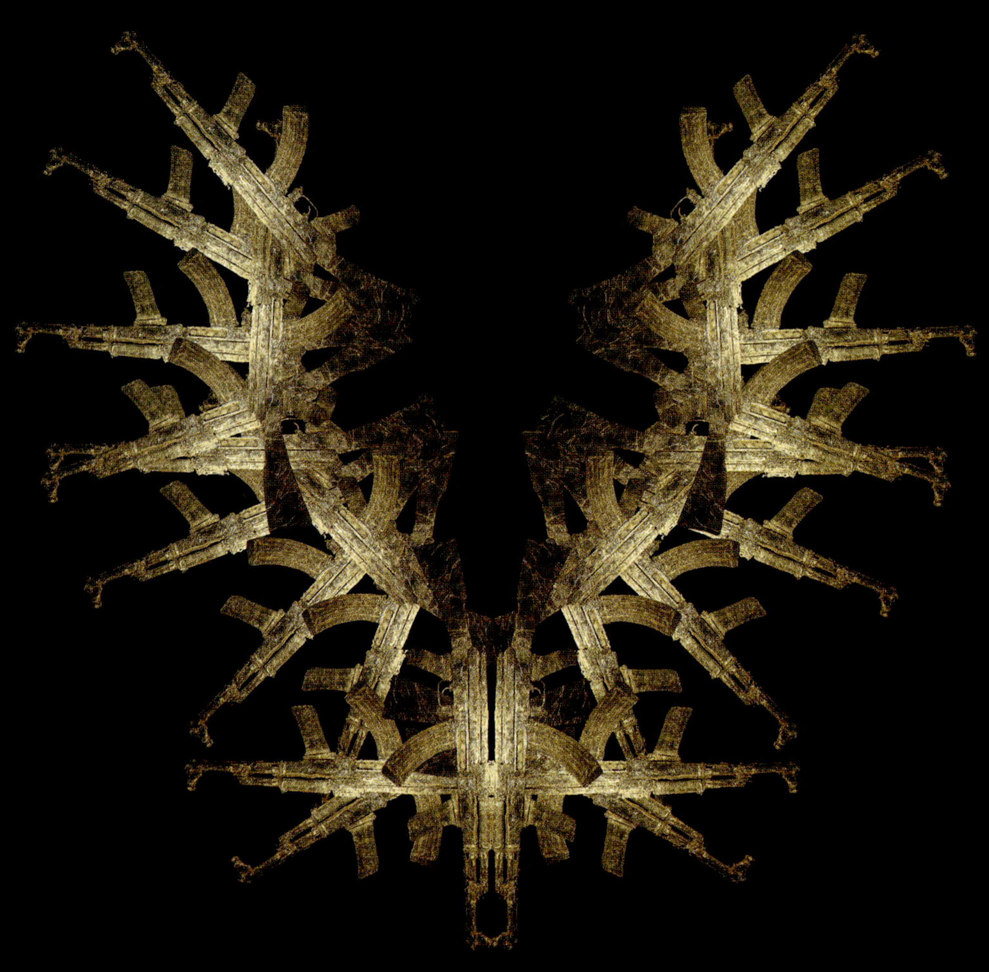

Yosman Botero
Postcolombino 17, 2016
gold leaf on Plexiglas
7¼ × 47¼ × 2¼ in.
Photo: Martha Elena Gomez

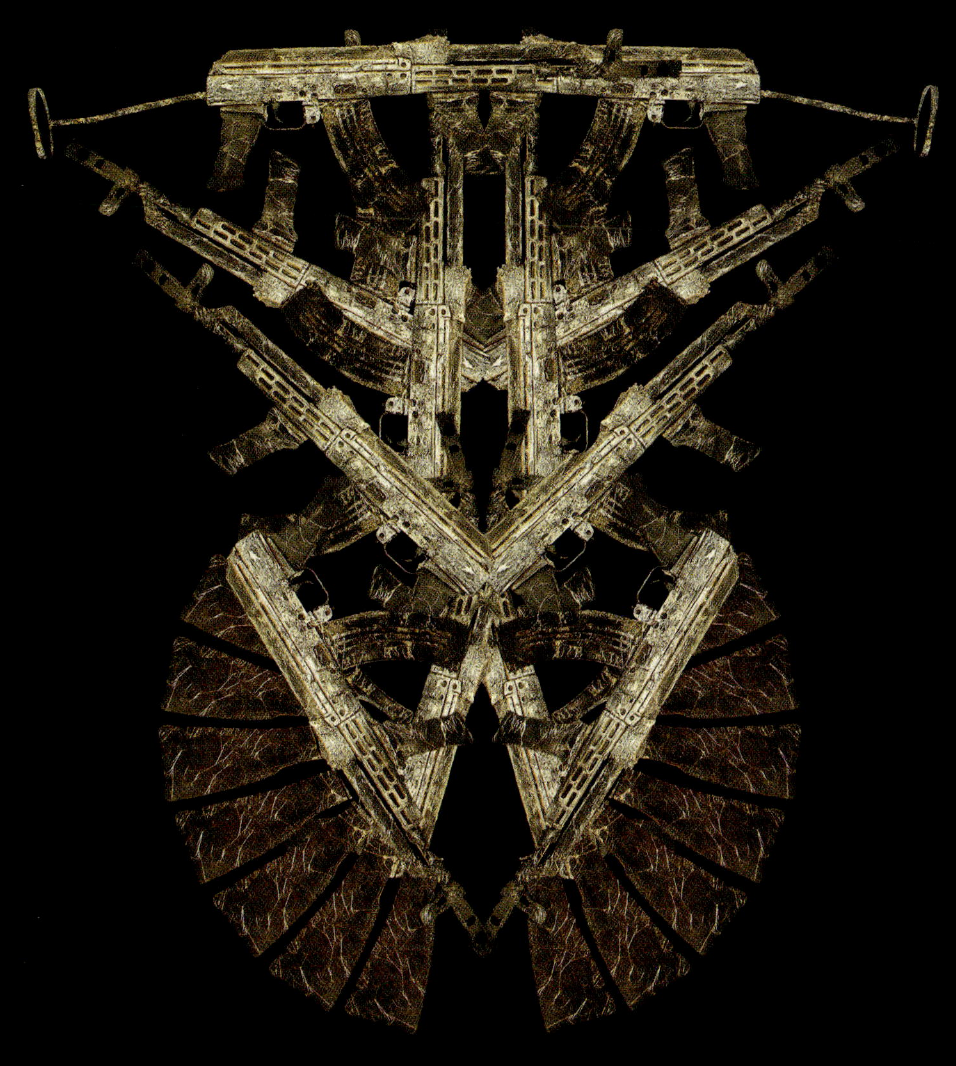

Yosman Botero
Postcolombino 3, 2016
gold leaf on Plexiglas
47¼ × 47¼ × 2¼ in.
Photo: Martha Elena Gomez

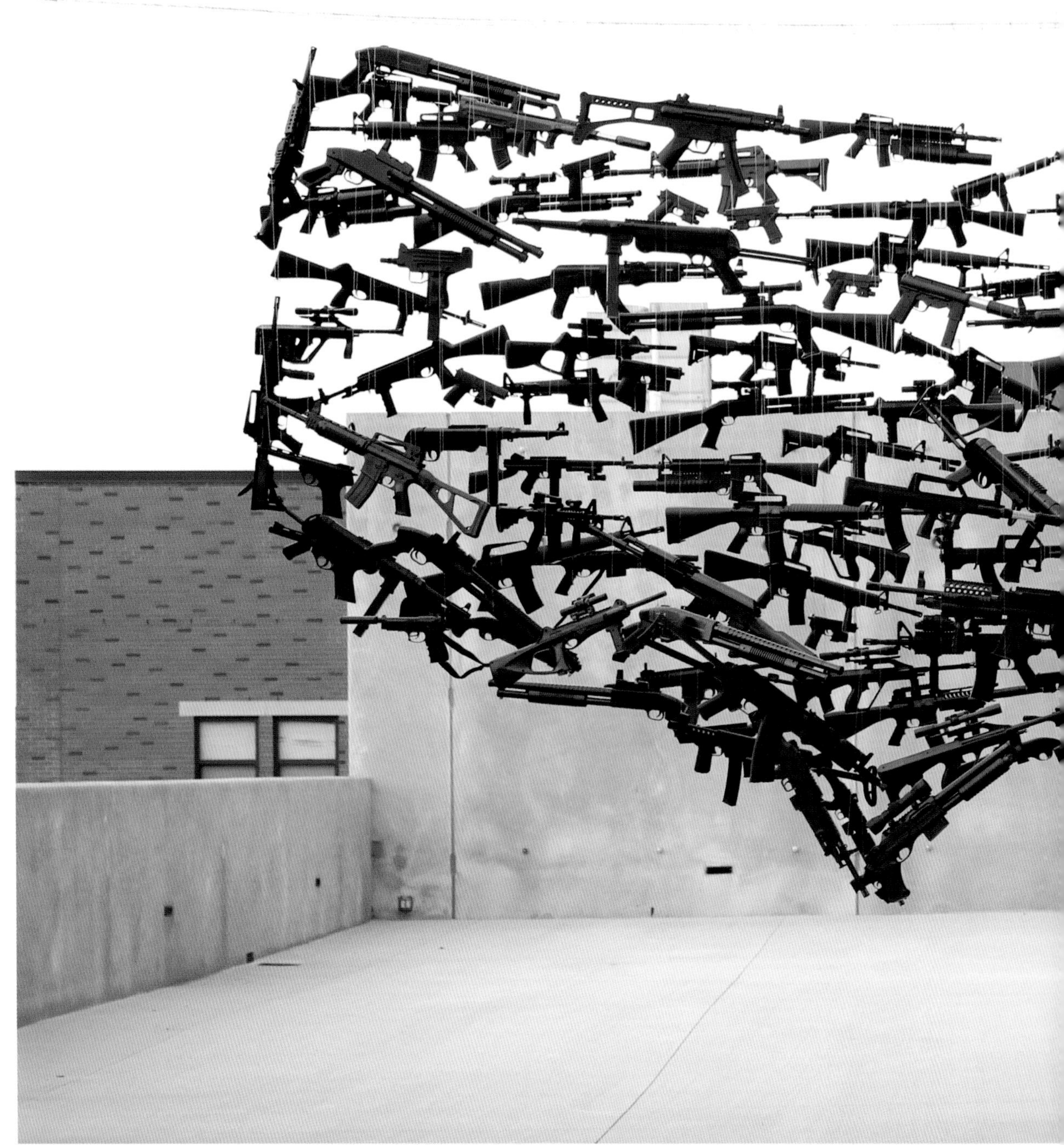

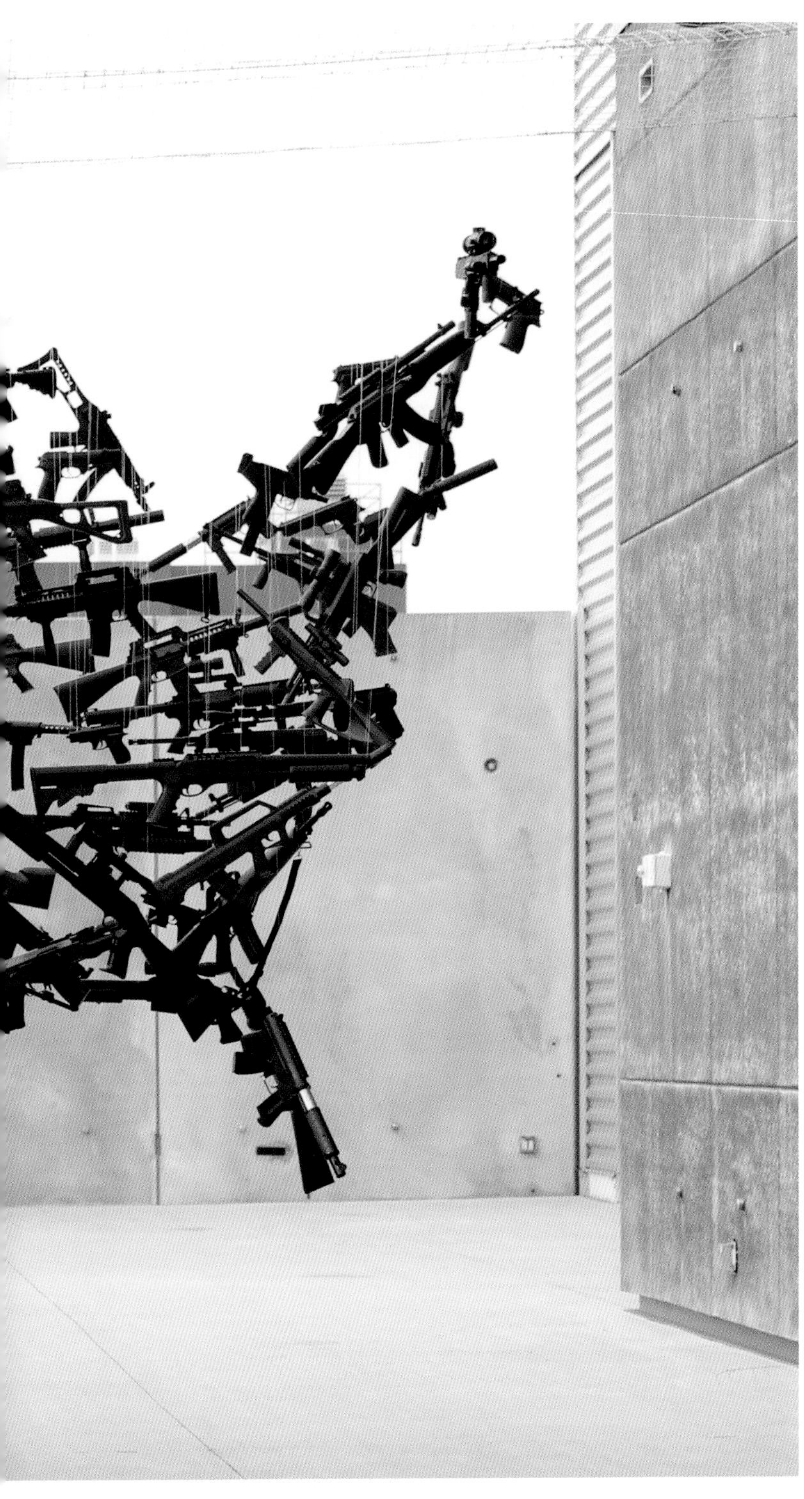

Michael Murphy
Gun Country, 2014
150 toy guns
12 × 20 × 12 ft.
Installation view, UICA roof Grand Rapids, MI

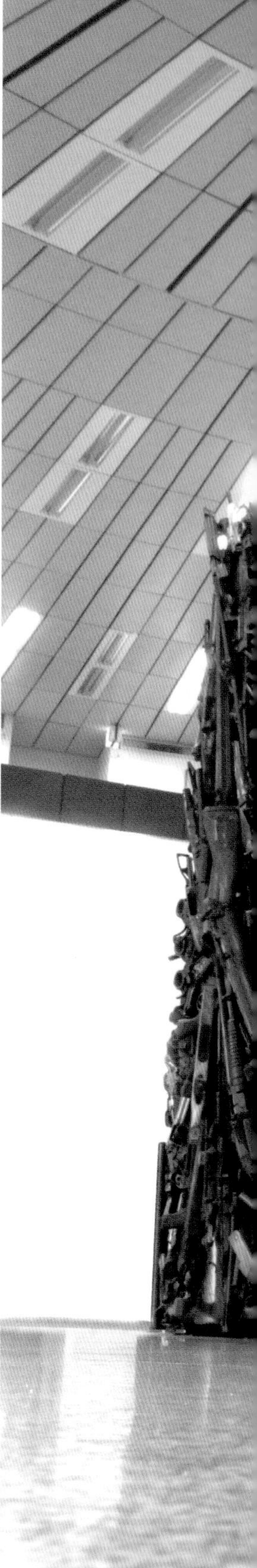

Sandra Bromley and Wallis Kendal
Gun Sculpture, 2000
7,000-plus deactivated weapons (including handguns, AK47s, rifles, landmines, and ammunition), steel, concrete
8 × 12 × 8 ft.
Partial Installation view from the International Vienna Centre (VIC), Vienna, Austria
Photo: Sandra Bromley

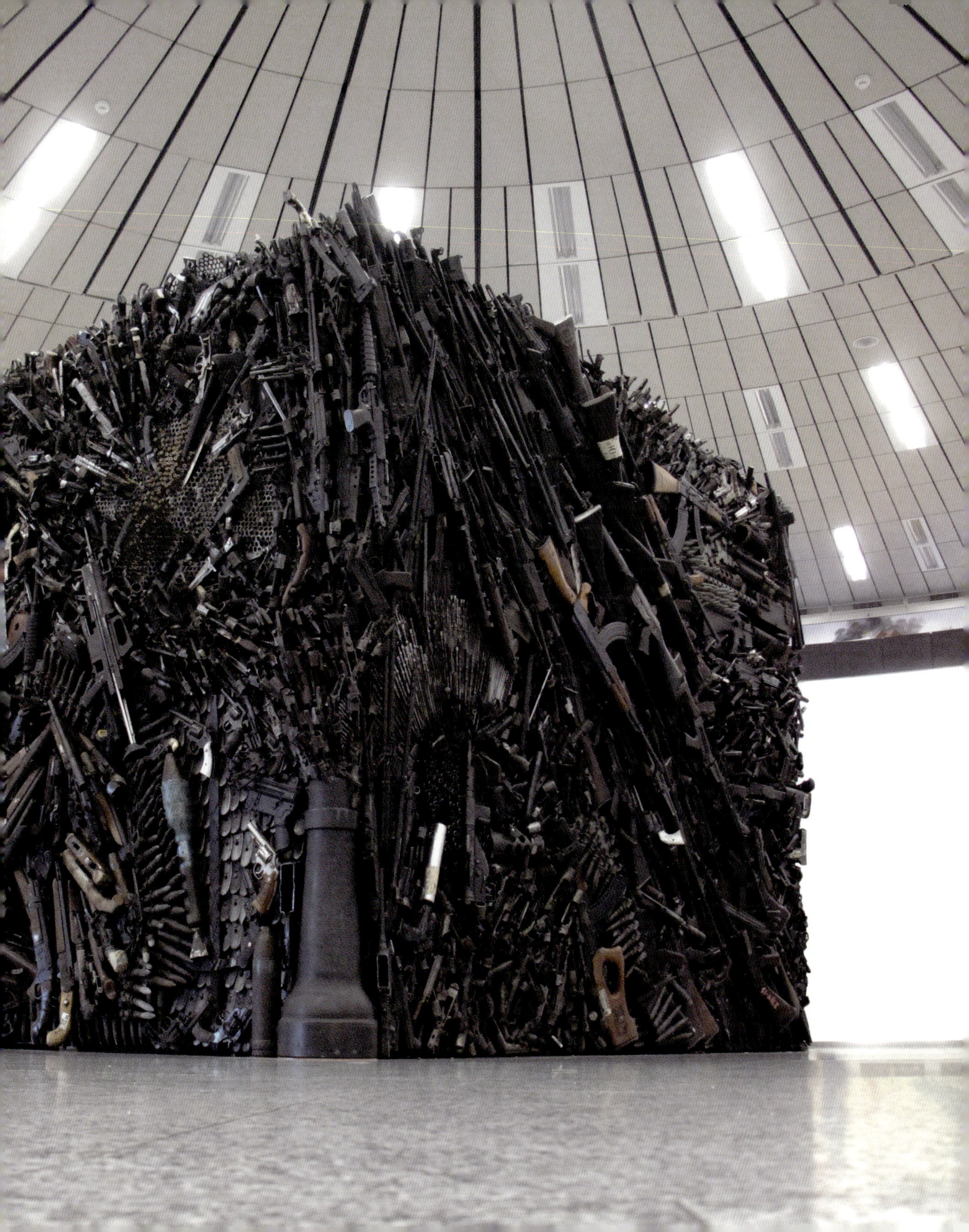

SELECTED BIBLIOGRAPHY

Bachelard, Gaston. *Fragments of a Poetics of Fire.* Dallas: Dallas Institute Publications, 1990.

Bally, Boris, ed. *I.M.A.G.I.N.E. Peace Now.* Providence, RI: Bally Humanufactured, 2016.

Browder, Laura. *Her Best Shot: Women and Guns in America.* Chapel Hill: University of North Carolina Press, 2006.

Diamond, Jared. *Guns, Germs, and Steel: The Fates of Human Societies.* New York: W. W. Norton, 1997.

Ferrara, Jonathan. *Guns in the Hands of Artists.* San Francisco: Inkshares, 2016.

Floyd, Nancy. *She's Got a Gun.* Philadelphia: Temple University Press, 2008

Fowler, Will, Anthony North, Charles Stronge, and Patrick Sweeney. *The Illustrated World Encyclopedia of Guns.* London: Anness, 2016.

Goudsblom, Johan. *Fire and Civilization.* London: Penguin Group, 1992.

Higonnet, Anne. *Pictures of Innocence: The History and Crisis of Ideal Childhood.* London: Thames and Hudson, 1998.

Hilpert-Stuber, Susanne, ed. *Ligen de Mire (Line of Sight).* Lausanne, Switzerland: Musée de design et d'arts appliqués contemporains, 2018.

Lee, Robert M., and R. L. Wilson. *The Art of the Gun: Selections from the Robert M. Lee Collection.* 5 vols. Sparks, NV: Yellowstone, 2013.

Pyhrr, Stuart W. *Firearms from the Collections of the Prince of Liechtenstein.* New York: Metropolitan Museum of Art, 1985.

Shorr, Kathy. *SHOT: 101 Survivors of Gun Violence in America.* Brooklyn, NY: PowerHouse Books, 2017.

Supica, Jim. *Guns.* Surrey, UK: TAJ Books, 2005.

Supica, Jim, Doug Wicklund, and Philip Schreier. *The Illustrated History of Firearms.* New York: Chartwell Books, 2011.

———. *Treasures of the NRA National Firearms Museum.* New York: Chartwell Books, 2013.

Wilson, R. L. *History and Art of the American Gun.* New York: Chartwell Books, 2015.

ARTIST INDEX

Suzanne Ramljak, a writer and art historian, is currently a curator at the American Federation of Arts, New York. She was formerly editor of *Sculpture* and *Metalsmith* magazines. Ramljak has authored several books on contemporary art and design, including *Natural Wonders: The Sublime in Contemporary Art* (Rizzoli), *On Body and Soul: Contemporary Armor to Amulets* (Schiffer), and *Unique by Design: Contemporary Jewelry in the Donna Schneier Collection* (The Metropolitan Museum and Yale University Press). She has contributed to numerous publications, and her writing on art has appeared in the *New York Times Book Review*, *Utne Reader*, and other periodicals. Among the exhibitions she has curated are "Playtime: Toys for Adults," "Romancing the Brain," "Divine Flesh: Contemporary Goddess Imagery," and "Case Studies: Art in a Valise."

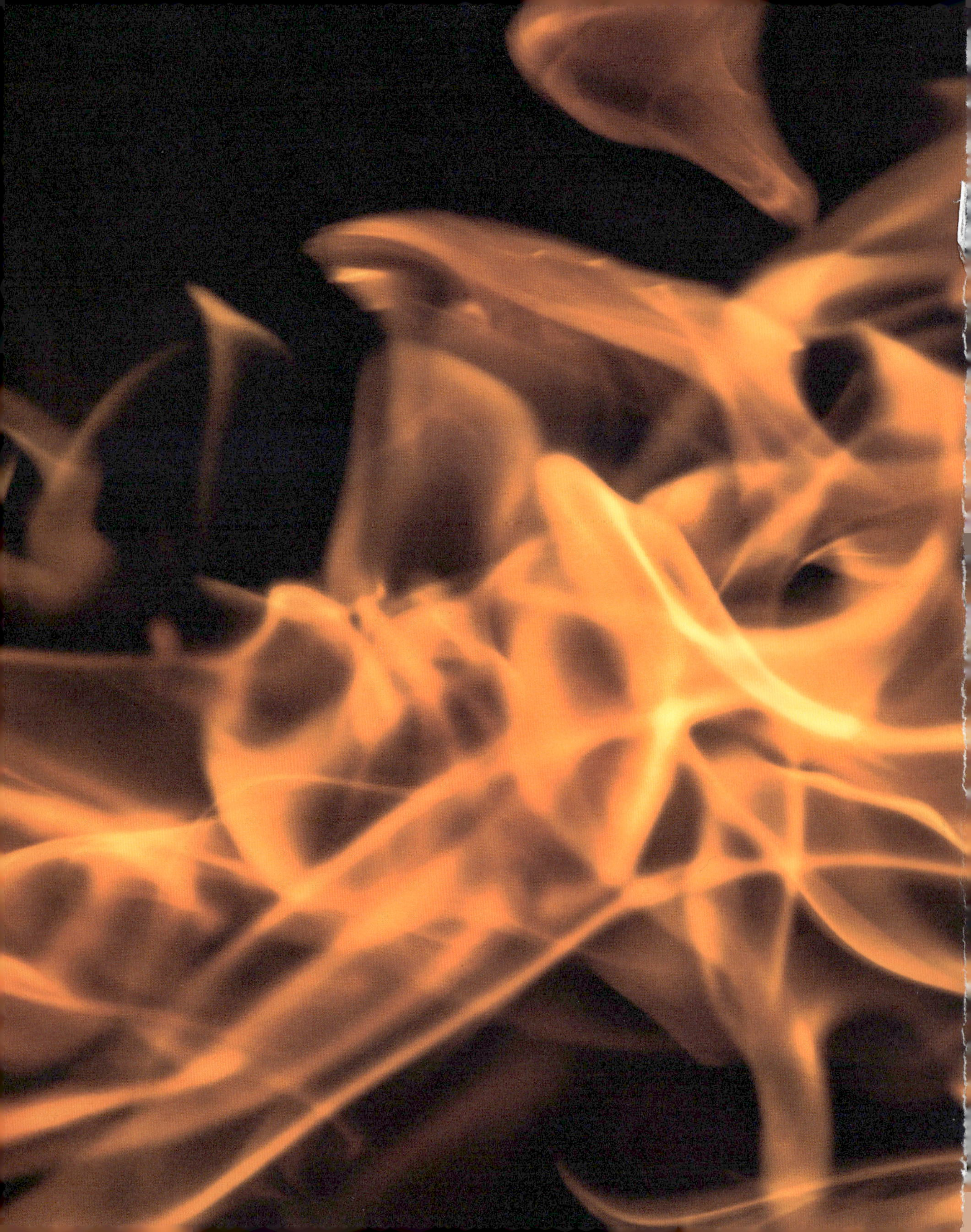